A LINGUISTIC INVESTIGATION OF APHASIC CHINESE SPEECH

STUDIES IN THEORETICAL PSYCHOLINGUISTICS

VOLUME 18

The titles published in this series are listed at the end of this volume.

A LINGUISTIC INVESTIGATION OF APHASIC CHINESE SPEECH

by

JEROME L. PACKARD
University of Illinois, Urbana

SPRINGER-SCIENCE+BUSINESS MEDIA, B.V.

Library of Congress Cataloging-in-Publication Data

Packard, Jerome Lee, 1951-
A linguistic investigation of aphasic Chinese speech / by Jerome L. Packard.
p. cm. -- (Studies in theorectical psycholinguistics ; 18)
Includes index.
ISBN 978-94-010-4903-0 ISBN 978-94-011-2040-1 (eBook)
DOI 10.1007/978-94-011-2040-1
1. Chinese language--Psychological aspects. 2. Aphasia.
I. Title. II. Series.
PL1071.P36 1993
495.1'01'9--dc20 93-28051

ISBN 978-94-010-4903-0

Printed on acid-free paper

For my mother,
Eda Ada Casucci Packard

. . . mille baci. . .

Contents

List of Figures

List of Tables

Preface

This work is a description and analysis of the elicited natural speech output of four aphasic speakers of Mandarin Chinese. As part of this study, I offer explanations for my findings which comport with certain theories of aphasia, linguistics and cognitive science. I would ask the reader to keep in mind that this is not a study in which different theories of aphasia are rigorously evaluated using experimental design features and controlled variables. Rather, the hypotheses offered here should be seen as an initial step toward understanding a body of naturally-occurring aphasic speech data.

This book is the product of five years' effort, and has benefitted along the way from the help and advice given to me by numerous individuals.

For extensive comments on the manuscript I owe a large debt of gratitude to Jim McCawley, Lise Menn, Loraine Obler, Michel Paradis, Richard Sproat, Edgar Zurif and the anonymous reviewers at Kluwer. Also providing helpful feedback and discussion of issues were Barb Finlay, Eleanor Saffran, Mike Kelly, Laura Koenig, Mitch Marcus, Bob Frank, Harold Goodglass, Eva Kehayia, Iosef Grodzinsky, Gonia Jarema, Rich Janda and Jack Hoeksema. My thanks to Ken Wexler for encouragement during the initial stages of the project, to Barbara Lust and Suzanne Flynn for encouragement and advice, and to Jim Forman for proofreading the manuscript. Special thanks to Ovid Tzeng for his continual assistance, advice and support.

My thanks go out to the community of Chinese linguistics scholars for providing support and helping me develop my ideas over the past several years. I especially thank Tom Ernst, Shou-hsin Teng, Thomas Lee, Galal Walker, Chung-yu Chen, Yung-O Biq, Ron Walton, Jim Tai, Moira Yip, Neil Kubler, Eric Zee, Margie Chan, John Dai, Bill Baxter, Jim Huang, Bob Sanders, Bill Wang, Chilin Shih, San Duanmu, Audrey Y-H. Li and Claudia Ross.

In Taipei, for help in locating and interviewing subjects, my thanks go to Yu-mei Chung, Show-er Li, Fu-mei Hsieh, Drs. Ming-shung Su and Zin-an Wu, and, most especially, Sylvia Chen. In Beijing, my heartfelt thanks to Drs. Yonglian Zhu, Chaoqun Hu and Xintian Li for helping me with my research, and for making the time spent there pleasant for my family and me.

For various forms of support at the University of Illinois at Urbana, my thanks go to Tom Havens, Jerry Morgan and the Beckman Institute, Linda May, Doug McDonald, Chin Wu Kim, Howard MacClay, Zhijun (Judy) Mu, Jan Davis, Gary Dell and C.C. Cheng. At the University of Pennsylvania, I thank David Murray, Pao-Yuan Chen, Xiaoyu Chen, Shengli Feng, Peggy Guinan, and Mark Steedman.

My greatest thanks must be reserved for my family—Carol, Errol, Sam and Eric Packard—for their love and patience over the long haul.

Chapter 1

Introduction

This book is an investigation of the natural speech output[1] of four speakers of Mandarin Chinese who suffered aphasia following brain damage. The method of investigation is a careful analysis of transcribed audiotapes recorded in interview situations. The resulting speech corpora (presented in full in the Appendix) are analyzed for their phonological, morphological, syntactic, discourse and pragmatic linguistic content.

The objective of this study is to determine how aphasic spoken language production deficits are manifest in Chinese, a language that is different in many ways from languages in which aphasia has been investigated most often[2]. Historically, analysis of aphasic speech has been largely restricted to languages spoken in western Europe. By investigating aphasic speech breakdown in Chinese, we may offer a new perspective on aphasia in the more commonly-analyzed languages, thereby increasing our understanding of potential universals in aphasia theory. In the course of this investigation, we shall also uncover language-specific characteristics that are valuable in diagnosing aphasia in Chinese, and obtain new insights into Chinese grammatical structure. The results advance our understanding of the relationship between language and the brain, thus constituting a worthwhile contribution to the cognitive and linguistic sciences.

[1] This work does not discuss Chinese character orthography production or perception deficts in aphasic patients. For a good summary of these studies, see Hoosain (1991) or Paradis et al. (1985).

[2] Most previous work on aphasia in Chinese speakers has not included detailed discussion of patients' speech production problems (for a review, see Hoosain 1991). Exceptions to this are experimental studies by Tzeng et al. (1991), and Bates et al. (1991), whose results will be discussed as they become relevant to our investigation.

1.1 Recasting Typology-dependent Theories

The classical aphasia syndromes have been defined based on an restricted range of language types. The classical syndromes are *Broca's* (also called

symptom	Broca's	Wernicke's
fluent	no	yes
meaningful	yes	no
effortful	yes	no
functor omission	yes	no
word formation	poor	good
phrase length	reduced	normal
complex syntax	no	yes
phonetic distortions	yes	some
intonation	abnormal	normal
word substitution	some	yes
neologism	no	yes
comprehension	good	poor
discourse structure	fair	poor

Table 1.1: Some Features of Classical Aphasia Syndromes

'non-fluent' or 'motor') aphasia, and *Wernicke's* (also called 'fluent' or 'sensory') aphasia, defined by dysfunctions affecting the language characteristics seen in Table 1.1. Some of the language characteristics that define the classical syndromes are independent of the particular language being ob-

• fluency	• semantic content
• ease of articulation	• phrase length
• syntactic complexity	• phonological accuracy
• use of correct word	• discourse structure

Table 1.2: Typology-Independent Aphasia Characteristics

served. These generic, non-language-specific linguistic factors include such phenomena as (see Table 1.2) speed of speech output, amount of speech,

- function words
- inflection
- neologisms
- word formation
- word prosody
- sentence prosody

Table 1.3: Typology-Dependent Aphasia Characteristics

and ease of articulation[3]. However, other criteria that are quite dependent on language typology (see Table 1.3) are also used to identify and classify syndromes. These non-universal criteria include the use of function words (the definition of which is often language-specific[4]), grammatical inflection (the nature of which varies from language to language), word formation (since the definition of 'word' is elusive and word structure varies from language to language), and tone production (which depends upon the linguistic function of tone in a given language).

As seen in Table 1.4, Chinese differs from what are considered more

• no grammatical agreement	• no gender inflection
• no case inflection	• no number inflection
• verb-like prepositions	• topic vs. subject prominence
• verb-like adjectives	• lexically contrastive tone

Table 1.4: 'Unusual' Typological Characteristics of Chinese

'typical' (usually, western European) languages in many of these characteristics (described in detail in Chapter 2). This being the case, how will a

[3]Edgar Zurif has pointed out that these non-language-specific factors may reflect general cognitive capacities shared by the language faculty.

[4]For example, Mandarin has a grammatical category often called 'coverb', which may be considered a function word depending on how it is used in a given context (see section 2.3.1).

given syndrome which has a defined effect on these speech characteristics appear in Chinese? This question is even more striking when a syndrome is defined largely based features that exist in only a subset of languages. In a language which does not have the features in question, will the aphasia symptom fail to appear?

For example, a hallmark symptom of Broca's aphasia is precisely the misuse of grammatical inflection. However, Chinese is said to have no inflection[5]. If there is no inflection in Chinese, then how will the 'inflection misuse' symptom manifest itself in Chinese speakers who exhibit other symptoms of Broca's aphasia?

There are at least two answers to this question. One is that the 'inflection misuse' symptom will simply not appear. Another is that it will appear, but in a different form. The first possibility implies that speakers of certain languages may be less subject to aphasic deficit than speakers of other languages. If this strikes the reader as odd, it may be because of the intuition that the specific language deficits seen in aphasia are merely surface manifestations of a general, underlying language dysfunction. It seems unlikely that a person might escape the linguistic consequences of neurological damage simply by being a speaker of one language rather than another. If on the other hand we observe the inflection deficit in Chinese in a different but related way, then we may conclude that Broca's aphasia is a general language dysfunction whose specific symptoms appear differently in different languages. This would suggest that there is an underlying universal language capacity at some level of representation.

Even though Chinese has many characteristics that are different from more commonly investigated languages, it can hardly be considered an 'outlier' among the languages of the world, since it is spoken by one-fourth of the earth's population. Any accounting of the nature of language, including theories of language deficit in aphasia, must deal with Chinese as a significant entity. Since Chinese is so different from the European languages upon which traditional descriptions of aphasia are based, it is likely that many Chinese findings will not be fully explained by current aphasia theory. The Chinese data should be considered a litmus test for classical theories of aphasia. To the extent that these theories account for the Chinese findings, their validity is upheld. To the extent that they fail to account for the data, the theories must be modified or discarded. The result is a new, broader perspective on aphasic disorders. Analyses of aphasia in Hebrew (Grodzinsky, 1984) and Italian (Miceli et al., 1983) revealed that in agrammatism, what were thought to be omissions of inflectional endings are more likely

[5] In section 2.3.11 we discuss the possible existence of inflection in an abstract sense in Chinese, manifested in an abstract INFL node in Chinese syntactic theory.

improper selections of the 'zero' member of the inflectional paradigm, and that agrammatic speakers are constrained to produce real words (Grodzinsky 1984). Cross-linguistic studies by Bates and her colleagues (e.g., Bates et al. 1987, Bates and Wulfeck 1989b) and by Menn and Obler (1990) have also shed new light on aphasia research. In the same way, accounting for the Chinese data in the present study will result in a fuller and more accurate theory of aphasia.

1.2 Issues in Aphasia Theory

Data from Chinese aphasia are likely to offer new perspectives and fresh insights into current issues in aphasia theory. I outline some of these issues in the sections that follow.

1.2.1 The Nature of Agrammatism

A language disorder known as *agrammatism* is often seen in Broca's aphasia. Agrammatism is commonly defined as a grammatical deficit which results in simplified syntactic structure, and the omission or otherwise misuse of free-standing grammatical function words and bound grammatical morphemes (such as inflection). Since agrammatism rarely occurs in a patient who does not have the other symptoms of Broca's aphasia (but see, e.g., Miceli et al., 1983, and Berndt and Caramazza, 1980), the two are often treated as equivalent.

Syntactic Explanations of Agrammatism

Most researchers have described the deficits in agrammatism as being syntactic in nature, because the phenomena of function word omission, simplification of syntactic structure and misuse of grammatical inflection lend themselves quite readily to syntactic explanations. Below are some examples of syntactic explanations of agrammatism. The list is not exhaustive, but gives an overview of what types of syntactic explanations have been offered to account for agrammatic speech output (for a review and discussion of syntactic approaches to agrammatism, see Schwartz, Linebarger and Saffran, 1985).

Zurif and Caramazza (1976) postulate that agrammatism is the result of a central syntactic disorder. Citing comprehension data and performance on linguistic judgement tasks, they suggest that in agrammatism, deficits affect the underlying knowledge of language, resulting in language abnormalities at both comprehension and production levels. Zurif and Blumstein

(1978), relying on evidence from both comprehension and production, argue that the inability of Broca's aphasics to recover syntactic facts implicates a deficit in syntactic processing. Berndt and Caramazza (1980) propose that agrammatism is a syntactic deficit which is dissociable from the articulatory output deficit with which it often cooccurs. They suggest that the cooccurrence of these two types of deficit constitutes Broca's aphasia, and that the reason for the cooccurrence of these two deficits is neuroanatomical. They argue that Broca's area is responsible for the functioning of a syntactic parser, and that this parser is disrupted when Broca's area suffers damage. The authors provide a good overview of the evidence supporting a syntactic deficit in agrammatism.

In their *closed-class hypothesis* of agrammatism, Bradley, Garrett and Zurif (1980) propose that function words have a privileged role in the formation of syntactic structure, and that in agrammatism, difficulty in accessing function words causes problems in building syntactic structures. Marcus (1982) frames this closed-class hypothesis in terms of a computational parsing mechanism for sentence comprehension, and demonstrates how agrammatic speech may result from disruption to that computational system.

Saffran, Schwartz and Marin (1980a) propose a combination of syntactic and phonological factors in their explanation of agrammatism. These investigators argue that there is a dissociation between two separate processes: one a syntactic process involving word order and other sentence construction processes, and the other a 'morphological' process involving the finalization of phonological form, which affects the use of bound and free grammatical morphemes. Miceli et al. (1983) also posit impairments to both syntactic (sentence construction) and morphological (inflection and function word) processes. In a study of agrammatic production, Saffran, Schwartz and Marin (1980b) posit difficulties in the computation of syntactic argument structure in agrammatism, and propose that agrammatic patients are unable to map underlying semantic structure onto the 'noun-verb-noun' structure of a sentence.

Schwartz, Linebarger and Saffran (1985) explain both production and comprehension deficits in agrammatism with their *mapping hypothesis*, in which they argue that agrammatic patients are deficient in performing translations between sentence form and sentence meaning. Caramazza and Berndt (1985) offer what they term a *multicomponent* view of agrammatism, in which they focus on the loosely specified constellations of symptoms which typically characterize the disorder. In this approach, the authors describe four different symptom patterns, which involve word order, comprehension and grammatical marker deficits to varying degrees. The authors contend that there is no single explanation for the disorders, but suggest that several accounts are possible, all of which must take into account the specifically expressive nature of the disorder. Caplan (1985) argues that agrammatism may be characterized in terms of impoverished syntactic structures. Specifically, Caplan proposes that only major lexical category labelling, but not syntactic structure per se, is available to the agrammatic speaker.

Based on a cross-linguistic study of agrammatic speech in 14 languages, Menn and Obler (1990) conclude that the syntactic processing difficulties in agrammatic speech are the result of 'blurred' morphosyntactic markers in underlying sentence frames. These 'blurred' markers fail to properly specify which inflections and function words are to be inserted into final surface sentence forms. Goodglass (1990) suggests that the deficit in agrammatism is reducible to an access difficulty for the oral production of grammatical morphemes.

Grodzinsky (1990) proposes that agrammatic speakers produce an abstract S-structure (see, e.g., Chomsky 1981) which contains a complete set of phrase marker nodes (i.e., syntactic form class category markers), but that the nodes are not *lexically* specified (i.e., the nodes contain abstract grammatical feature marking but not actual 'words'). Since the lexical content of the nodes is unspecified, agrammatic speakers are subsequently unable to assign a phonological form to the nodes. Specifically mentioned by Grodzinsky among these non-lexical nodes are the agreement (Agr) and tense nodes under the INFL node. Since most inflections, grammatical function words and null anaphors are specified at the abstract S-structure level, according to Grodzinsky it is just those elements that are not produced by agrammatic aphasics.

What the preceding explanations of agrammatism have in common is that they posit the primary dysfunction to lie in syntactic representation or processing, and assume that the inflection deficit occurs as the result of a defective syntax.

Morphological Explanations of Agrammatism

Lapointe (1983) implicates a defective mophological component in his theory of agrammatism, arguing that omitted and spared elements are distinguished by morphological criteria. Lapointe adopts the word formation theory of Selkirk (1984), which provides structural criteria distinguishing three morphological classes: inflectional morphemes, derivational morphemes attached via word boundary suffixes (#), and derivational morphemes attached via morpheme boundary suffixes (+). Word boundary derivational affixation is nonproductive affixation (resulting in a form he terms the *minimal stem*). Word boundary inflectional affixation he considers to be productive affixation, occurring outside of the minimal stem. Morpheme boundary derivational affixation is non-productive, and occurs within the minimal stem.

Based on this framework, Lapointe proposes that the elements retained in agrammatism are just those stem-level items (of major categories) that are inserted into morphosyntactic structures during lexical insertion. In other words, Lapointe proposes that *minimal stems are retained in agrammatism.* Lapointe opts for a morphosyntactic rather than a purely morphological explanation, because he assumes that the functor deficit involves their use within syntactic contexts rather than their lexical storage and retrieval (c.f., e.g., Bradley, Garrett and Zurif 1980).

Miceli et al. (1983) and Saffran et al. (1980a) posit the dissociation of syntactic and morphological aspects of agrammatism, but both studies define 'morphological' somewhat loosely by including free grammatical morphemes (i.e., function words) in their definitions.

Regarding the possibility of a morphological deficit in agrammatism, it is worth noting that Grodzinsky's syntactic theory of agrammatism (1990, p. 60) predicts that there will be no deficit in derivational morphology or any other aspect of word formation not demonstrably related to syntax. Non-syntactic morphological processes are predicted to remain intact, according to Grodzinsky's theory.

One important fact about morphology that is seldom mentioned in discussions of agrammatism is that inflection errors *all necessarily involve complex word formation.* Because of the obvious syntactic problems associated with agrammatism, there is a tendency to consider all agrammatic inflection problems to be syntactic in origin. We should not, however, overlook the possibility that at least part of the inflection problem in agrammatism is due to difficulties in the construction of complex words per se. Given the unequivocal existence of a syntactic deficit in agrammatism, it is natural to expect the syntax to be deficient in specifying correct inflectional affixes. However, the portion of the inflection problem which is attributable to syntax is logically dissociable from a portion which may be attributed to the construction of words. In other words, syntax and word formation are two potentially independent sources of inflection error in agrammatism.

Investigators have generally not paid much attention to the formation of complex words in agrammatic speech[6], but non-inflectional word formation deficits nonetheless have been observed. These deficits have been noted in Italian (Badecker and Caramazza 1989), German (deBleser and Bayer 1985, 1990) and English (Libben 1990). These investigators found that complex

[6] A notable exception to this is Miceli et al. (1983), who observe that "Derivational morphology appears to be spared..." in their two mildly agrammatic Italian-speaking patients.

word formation errors do occur in agrammatism, and are based on the structural properties of the complex words.

Our investigation of aphasic Chinese speech should shed light on the issue of syntactic versus morphlogical factors in agrammatism. If it is true that the inflection deficit in agrammatism is solely syntactic in origin, then complex words in Chinese agrammatics should escape deficit, since complex word formation in Chinese is not demonstrably related to syntax[7]. Otherwise, the inflection deficit might be seen as involving a defective word formation component in addition to a defective syntax.

Phonological Explanations of Agrammatism

Kean (1977, 1980, 1982) proposes that agrammatism is due to a phonological deficit which affects syntactic structure. Kean's analysis assumes a broad interpretation of what constitutes phonology, and in fact relies on the use of syntactic criteria to determine word boundaries. According to Kean, word boundaries attach to the right and left of major syntactic phrase categories (noun, adjective and verb). Following this operation, Kean defines a *phonological word* as any string which itself contains no word boundary, and claims that phonological words are retained in agrammatism. *Phonological clitics* are those items attached to phonological words via word boundaries, and are posited to be just those items omitted in agrammatic speech. In addition, Saffran, Schwartz and Marin (1980a) also consider agrammatism to be partially attributable to a phonological deficit (see page 6).

1.2.2 Linguistic Modularity

A common assumption in cognitive science is that the different cognitive faculties are independent computational systems, or 'cognitive modules' (Fodor 1983[8]). This 'modularity hypothesis' extends to the linguistic system (see, e.g., Levelt 1989, pp. 14-22), which comprises autonomous components representing the different linguistic capabilities (e.g., phonological encoding, word formation, syntactic structure formation). The linguistic components are posited to possess certain common properties which characterize their operation. They are highly ***task-specific*** (i.e., the types of operations they perform are limited) and take *characteristic I/O* (Levelt 1989, p. 15). This means that modular input and output occurs in a form which is maximally restricted, and specific to a given component.

[7]Possible exceptions to this are discussed in section 2.3.11.

[8]Fodor posits the perceptual systems ***plus language*** (p. 44) as candidates for modular systems.

Components are posited to be *informationally encapsulated*, i.e., they exchange information only at the point of component I/O, and their internal processes are minimally affected either by 'executive control', or by the operation of other components[9]. Component-internal processes are *automatic* and *reflex-like*, and not subject to intention or conscious awareness. This makes component-internal processes very fast and efficient, but inflexible and difficult to alter.

Linebarger (1989, 1990) considers the nature of speech deficits in aphasia as evidence supporting the hypothesis of linguistic system modularity. Linebarger makes a convincing case that the selective loss and preservation of lexical, syntactic and semantic capabilities in aphasic patients indicates that these capabilities are under separate, modular control. Caramazza and Berndt (1985) also use a modular approach in their analysis of aphasic speech, proposing that agrammatism is a *multicomponent deficit* which reflects the structure of the various components implicated in sentence processing. Like Linebarger, Caramazza and Berndt consider the symptoms identified in agrammatism to be evidence that independent functional systems are implicated in sentence processing.

Unless the cooccurrence of language deficits that constitutes aphasia syndromes is merely random, the syndromes must be explicable in terms of unifying, non-random factors. The modular linguistic system, with its set of self-contained but interacting components, is a plausible candidate in the search for such factors.

Fractionation of Components

If we assume the existence of autonomous linguistic components, there are different possible ways to conceive of linguistic system breakdown in aphasia. For example, damage could extend across component 'boundaries', affecting processes in different components. Alternatively, damage could result in the *fractionation* of components along linguistically (or, psycholinguistically) significant lines, resulting in the total and selective disruption of one or more components. As it turns out, such fractionation along component boundary lines seldom occurs (see discussion in Caramazza and Berndt, 1985).

---

[9] Fodor's focus is on the unavailability of module-internal information to *central consciousness* (1983, p. 55). However, this information is also posited to be relatively inaccessible to *other modules* (see discussion in Levelt 1989, pp. 276-282). As an example, consider the Lexical Integrity Hypothesis (LIH, Jackendoff 1972). According to the LIH, the syntax may not refer to the internal structure of a word ('once a word, always a word'). Intermediate stages of word representation or processing are therefore inaccessible to syntactic operations, meaning that the syntactic component has no access to the intermediate representations within the word formation component.

1.2.3 Validity of the Notion 'Syndrome' in Aphasia

Some investigators have called into question the theoretical and functional validity of aphasia syndromes (including agrammatism). They argue that the syndromes are neither functionally nor cognitively defined (e.g., Badecker and Caramazza 1985, Marshall 1982), and that the choice of subjects according to cooccurrence of clinical symptoms results in a clinically determined selection bias (e.g., Badecker and Caramazza, ibid.). The latter investigators suggest that subject selection for a given study should proceed according to symptoms affecting a specific cognitive component or nexus of cognitive components, rather than on the constellations of symptoms that traditionally define the major syndromes.

The present investigation relies upon linguistically-defined criteria in selecting subjects to avoid clinical bias based on a pre-defined syndrome profile. Furthermore, we investigate the specifically cognitive basis of the syndromes by exploring the nature of the relationship between the aphasia syndromes and the modular structure of the cognitive linguistic system.

1.2.4 Non-distinctiveness of Syndromes

Some investigators have argued that the speech deficits observed in the classical aphasia syndromes have more similarities than differences, with processing or other factors accounting for the differences. Heeschen (1985) argues against a distinction between paragrammatic (Wernicke's) and agrammatic (Broca's) speech, arguing that agrammatics avoid sources of potential trouble, while paragrammatics do not. Bates and Wulfeck (1989a) offer a similar proposal, arguing that the only difference between the fluent and non-fluent groups is in sentence planning. They suggest that non-fluent speakers attempt to avoid grammatical complexity, while fluent speakers 'barge ahead', trying unsuccessfully to produce complex constructions. During the course of our investigation, we will survey the Chinese data with an eye toward determining whether significant differences between the syndromes do in fact exist.

1.2.5 Representation versus Processing

Language production and comprehension is an exceedingly complicated affair that undoubtedly involves not only abstract knowledge of language but also the on-line implementation of that knowledge. The ideal explanation of agrammatism may involve the interaction of linguistic knowledge structures and the psycholinguistic processing mechanisms that operate on those knowledge structures in real time. Zurif and Blumstein (1978) make the point that the representation of linguistic knowledge and its on-line processing may not be neurologically independent. Levelt (1989, p. 17) states that processes and representations cannot be studied independent of one another, since the kind of processing algorithm we assume places theoretical limits on the types of representations that we posit.

The approach followed here is to consider how the linguistic system could suffer a generalized deficit which would result in the types of problems seen in agrammatism, while remaining agnostic on the issue of whether the deficit necessarily involves the distinction between processing and representation. Rizzi (1985) argues that a valuable approach toward the analysis of pathological language is to

> determine whether the relevant data can be organized into natural classes in terms of modular structure, that is to say, whether properties of pathological behavior can be deduced from the theory by assuming impairment in one or more modules (pp. 154-155).

I propose to follow this approach, in which a distinction between independent processing and representation factors is considered likely but for the moment is not assumed. It may be possible to offer the most optimal explanations of language deficit by making explicit reference to the distinction between knowledge structures and their implementation. If such a distinction falls out naturally upon consideration of the data and serves to explain the observed phenomena, then we have good empirical justification for enriching the theory in this way.

Also, we must keep in mind realistic, psychologically plausible models of linguistic representation that may be used in conjunction with processing models to come up with a viable overall model of speech production and aphasia. For more on the issue of representation versus processing in aphasia, see Sproat (1985) and Kean (1982).

1.3 Language Structure Reconsidered

Our observations on Chinese aphasia will provide us with a different perspective on linguistic structure in general, and on the structure of the Chinese language in particular. The form that language takes when it malfunctions provides insights into its structural properties. In the case of Chinese, these insights may well differ from traditional views of grammar.

1.3.1 The Value of 'System-External' Evidence

For the past several decades, a major goal of linguistic science has been to determine the form of knowledge that represents human natural language competence. In this context, native speaker intuition is considered primary data, and the structure of language is seen as the abstract form the grammar of a language must take to account for the fact that children acquire it so quickly with exposure to limited data.

It is often assumed that linguistic system-internal evidence (i.e., that evidence which is adduced from the grammatical system of the language) represents a purer form of language competence than does system-external evidence (i.e., that evidence which is adduced from language acquisition, aphasia, speech errors, etc.). The argument is that in considering only system-internal evidence, 'performance' factors such as memory, psychological processing, false starts and restarts, fatigue and so forth are factored out, yielding a more perfect representation of the language competence in the mind of the speaker.

As Comrie (1990) points out, choices between competing linguistic analyses that are undecidable on the basis of purely internal evidence may be resolved with system-external evidence. When linguistic analyses reach the point of diminishing returns using system-internal evidence, it is wise to shift the approach and consider alternative forms of language data. In the present work, evidence from aphasic speech is used to constrain theories of linguistic structure.

1.3.2 Deficit as Evidence of Structure

The structure and composition of a vase may not be apparent until it is broken. The performance of a computer operating system gone awry due to a defective hardware circuit may give us information about the design structure of that system. System abnormalities are often used to infer characteristics of system structure. In cell biology, information about the structure of normal cells is often obtained by considering the characteristics of pathological cells. The occurrence of brain tumors that cause visual system deficits provides information on how visual information is processed in the normal brain. In reading psychology, the existence of different reading pathways (such as the 'phonetic' versus 'whole word' pathways) was discovered by investigating dyslexia and other reading disorders. Likewise, aspects of language structure may be inferred by analyzing abnormal speech. One example is the analysis of speech errors (e.g., Fromkin 1972, Cutler 1980, Garrett 1980, Dell 1984). Another example is the work of Kean (1977, 1980, 1982), who explained language deficits in Broca's aphasia with a theoretical concept—the phonological word—which cut across language components as traditionally defined by structural linguistic analysis, offering a new perspective on language structure.

If a goal of linguistics is to determine the structure of language and uncover the nature of human natural language competence, then the analysis of aphasic speech fits neatly into the research paradigm. The use of both normal and dysfunctional language is likely to provide converging evidence supporting theories of linguistic structure.

1.4 Summary of Goals

Natural language provides us with a unique perspective into how the human mind is structured. The form language takes when it malfunctions shows us the possible ways the system can go wrong—insights which may not be available through observation of the intact system. The evidence from Chinese is particularly valuable because it is so different from languages upon which traditional theories of aphasia are based. Our investigation of aphasic Chinese speech will reveal whether aphasia syndromes as presently conceived are a universally correct characterization of language deficits which occur following brain damage. Our investigation may also provide new insights into the linguistic structure of Chinese: when the Chinese language breaks down, does it do so along the lines assumed by traditional grammatical analyses of Chinese? Or will the types of deficits observed suggest an analysis more akin to, for example, Indo-European languages? The answers to these questions constitute valuable and interesting contributions to the fields of linguistics and cognitive science.

1.4.1 Plan of Exposition

Following this introductory chapter, Chapter 2 provides the reader with enough background on the Chinese language to understand the description of language deficits that follows. Chapter 3 contains a detailed linguistic description and analysis of deficits in the speech of four aphasic speakers of Chinese. In the final chapter, a set of speech characteristics helpful for aphasia diagnosis is offered for Chinese, and an explanation of aphasia syndromes based on the theory of linguistic modularity is proposed.

Chapter 2

A Brief Mandarin Grammar

Different forms of the Chinese language are spoken throughout China, ranging from the Mandarin common in the north to the Cantonese spoken in the south. Although linguistically they may be considered different languages rather than dialects (because they are mutually unintelligible), they are usually referred to as 'dialects' dialects because they are historically related, share a common script and exist within one unified political entity. The Mandarin dialect is the *lingua franca* of China, since it is nearly universally understood and spoken throughout the country. Mandarin itself has many local varieties, or 'subdialects', with the major differences being in phonology and lexicon. The four patients in this study (presented in Chapter 3) are speakers of different subdialects of Mandarin. Where their speech differs from the description of standard Mandarin presented in this chapter, those differences will be pointed out and explained if they are relevant to the analysis.

The following description of Mandarin grammar is intended to give readers enough information to understand the findings presented in subsequent chapters. Such a treatment necessarily glosses over many important details of the language and sidesteps many interesting theoretical questions on Chinesegrammar. For those who want a more detailed account of Chinese grammar, it is suggested that Li and Thompson (1981) and Chao (1968) be consulted. For a theoretical account of Mandarin phonology the reader is referred to Cheng (1973) for segmental phonology, Shen (1990) for tonal phonology, and Bao (1990) and Duanmu (1990) for syllable structure. For theoretical aspects of word formation in Mandarin, see Thompson (1973),

Li, Yafei (1990), or Packard (1990b). For more information on theoretical Chinese syntax see Huang (1982a), or Li, Audrey Y-H. (1990). For more general information on all aspects of the Chinese language, the reader is referred to Norman (1988), Ramsey (1987) or DeFrancis (1984).

2.1 Phonology: The Mandarin Sound System

A discussion of the sound system of Mandarin is important for the description of aphasia in Chinese. I will discuss different aspects of segmental phonology (consonants and vowels), tonal phonology and syllable structure.

2.1.1 Segmental Phonemes

Phonetically, Standard Mandarin has twelve vowels and 22 consonants[1]. In the consonants (as seen in Table 2.1) there are labial, dental, apical, palatal, retroflex and velar series. An interesting fact about the Mandarin

labial	p	p'	m	f		b	p	m	f	
dental	t	t'	n		l	d	t	n		l
apical	c	c'		s		z	c		s	
palatal	tφ	tφ'		φ		j	q		x	
retroflex	c̣	c̣'		ṣ	ṛ	zh	ch		sh	r
velar	k	k'	ŋ	x		g	k	ng	h	

Table 2.1: Mandarin Consonants: Phonetic Values (left) and *Pinyin* Equivalents (right).

consonantal system is that the palatal series is in complementary distribution with three other phonetic series: the apicals, retroflexes and velars. Palatal consonants only occur before high front vowels, while the apical, retroflex and velar consonants never do.

The vowel system (see Table 2.2) phonetically consists of five high vowels ([i], [ü], [ɿ][2], [ʅ][3] and [u]), five mid vowels ([e], [ə][4], [ɤ][5], [o] and [ε]), and two low vowels ([a] and [ɑ]).

[1] Much of this discussion is based on Cheng (1973).

[2] [ɿ] represents the high front unrounded apical vowel, as in the word for 'four' *si*.

[3] [ʅ] represents the vowel that occurs with retroflex initials.

[4] [ə] represents schwa.

[5] [ɤ] represents the back mid unrounded vowel as in *de* 'virtue'.

ı	ɩ	i	ü				u
		e			ə	ɣ	o
			ɛ				
				a		ɑ	

Table 2.2: Mandarin Vowels

Pinyin orthography[6] represents a phonemicized version of this vowel system. In *pinyin*, there are three high vowels: /i/ (which represents [i], [ɩ] and [ı] in different phonetic environments), /u/ and /ü/; two mid vowels: /e/ (which represents [e], [ə], [ɣ] and [ɛ] in different environments) and /o/; and one low vowel /a/ (which represents [a] and [ɑ] in different environments).

2.1.2 Tonal Phonemes

Mandarin Chinese is a lexical tone language, meaning that a small number of basic pitch contour patterns ('tones') are phonologically contrastive, and therefore distinguish lexical items. Mandarin has four such lexical tones: high-level (*shū* 'book'), mid-rising (*shú* 'ripe'), low-rising (*shǔ* 'mouse') and high-falling (*shù* 'tree'). These lexical tones are considered to be associated with the nuclear vowel of the syllable (see 2.1.3 below). An interesting question about the production of these tones in aphasic speech is whether these 'tonal phonemes' are affected in the same way non-tonal phonemes are affected, i.e., do aphasic Chinese speakers make tonal mistakes, just as they improperly produce consonants and vowels? This question arises because certain aspects of pitch production have been thought to be relatively spared in certain categories of aphasia (see e.g., Danly and Shapiro 1982, Gandour 1987).

Lexical tones change their phonetic shape in connected speech. The changes involve variation in length, amplitude and fundamental frequency (F_0) value. For example, in normal connected speech, the maximum F_0 value of all tones is reduced, and the minimum value is raised, resulting in a narrower F_0 'envelope'. Another example is in questions formed with the sentence-final question particle *ma* (see examples 2.44-2.45). In this type of question, the F_0 value of the entire sentence is raised (see, e.g., Shen 1990 and Kratochvil 1968).

[6] When not referring specifically to phonetic forms, *pinyin* romanized Chinese is used throughout the book.

Considering other aspects of F_0 in speech production, Mandarin Chinese may be considered more a 'stress-timed' than a 'syllable-timed' language. This means that syllables are produced with different degrees of prominence (marked by differences in F_0, amplitude or duration)[7], and these prominence relations determine the timing or cadence with which words, phrases and sentences are produced (see, e.g., Selkirk 1984, p. 41; Hoequist 1983).

2.1.3 Syllable Structure

The structure of the Mandarin syllable, very simple when compared to that of many other languages (e.g., English), is depicted in linear form in Figure 2.1, and in hierarchical form in Figure 2.2. A Mandarin syllable may

(c)(g)v(s)

Figure 2.1: Mandarin Syllable Structure (linear)

minimally consist of a vowel ('nuclear vowel') and one of the four contrastive tones, e.g., *wù* (phonetically [ù]) 'fog'. The nuclear vowel (*v* in Figures 2.1 and 2.2), is, together with the associated tone, the only obligatory part of

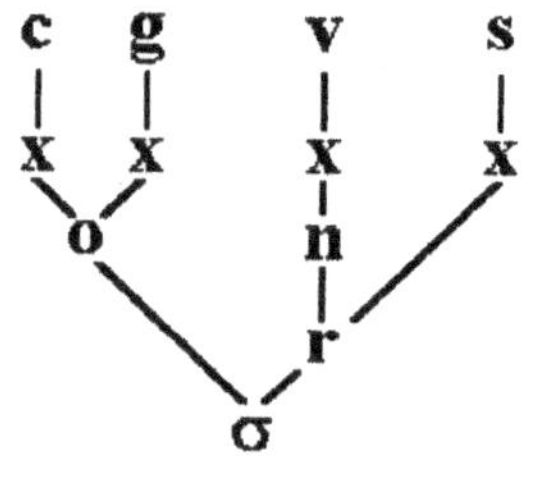

Figure 2.2: Mandarin Syllable Structure (hierarchical)

the syllable. Optionally occurring as constituents of the Mandarin syllable are a syllable-initial consonant (*c* in Figures 2.1 and 2.2), a medial glide,

[7] As Richard Sproat points out, this is more true in the northern than southern subdialects of Mandarin.

which occurs between the initial consonant and the nuclear vowel[8] (*g* in Figures 2.1 and 2.2), and a syllable-final, sonorant (i.e., either a vowel or the apical nasal consonant *n*), 'coda' (seen as *s* in Figures 2.1 and 2.2). Any of the vowels may occur as nuclear vowels, only [i], [ü] and [u] may occur as medial glides, and only [i] and [u] may occur as coda vowels.

The simple structure of the Mandarin syllable plus the fact that Mandarin consonants and vowels are relatively few in number, together mean that the set of possible syllable shapes in Mandarin is somewhat restricted in size. There are only about 1200 distinct syllable shapes in Mandarin, and only 400 or so if the four tones are not taken into account. This means that the occurrence of homophones (for monosyllabic words) is much more common in Mandarin than in most other languages.

For aphasic speech analysis, an important practical consequence of the restricted set of syllable shapes is that if a syllable with the proper form is produced, it is more difficult than in other languages to tell whether the produced form is a real word or not. This is because (unlike, e.g., in English) almost all of the 1200 syllables in Mandarin are possible words. Therefore our analysis must rely heavily on context, and precise criteria are needed to identify paraphasias, jargon and neologism in Mandarin (see Chapter 3).

2.2 Morphology: Word Formation in Mandarin

Chinese often has been described as 'monosyllabic', with the false implication that most words in the language are one syllable long[9]. Monosyllabic words *are*, however, common, with most of the words in some classes (e.g., particles, determiners, classifiers (see 2.2.1) and prepositions (also known as 'coverbs'; see 2.3.1) consisting of only one syllable. However, most words in Mandarin are *complex*, i.e., more than one syllable/morpheme long (Kra-

[8] The analysis of Mandarin syllable structure depicted in Figure 2.2 follows Duanmu (1990) in representing the pre-nuclear glide as under the domination of the onset. This is different from traditional analyses of the Chinese syllable, nearly all of which consider the pre-nuclear medial glide to be part of the *rime* (*r* in Figure 2.2). Two reasons for associating the glide more closely with the onset than with the rime (Duanmu, personal communication) are first, that the pre-nuclear glide has a relatively short duration in the presence of an initial consonant, but has the duration of a regular segment when there is no initial consonant (Howie, 1976). This follows if the glide is part of the onset. Second, the glide does not change the 'weight' of the rime for stress and tone purposes.

[9] This is probably because individual Chinese written characters are often (wrongly) considered to be individual words, and characters virtually all represent one syllable.

tochvil 1968 p. 64)[10]. The term 'morphosyllabic' is accurate, since most morphemes in Mandarin consist of one syllable and vice-versa (see discussion in DeFrancis, 1984).

Complex words are formed by combining morphemes through *affixation* and *compounding*. Affixation is the *productive* attachment of a *bound* morpheme which occupies a *consistent position* in a word, and results in a *consistent change in meaning*. Some examples of prefixes are *ke-* '-able', *dan-* 'uni-', *shuang-* 'bi-', *wěi-* 'pseudo-' and *wèi-* 'micro-'. Some examples of suffixes include *-jia* '-ist' or '-ian', *-men* human pluralizer, *-xing* '-ness' or '-ity', *-hua* '-ify' or '-ize', *-zhe* '-ing', *-de* '-ly', *-guo* a verbal aspect marker indicating experience, and *-le*, a verbal aspect marker indicating completion.

Compounding is the most common word formation process in Mandarin. A compound is a word composed of morphemes which do not fit the criteria for affixation listed above[11]. Compounds are formed by combining morphemes from virtually every form class category in many different orders. However, the rules used to form compounds differ greatly in their productivity. Furthermore, compounds are not equally subject to certain grammatical operations and their constituent morphemes are not bound to an equivalent degree.

For compound nouns the most common form is $[\text{N-N}]_N$ as in *pibao* (leather-bag, 'wallet'), *fumu* (father-mother, 'parents') and *niunai* (cow-milk, 'milk'). For compound verbs the most common form is $[\text{V-V}]_V$, as in *xihuan* (like-joy, 'like'), *jiejue* (dissolve-decide, 'solve') and *taolun* (discuss-talk, 'discuss'). Most compound nouns have a noun as the right hand member of the compound ($[\text{X-N}]_N$), and most compound verbs have a verb as the left hand member of the compound ($[\text{V-X}]_V$). For this reason, compound nouns may be considered canonically right-headed (see Packard 1990b), and compound verbs may be considered canonically left-headed (see Li, Y-F. 1990, Packard 1990b). Compounds which do not conform to these canonical headedness conventions receive special treatment in the word formation grammar of Mandarin (see 2.2.1 below, and also Packard 1990b).

A special type of compound verb in Mandarin is the *resultative compound*. In a resultative compound, the first member of the compound is a regular active verb, and the second member is a verbal ending which

[10] This was probably not true for the classical Chinese language (e.g., the Chinese spoken during the Han dynasty at the turn of the millenium). At that time, most words probably were one syllable long.

[11] I will follow Chinese linguistic tradition and use the term *compound* for the class of words described here, even though the more common meaning of compound in linguistics is 'a word formed from two (or more) free forms'. In the traditional Chinese usage of the term, the constituents of a compound are not necessarily free forms.

indicates the result of the action of the first verb. The second member is from a closed class of (usually active) verbs, e.g., *wan* 'to finish', *dong* 'to understand' or *dao* 'to arrive/attain'. Thus *kan* 'to see' becomes *kanwan* 'to finish seeing' or *kandong* 'to understand through seeing', and *zhao* 'to seek' becomes *zhaodao* 'to find'. The insertion of a 'potential affix', either *-de-* 'attain' or *-bu-* 'not', between the two members of a resultative compound indicates the ability or inability respectively of the verbal action to take place (e.g, *zhaodao* 'to find', but *zhaodedao* 'to be able to find', and *zhaobudao* 'to be unable to find').

Mandarin words are not the structurally simple monoliths they are often portrayed as. Rather, they contain significant structural complexity which affects their operation within the grammar. There are major differences among classes of complex words in their ability to undergo certain grammatical operations. Also, there are differences in the productivity of word formation processes, and in the word-forming productivity of individual morphemes. In addition, Chinese words vary considerably in the strength with which their constituent morphemes are bound together.

Most treatments of word formation in Mandarin (e.g., Lu 1964, Chao 1968, Thompson 1973, Li and Thompson 1981) are descriptive accounts of what processes combine which types of elements to form words of various form classes. Analyses such as these generally had not addressed the abovementioned productivity differences and cooccurrence restrictions. They are, however, accounted for by applying the theory of Lexical Phonology and Morphology to Mandarin word formation.

2.2.1 An LPM Analysis of Mandarin

The basic insight of Lexical Phonology and Morphology (LPM; see, e.g., Kiparsky 1982; Halle and Mohanan 1985; Mohanan 1986) is that word formation rules fall into classes based on rule type, the nature of the morphemes used in the rules, and the classes of phonological rules which apply[12]. These rule classes are ordered in the lexicon according to order of operation. This notion of ordered blocks of word formation rules is formalized by positing a lexicon composed of hierarchically-ordered *levels* or *strata* within which the different word formation processes occur. Words are 'built up' by moving from earlier 'lower' levels where rules are least productive and word constituents are most tightly bound, to later 'higher' levels where the rules are highly productive and word constituents are least tightly bound. Words pass from one lexical level to the next, with processes

[12] We will not focus on the phonological aspects of LPM here. For a discussion of the phonological aspects of LPM in Mandarin, the reader is referred to Chan (1984) and Packard (1992).

at any given level being unavailable at subsequent levels. In this way, certain classes of words are not subject to certain word formation processes.

For example, in English there are three different classes of affix: class 1 derivational affixes, class 2 derivational affixes and inflectional affixes. Briefly, class 1 derivational affixes (such as *-ity*) attach to stems, often change the form class of the words they affix to and often change the stress pattern (e.g., áctive → actívity). Class 2 derivational affixes (such as *-less*) often change a word's form class, but not its stress pattern (actívity → actívityless). Inflectional affixes (such as *-s*) change neither form class nor stress pattern (actívity → actívities).

These three types of affix apply to words in a given order, namely, class 1 affixes followed by class 2 affixes and then inflectional affixes. For example, the class 1 affix *-ate* must attach before the attachment of the class 2 affix *de-* : active → activate → deactivate, *versus* active → *deactive → deactivate. In the same way, the affixation of third person singular *-s* may not precede the affixation of *-ate*, or the incorrect form results: active → activate → activates, *versus* active → *actives → *activesate.

The order in which these three classes of affix apply to words is correlated with their productivity as word-forming operations. Inflection (e.g., *-s, -ed, -ing*) applies nearly without exception to all (regular) words, and hence is the most productive. Class 2 affixes (e.g., *re-, de-, -less, -ful*) are less productive than inflection (e.g., *hateful* is fine but **loveful* is not), but highly productive nonetheless. Class 1 affixes (e.g., *a-, in-, -tion, -ity*) are the least productive, disallowing rule application in many cases: active → activity, but abortive → *abortivity; suck → suction, but buck → *buction; frequent → infrequent, but rare → *inrare.

The order and productivity of the affixes are also correlated with the strength with which they are bound to the words they form. Thus, the inflectional suffixes *-s* and *-ed* intuitively seem less strongly bound to a word than the derivational suffixes *-ity* and *-tion*.

The proposed structure of the Mandarin lexicon analyzed in an LPM framework is as follows (see Packard 1990b for a complete version of the theory). At level I (the 'deepest' or 'innermost' level, analogous to the level of class 1 derivational affixes in English) are the words which are formed using the least productive of the word formation processes in Mandarin. These words have only vaguely discernable or no internal structure, such as the conjunctions *suiran* 'although', *keshi* 'however', and the adverbials *yiqian* 'before' and *yihou* 'after'. Also at this level are words that belong to the class of non-productive resultatives (Chao 1968, p. 435), and also complex words that are *exocentric*[13]. At level II (roughly akin to the level of

[13] A word is considered exocentric if its form class does not match the form class of

class 2 derivational affixes in English) are compounding and affixation processes that are more highly productive, such as regular (i.e., non-exocentric) nominal compounding, the affixation of classifiers to numbers and determiners (see 2.3.2), and regular resultative verb compound formation. Also at this level are the resultative verb affixation process, and the affixation of nominal suffixes such as *-zi*, *-r* and *-tou*. At level III are all regular and stative verb compounding processes, and also the question formation reduplication and affixation processes. Finally, level IV contains the most productive affixation processes in Mandarin, such as the continuation suffix *-zhe*, the experiential aspect marker *-guo*, the perfective aspect marker *-le*, the verbal suffixes *buliao* and *deliao* which indicate inability and ability respectively, and the human plural marker *-men*. The attachment of aspect makers like *-guo* and *-zhe* in the lexicon is supported by Huang's (1982a, p. 165) analysis, according to which these markers are suffixed to verbs in the lexical component of the Mandarin grammar.

2.2.2 LPM as an Approach to Morphological Deficit

The LPM analysis of Mandarin presented here was undertaken in order to demonstrate the richness of Mandarin word formation data, and also to account for Mandarin compounding deficits in aphasia, since LPM had shown promise in explaining aphasic affixation deficits in other languages.

In a study on derivational affix repetition by English-speaking agrammatics, Kehayia, Caplan and Piggott (1984) found differences which they said suggested a level-ordered representation of the productive component of morphology. Futter and Bub (1986) first proposed using the level-ordered theory of LPM to account for some complex morphological reading errors found by Patterson (1980). The authors proposed a disturbance whereby the lower in the lexical level hierarchy the complex word was formed, the more the word would be subject to deficit. deBleser and Bayer (1990) used Futter and Bub's proposal to analyze morphological reading errors in a German patient, and found that the theory had rather more predictive power when the hierarchy was reversed, viz., that the words were more prone to error the shallower in the lexicon they are formed. deBleser and Bayer suggested this might be due to the 'feeding relation' postulated in LPM, whereby lower lexical levels feed into upper ones, but not vice-versa.

deBleser and Bayer's findings comport with the results of Miceli and Caramazza (1988; see also Badecker and Caramazza 1989), who found that inflectional errors (formed at level IV in LPM) far outnumber derivational errors (formed at levels I and II) in an aphasic Italian patient. Caramazza

---

the morpheme in canonically-defined head position; see Packard (1990b).

and his colleagues interpreted their findings as evidence that inflectional and derivational word formation processes are both located in the lexicon, and that they constitute autonomous lexical subcomponents. Miceli and Caramazza specifically suggested the theory of LPM as a plausible candidate for formally distinguishing inflectional and derivational morphology as two autonomous subcomponents of the lexicon. Previous theoretical work on agrammatism by Kean (e.g., 1982, p. 190) had predicted that inflectional and derivational morphological processes would be differentially affected in agrammatic aphasic speakers, with derivational processes being less subject to deficit.

Therefore, an LPM analysis of Mandarin word formation was included in this investigation because the theory accounts for Mandarin word formation facts, and because it had shown promise in explaining morphological deficit in other languages.

2.3 Syntax

I will first present information on basic sentence constituent order, followed by descriptions of noun and verb phrases. I will then discuss other syntactic phenomena, including derived word orders and theoretical issues.

2.3.1 Sentence Word Order

The basic order of constituents in a simple Chinese sentence is subject-verb-object, with nearly all sentential modifiers (with some exceptions, such as sentence-final aspect marking) occurring between the subject and the verb,

[SUBJECT] [MODIFIER] [VERB] [OBJECT]

Figure 2.3: Mandarin Word Order

as schematized in Figure 2.3.

Included under the rubric 'sentential modifiers' are all adverbial phrases: time (2.1), place (2.2), frequency (2.3), scope (2.4), negation (2.5) and manner (2.6).

2.1	Ni	shier dian	chi	zhongfan.
	you	twelve o'clock	eat	middle-food

You eat lunch at noon.

2.2	Ni	zai jia[14]	chi	zhongfan.
	you	at home	eat	middle-food

You eat lunch at home.

2.3	Ni	chang	chi	zhongfan.
	you	often	eat	middle-food

You often eat lunch.

2.4	Nimen	dou	chi	zhongfan.
	you-PL	all	eat	middle-food

You all eat lunch.

2.5	Ni	bu	chi	zhongfan.
	you	not	eat	middle-food

You don't eat lunch.

2.6	Ni	manmande	chi	zhongfan.
	you	slow-slow-ADV	eat	middle-food

Eat lunch slowly.

Also occurring in the 'sentential modifier' position are *coverbs* (2.7-2.11) and auxiliary verbs (2.12 and 2.13). Coverbs are words used to express location, direction, instrumentality, and other modes of predicate action. They usually translate into English as prepositions. However, unlike English prepositions, some coverbs may function as the main verb of a

$$[[\text{Coverb}]\ [\text{NP}]]_{CP}$$

Figure 2.4: Coverbial Phrase Structure

sentence[15]. Coverbs possess properties that cause them to pattern exclusively neither with verbs nor with prepositions (see Ross 1991, McCawley 1992). The (surface) structure[16] of the coverbial phrase (CP) is a coverb followed by a noun phrase (NP) indicating location, direction, etc., as seen in Figure 2.4. The examples below illustrate the use of coverbial phrases

[14] This is actually a coverbial phrase, discussed below.

[15] McCawley (1992) argues that most coverbs are prepositions, and that few coverbs can actually pass certain tests of verbhood.

[16] More complex, abstract structures have been posited. See, e.g., Ross (1991) and A. Y-H. Li (1990).

2.7 Wo [dui haizi]$_{CP}$ shuo hua.
I toward children speak speech
I talk to the children.

2.8 Wo [zai zher]$_{CP}$ chi zhongfan.
I at here eat middle-food
I eat lunch here.

2.9 Wo [yong kuaizi]$_{CP}$ chi fan.
I use chopsticks eat food
I eat with chopsticks.

2.10 Wo [gei ta]$_{CP}$ zuo fan.
I give him make food
I cook for him.

2.11 Wo [gen ta]$_{CP}$ chi fan.
I with him eat food
I eat with him.

indicating direction (2.7), location (2.8), instrument (2.9) benefaction (2.10) and accompaniment (2.11). The structural relation of the coverbial phrase to the main verb phrase (A. Y-H. Li 1990, p. 6), is seen in Figure 2.5 (c.f., Ross 1991, p. 93).

$$[[[\mathrm{COVERB}]\ [\mathrm{NP}]]_{CP}\ \mathrm{V}\ \mathrm{O}]_{VP}$$

Figure 2.5: Verb and Coverbial Phrase Structure

The usage of auxiliary verbs is straightforward, and is seen in 2.12 and 2.13 below.

2.12 Ta keyi chi zhongfan.
he may eat middle-food
He may eat lunch.

2.13 Ta yao chi zhongfan.
he want eat middle-food
He wants to eat lunch.

An example of a sentence containing time, scope and coverbial modifiers, and an auxiliary verb, is seen in 2.14. The order of elements within the modifier slot is generally quite free, with the few restrictions on their order largely a matter of semantic coherence.

2.14	Women	[xianzai]$_{time}$	[dou]$_{scope}$	[keyi]$_{aux}$	[gen	ni]$_{cp}$	qu.
	we	now	all	may	with	you	go

We may all go with you now.

One fairly rigid restriction, however, is that if a sentence has a coverbial phrase, it must generally occupy the rightmost position in the modifier slot (i.e., directly to the left of the verb). The negative marker *bu* negates any constituent in this slot by occurring to its left (except for time adverbials, which are usually not directly negated).

2.3.2 Complex Nominals

A complex noun phrase (NP) may consist of a bare noun (N), a noun plus a 'quantifying' modifier (e.g., a determiner like *nei* 'that' and/or a number), and a noun with a 'descriptive' modifier[17] (such as a possessive noun, an adjective, or a complex predicate acting as a relative clause; see 2.19-2.23)[18]. When a 'quantifying' modifier is used, a *classifier*[19] is required.

A classifier is a bound morpheme[20] which often matches certain semantic features of the noun it modifies. Classifiers by themselves do not normally occur as independent words (and therefore are not considered function words per se), but they do form function words by combining with 'quantifying' modifiers in the lexicon (at level II, see 2.2.1)[21]. There are well over one hundred different classifiers, but by far the most common, 'general-purpose' classifier is *-ge* (see examples in 2.15-2.18 below; for comprehensive lists, see Chao 1968 or Li and Thompson 1981).

2.15	sange	xuesheng
	three-C	student

three students

2.16	zheitiao	lu
	this-C	road

this road

[17]For possible orderings of these modifiers, see Figure 2.6, and also examples 2.24 and 2.25.

[18]As Jim McCawley points out, a noun by itself or together with a modifier makes up an $\bar{N}$.

[19]The term *classifier* includes both classifiers per se (which match salient perceptual properties of the modified noun) and *measures* (which refer to the quantity of the noun). For a further discussion of this distinction, see Tai and Wang (1990).

[20]NB: it is bound to the preceding quantifier, not the noun it modifies.

[21]For this reason, in the descriptions of aphasic speech that occur in Chapter 3, the use of classifiers is discussed both under word formation (because they are important word forming elements) and in the section on syntax under 'function words' (because when used in conjunction with quantifiers they form function words, and constitute important constituents of complex noun phrase syntax).

2.17 neidong fangzi
that-C house
that house

2.18 neisantiao lu
that-three-C road
those three roads

Classifiers are almost completely redundant as grammatical elements, since their appearance is predicted by the occurrence of a noun plus a number and/or determiner, and because semantically classifiers either add no information or redundantly agree with semantic features of the noun they modify[22]. Classifiers are also required for the quantification of certain nouns in English, i.e., the so-called 'non-count' nouns (e.g., *one bread vs. one *loaf* of bread).

When a 'descriptive' modifier modifies a noun, the use of the prenominal modification marker *de* is generally required. As seen in the following examples, the modifier may be a noun (2.19), a stative verb[23] (2.20), a verb phrase (2.21), a coverbial phrase (2.22) or a sentence (2.23).

2.19 $[\text{wo}]_N$ de xuesheng
I MOD student
my student(s)

2.20 $[\text{hao}]_{SV}$ de xuesheng
good MOD student
good student(s)

2.21 $[\text{xihuan wo}]_{VP}$ de xuesheng
like I MOD student
students that like me

2.22 $[\text{zai zher}]_{CV}$ de xuesheng
at here MOD student
students that are here

2.23 $[\text{wo xihuan}]_S$ de xuesheng
I like MOD student
students that I like

[22]Richard Sproat points out that since classifiers must match semantic features of the nouns they modify, they are therefore the closest thing that Mandarin has to morphological agreement, and so may be considered analogous to agreement morphology in inflecting languages. Tzeng et al. (1991) make the same point.

[23]See section 2.3.3.

Grammatically, *de* is usually optional when the modifying element is adjectival or in some cases when it marks inalienable possession or intimate association. Functionally, since the modifier usually immediately precedes the noun, the presence of *de* is somewhat redundant in marking the modification relationship, unless the modifying element is verbal in nature (i.e., a verb phrase as in 2.21, a coverbial phrase as in 2.22, or a 'sentence' as in 2.23).

The prenominal modification marker *de* is the most frequently-occurring word in Mandarin (Liu et al. 1975, Suen 1979). In addition, it is a grammatical function word par excellence, because it is functionally not only completely grammatical, but also quite redundant, as explained in the paragraph above. Also, *de* always takes weak stress, another prototypical characteristic of function words.

The prenominal modification structure with *de* may occur in ***headless*** form, i.e., without an overt lexical noun in head (modified) position. This happens when the nominal referent is clearly understood from context or is non- specific. For example, *haode xuesheng* (good-MOD student) means 'the good student', while *haode* ϕ (good-MOD ϕ) means 'the good one'.

The 'quantifying' noun phrase modifier may either precede or follow the 'descriptive' modifier. In the former case, the quantified amount is

$$[[\text{NUM}] \quad [\text{CLAS}] \quad [\text{modifier} + \text{de}] \quad [\text{NOUN}]]_{\bar{N}}$$

$$[[\text{modifier} + \text{de}] \quad [\text{NUM}] \quad [\text{CLAS}] \quad [\text{NOUN}]]_{\bar{N}}$$

Figure 2.6: Modifiers within a Complex Nominal

taken to be part of a larger set, while in the latter, the quantified amount is considered a set unto itself. Those two possible orderings are seen in Figure 2.6, and in examples 2.24 and 2.25 respectively.

2.24 $[[\text{san}]_{num}$ $[\text{kuai}]_{clas}$ $[\text{wode}]_{mod}$ $[\text{qian}]_{noun}]_{\bar{N}}$
three CLAS me-MOD money
three of my dollars

2.25 $[[\text{wode}]_{mod}$ $[\text{san}]_{num}$ $[\text{kuai}]_{clas}$ $[\text{qian}]_{noun}]_{\bar{N}}$
me-MOD three CLAS money
my three dollars

As in most languages, in Mandarin a sentence can act as a noun when it is embedded in a matrix sentence, occurring as an argument of certain verbs (such as 'believe' (*xiangxin*), 'know' *zhidao*, or 'want' *yao*). A. Y-H. Li (1990) motivates a distinction between finite and non-finite clauses in Mandarin based on various properties of these embedded sentences (see footnote 32).

Nouns in general, and especially pronouns, are more subject to omission in Chinese than in many languages (see Li and Thompson 1981 pp. 657-675 for a good summary). In addition to standard noun phrase omissions (such as the 'gap' in a relative clause which is coreferential with the head of the relative), Chinese also freely allows pronoun omission, in both subject and object positions, under the following conditions: first, when the referent of the pronoun is clear from context, and that referent need not be highlighted for reasons such as contrast or shift of discourse topic; and second, when the referent is third person and non-human (i.e. in general where the English pronoun 'it' would be used). Exceptions to these two conditions (Li and Thompson 1981, p. 675) are that a pronoun (or any noun) which is the object of a preposition (i.e., the noun in a coverbial phrase; see 2.3.1) may never be omitted, and a pronoun (or any noun) which acts as a 'pivotal NP' (i.e. one that is both the direct object of one verb and the subject of a second verb in the same sentence) may not be omitted.

Chinese has one pronoun each for first (*wo*), second (*ni*) and third (*ta*) person singular, with the plural formed by addition of the human plural suffix *-men*[24].

NP coordination in Mandarin most commonly occurs by juxtaposition of the elements to be coordinated, as seen in 2.26.

2.26	Zhangsan,	Lisi	dou	yao	qu.
	Zhangsan	Lisi	all	want	go
	Both Zhangsan and Lisi want to go.				

Alternatively, a coordinating conjunction such as *gen* or *he* may be used, as seen in 2.27.

2.27	Zhangsan	gen	Lisi	dou	yao	qu.
	Zhangsan	and	Lisi	all	want	go
	Both Zhangsan and Lisi want to go.					

If the coordinated nouns constitute the direct object NP, the coordinating conjunction is obligatory if the NP remains in post-verbal direct object position.

---

[24]In addition, in standard Mandarin as well as the Beijing subdialect, the pronoun *zanmen* 'we' is used as a first person plural form that excludes anyone not being directly addressed.

2.28	Wo	yao	shu	gen	bi.	
	I	want	book	and	pen	

I want a book and pen.
(c.f. *Wo yao shu, bi.)

More commonly, however, the coordinated nouns acting as the direct object are topicalized, and the coordinating conjunction is optional, as seen in 2.29.

2.29	Shu	(gen)	bi	wo	dou	yao.
	book	(and)	pen	I	want	both

I want both a book and pen.

2.3.3 Verb Phrases

There are two large classes of verb in Mandarin, *active* verbs and *stative* verbs. Active verbs are those verbs that do not express an adjectival state. Stative verbs are like adjectives in many languages, but are considered main predicates in Mandarin because they are directly negated, take verbal aspect, and can stand alone as the main verb of a sentence. So for example the sentence *Ta hao* (lit. 'he good') means 'he is well', without the need for an empty copula to mark the adjective as a 'predicate adjective' as in English. Stative verbs are obligatorily intransitive, but may take an object complement expressing qualities such as frequency or extent, seen as COMP in 2.30 and 2.31.

2.30	Ta	haode	[shei	dou	xihuan	ta]$_{COMP}$
	he	good-ADV	who	all	like	him

He's so good that everyone likes him.

2.31	Ta	haole	(you)	[san	tian]$_{COMP}$
	he	good-ASP	(have)	three	day

He's been well for three days.

The basic structure of the Mandarin VP is a verb followed by an optional direct object or complement[25]. Mandarin does not distinguish finite and infinitive verb phrases[26], and has no complementizer that introduces a sentence complement. Furthermore, verb or verb phrase coordination takes place through juxtaposition, with no coordinating conjunctions. One consequence of these facts is that verbs and verb phrases often occur directly

[25] Although it does not affect the analysis here, an interesting constraint on the Mandarin VP is that only one major constituent, whether it be the object or a complement (such as a manner adverbial, see 2.3.6), may follow the verb. For further discussion of this phenomenon, see Huang (1982a), or A. Y-H. Li (1990).

[26] At least not on the surface. A. Y-H. Li (1990), however, argues that an underlying ±finite distinction exists in the grammar of Chinese (see footnote 32).

2.32	Ta	chang	ge	xie	xin.
	he	sing	song	write	letter

He sings songs and writes letters.

2.33	Wo	qing	ta	xiexie	laoshi.
	I	ask	he	thank	teacher

I asked him to thank the teacher.

2.34	Wo	zhidao	ta	shi	laoshi.
	I	know	he	be	teacher

I know (that) he is a teacher.

juxtaposed in a 'serial' construction, with no intervening function words such as the infinitive 'to', a complementizer 'that' or coordinating conjunctions[27]. For example, in 2.32 we see two verb phrases coordinated through juxtaposition. In 2.33 we see a verb phrase that would be marked as infinitival in other languages merely juxtaposed to a main verb, and in 2.34 is an example of a juxtaposed sentence complement. Such complements are introduced with a complementizer (such as 'that' in English) in many languages.

2.3.4 Direct Object Movement

The most common departure from basic SVO word order in Mandarin is the movement of the object to the left of the verb for purposes of topicalization, passivization or general focus. 2.35 is an example of a basic SVO sentence.

2.35	Zhangsan	maile	neiliangzhi	ji.
	(name)	sell-ASP	that-2-M	chicken

Zhangsan sold those two chickens.

2.36 and 2.37 show topicalized forms of that sentence. In 2.38 we see an example of the *ba* construction. If the direct object is 'old information'

2.36	Neiliangzhi	ji,	Zhangsan	maile.
	that-2-M	chicken	(name)	sell-ASP

Those two chickens, Zhangsan sold.

2.37	Zhangsan	neiliangzhi	ji,	maile.
	(name)	that-2-M	chicken	sell-ASP

Those two chickens, Zhangsan sold.

[27] See Li and Thompson pp. 594-622 for a detailed discussion of serial verbs.

2.38	Zhangsan	ba	neiliangzhi	ji	maile.
	(name)	OBJ	that-2-M	chicken	sell-ASP

Zhangsan sold those two chickens.

and definite[28], there is a strong tendency to move it to the left of the verb preceded by the object marker *ba*. 2.39 is an example of passivization in

2.39	Neiliangzhi	ji	bei	Zhangsan	maile.
	that-2-M	chicken	PASS	(name)	sell-ASP

Those two chickens were sold by Zhangsan.

Mandarin, with the object moved to the front and overtly marked as the patient with the passive marker *bei*. In current theories of Chinese syntax, the topic is taken to be base-generated rather than derived via movement rules (see, e.g., Huang 1984a).

2.3.5 Aspect Markers

Aspect markers are used to mark phenomena such as change of state, continuing action and completed action. The most common aspect marker in Mandarin is the particle *le*. The meaning of *le* varies depending on its scope of modification. Generally speaking, when the scope of *le* is limited to the

2.40	Wo	maile	sanben	shu.
	I	buy-ASP	three-M	book

I bought three books.

2.41	Wo	bu	mai	shu.
	I	not	buy	book

I don't buy books.

Wo	bu	mai	shu	le.
I	not	buy	book	ASP

I don't buy books anymore.

verb (as seen in 2.40), it indicates completion of the action associated with that verb. When *le* has scope over the entire sentence (i.e, when it occurs as a sentence-final particle), it indicates that the situation described by that sentence represents a change relative to some time in the past (as seen in in 2.41).

Other common aspect markers in Chinese are the verbal suffix *-guo*, which indicates that the verbal action has happened before, the verbal

[28] There are other restrictions as well.

suffix *-zhe*, which indicates that the verbal action is ongoing or continuing, and the adverb *zai*, which also indicates ongoing action.

In Chinese, 'tense' (i.e., the relationship between the time of speech and the time of main predicate action) is expressed by the use of time adverbs which provide a reference time for predicate action. Thus, for example, a sentence in Chinese is translated using past tense inflection in other languages if the time words *zuotian* 'yesterday' or *yiqian* 'previously' were used, and the same Chinese sentence is translated using future tense inflection if the time words *mingtian* 'tomorrow' or *jianglai* 'in the future' are used.

According to Huang (1982a, p. 165) aspect makers like *-guo* and *-zhe* suffix to verbs in the word formation component of the grammar. He considers the aspect marker *-le*, however, to be quite different. Huang considers the pre- and post-verbal position alternation between *-le* and *mei(you)* (see Wang 1965) as evidence that *-le* and *mei(you)* are both generated in INFL, with *-le* undergoing movement to its surface position as a verb suffix. Also generated in INFL according to Huang (1982a, p. 367) are words occurring in preverbal modifier position which indicate aspect, such as *zai* 'at' (progressive) and *hui* 'can' (future) (see 2.3.11).

2.3.6 Manner Adverbial Modification

Manner adverbials are used with the adverbial modifying particle *de*[29] suffixed to the verb, followed by a stative verb indicating manner, as seen in 2.42. A manner adverbial may also modify the verb in the pre-verbal slot, as seen in 2.43. In this type of manner modification, the *de* is suffixed to

2.42 Ta zoude kuai.
he walk-ADV fast
He walks quickly.

2.43 Ta hen kuaide zoule.
he very fast-ADV walk-ASP
He walked very quickly.

the modifying stative verb. When the adverbial phrase precedes the verb in this way, the aspectual meaning is punctive rather than habitual as in 2.42. Also, in preverbal adverbial modification the stative verb is often reduplicated and used as a suggestion or command (as seen in example 2.6).

[29]This is not the prenominal modifier *de*. Although the prenominal modification marker *de*, the adverbial *de* in 2.42 and the manner adverbial *de* in 2.43 are phonologically identical and functionally somewhat similar, they are considered different morphemes. This is because they have different historical origins and are written differently.

2.3.7 Conjunctions

In general, the presence of a coordinating conjunction is obligatory only when the coordination involves clauses, and specifically when it involves some sort of logical dependency between clauses. Examples of such clausal conjunctions would be *suoyi* ('therefore'), *erqie* ('moreover'), *keshi* ('however'), *yinwei* ('because'), *haishi* ('or'), *huozhe* ('or else'), *jiu* ('then') and *cai* ('only then'). At the discourse level, continuity is achieved through the use of such sentence-initial 'discourse conjunctions' as *na* or *nemmo* ('then'), *ranhou* ('afterward'), or *hai you* ('and then').

2.3.8 Question Formation

There are four ways to form questions in Mandarin. The first is with sentence-final question particles such as *ma* or *a* (seen in 2.45), which convert statements into questions.

2.44 Ni renshi ta.
you know him
You know him.

2.45 Ni renshi ta ma?
you know him Q
Do you know him?

The second is with question words such as *shenmo* 'what', *shei* 'who', *nar* 'where' and *zenmo* 'how', as exemplified in 2.46. These question words do

2.46 Ni renshi shei?
you know who
Who do you know?

not involve syntactic 'movement' rules as in English[30]. The third is the formation of disjunctive questions using either the 'A-not-A' predicate duplication form (as seen in 2.47) or the disjunctive conjunction *haishi* 'or'.

2.47 Ni renshi bu renshi ta?
you know not know him
Do you know him?

The fourth is with 'tag' questions (seen in 2.48), in which a statement is followed by either a predicate with a question particle, or a predicate within which a disjunctive question occurs.

[30] But see Huang (1982b) for a discussion of abstract *wh-* movement in the Logical Form component of the grammar of Mandarin.

2.48	Ni	renshi	ta,	dui	bu	dui?
	you	know	him	right	not	right

You know him, right?

2.3.9 Negation

Negation in Mandarin is marked by the adverb *bu*, which modifies verbs (and some adverbs) by occurring to their left. Two exceptions to the use of *bu* for negation are when the verb *you* 'have' is negated, and when events in the past are negated. In both these cases (as exemplified in 2.49-2.53 below), the negative *mei* is used in place of *bu*.

2.49	Ta	na	qian.
	he	take	money

He takes money.

2.50	Ta	bu	na	qian.
	he	not	take	money

He doesn't take money.

2.51	Ta	you	qian.
	he	have	money

He has money.

2.52	Ta	meiyou	qian.
	he	not-have	money

He doesn't have money.

2.53	Ta	mei	na	qian.
	he	not	take	money

He didn't take money.

2.3.10 Sentence-final Particles

There are many sentence-final particles used in Mandarin Chinese. These particles can have grammatical functions such as marking questions (*ma, a*) or aspect (*le, ne*), or they may provide pragmatic information such as emphasis (*a, la*), exclamation (*ya*) assertion (*ba, me*), or request for confirmation (*hei, ho*).

2.3.11 Theoretical Issues

Inflection in Mandarin

Due to the absence in Chinese of overt inflectional marking, the nature of abstract syntactic phrase structure nodes such as INFL (see, e.g., Chomsky 1981) is an important issue in Chinese syntax. This issue is relevant to our investigation because such theoretical constructs have been used to account for agrammatic speech output. Grodzinsky (1990, p. 59), for example, explains the misuse of function words and inflectional morphology in agrammatism by proposing that the content of all non-lexical phrase structure nodes (such as INFL) is deleted. According to this hypothesis (following Grodzinsky's definition 1 of non-lexical on p. 59), determiners, complementizers, adverbs, inflection, auxiliaries and case markers are subject to deletion in agrammatism.

Linguists differ on the nature of INFL in Chinese. There is general agreement that INFL occurs preceding and outside the immediate dominance of the VP[31]. Regarding the content of the INFL node, James C-T. Huang (1982a, p. 367) posits the occurrence of auxiliary verbs (which often express tense) such as *you* 'have' (perfective aspect), *zai* 'at' (progressive aspect), *hui* 'can/will' (future aspect), the perfective aspect suffix *le* (which attaches to the verb by means of a process such as English 'affix hopping'; Huang 1982a, pp. 164-165), and the negative *bu* (Huang 1988, p. 286) within INFL.

Y-H. Audrey Li (1990) does not specify exactly which surface elements the INFL node contains, but does propose that in Chinese the INFL of a tensed clause is a Case assigner, while the INFL of an infinitive clause is not[32]. Thus if, according to Grodzinsky, , non-lexical nodes such as INFL are devoid of content in agrammatism, then, for example, we might expect Case to (incorrectly) go unassigned in a tensed clause in Chinese agrammatism. Practically speaking, in examining the speech of non-fluent patients such as LXZ, the Case-assigning properties of INFL may be of little consequence, because in Chinese they arise mostly in the context of sentence embedding, and non-fluent patients such as LXZ rarely, if ever, produce embedded sentences.

---

[31] Although see Travis (1984), who posits an INFL node in sentence-final position in Chinese.

[32] Li argues for a distinction between infinitive and finite clauses in Chinese based on the properties of embedded clauses used with 'infinitive' verbs such as 'persuade' (*quan*) and 'force' (*bi*). Briefly, infinitives: 1. license aspect (e.g., *guo* 'have done') in the embedded clause, 2. allow negation markers in the matrix clause to license negative polarity item in the embedded clause, 3. do not allow future tense markers like *hui* 'will' in the embedded clause, and 4. do not allow lexical NPs in the subject position of the embedded clause.

The 'Sentential Modifier' Slot

The items that occur in the sentential modifier slot between the subject and the verb structurally occupy either the INFL node or a node (such as AUX or adverbial) that is under the immediate dominance of the VP. According to Huang (1982a, p. 184, fn. 23), adverbs are adjoined to VP, while auxiliary verbs are all in INFL (see 2.3.11 above). According to A. Y-H. Li (1990, p. 169), time adverbials occur outside the VP, while other adverbials occur within the VP. Also, coverbs occur within the VP according to Li, as seen by the structure in Figure 2.5.

2.4 Discourse and Pragmatics

The discourse structure of Mandarin is like that of many other languages, in that normally *topic succession* and *topic change* occur through the discourse, often overtly marked with optional *discourse connectives* (such as *nemmo*, see 2.3.7; see also Biq, 1990). Also, entities are usually introduced into the discourse in sentence-final (i.e., object) position, with sentence-intial (i.e., subject or topic) position generally reserved for 'old' or 'given' information (Prince, 1981). All of these devices are used to preserve *discourse cohesiveness* between two interlocutors[33].

A salient characteristic of Chinese discourse is the frequent absence of anaphoric topics in the discourse. The existence of such 'topic chains' (an antecedent topic in one sentence followed by 'empty' anaphoric topic positions in subsequent sentences; see Tsao, 1978 and Shi, 1989) in Chinese means that there are fewer overt coreferential NPs in a discourse than in many other languages.

In terms of linguistic pragmatics, in Mandarin it is common to use words which indicate the attitudes or beliefs of the speaker. In addition to the words listed in the previous section on sentence-final particles, there are words which indicate agreement with the interlocutor (e.g., *a, hm, hei*), or express doubt (*ei, o*), surprise (e.g., *aiya, aiyo*) and resignation (e.g., *ai, hai*). These may all be considered function words, and may occur in isolation, sentence-initial, or sentence-final position.

[33] For a good review of discourse production in aphasia, see Ulatowska et al. (1990), and Joanette and Brownell (1990).

Chapter 3

Speech Analysis

This chapter presents a detailed grammatical analysis of the speech deficits of four aphasic speakers of Mandarin Chinese, Li Xinzheng[1] (LXZ), Guo Jiande (GJD), Yang Xifeng (YXF) and Zheng Youjuan (ZYJ). LXZ, GJD and YXF were hospitalized in Taipei, Taiwan, and ZYJ was hospitalized in Beijing, China. They were referred by staff doctors and speech pathologists, and their speech was recorded in 1982-83. The original taping occurred as part of a subject selection protocol for a phonological study of tone production in aphasic Chinese speech (Packard 1984, 1986). These four patients were selected for this grammatical study because the speech sample from their interview (see following paragraph) was long enough and contained enough identifiable lexical and syntactic constituents to support a proper grammatical analysis. LXZ and YXF represent prototypical examples of Broca's and Wernicke's aphasia respectively, while GJD and ZYJ fit traditional diagnostic categories less closely.

The speech corpora were elicited in informal interview situations, during which the interviewer[2] encouraged the patient to produce as much spontaneous speech as possible. All patients except LXZ were also asked to describe a picture (depicting two children stealing cookies while their mother washes dishes, from Goodglass & Kaplan, 1972) as a means of eliciting speech. The speech samples were recorded in a quiet room on Sony CHF-60 cassette tapes, using a Sony TCM-141 cassette recorder equipped with a Sony ECM-16T Electret condenser microphone attatched to the patient's lapel. The resulting recordings were transcribed by the author into *pinyin*

[1] The patients' real names are not used here.

[2] My thanks to Sylvia Chen, who did most of the interviewing in Taipei, and Hu Chaoqun who did most of the interviewing in Beijing.

romanized Chinese with assistance from native-speaking informants[3]. The complete corpora of all four patients (in *pinyin*, including interlinear English translation) are presented in the Appendix, beginning on page 164.

The speech data in this chapter are organized by patient, with each patient's speech analyzed to determine its phonological, morphological, syntactic and discourse structure. For each patient a general characterization of their speech is presented, followed by a more detailed analysis and specific examples.

The following abbreviations are used for grammatical terms in the second line of the translation:

ADV	= Adverbial
AFF	= Utterance of Affirmation
ASP	= Aspect Marker
COMP	= Complement
DO	= Direct Object
EMP	= Particle indicating Emphasis
EXC	= Particle indicating Exclamation
HES	= Hesitation Filler
C	= Classifier
MOD	= Marker of Prenominal Modification
OBJ	= Direct Object Marker 'ba'
ORD	= Ordinal Prefix
PL	= Plural
Q	= Question Marker
SUG	= Particle of Suggestion

The following conventions are used in the transcription and translation of speech data for the examples in this chapter.

1. Utterances are divided into words, with complex words assigned to one of four lexical levels (following Packard 1990b; see also 2.2.1). The lexical level of each complex word is marked in the Appendix).

2. For all utterances in this chapter, the actual utterance is presented on the first line, a literal morphemic translation is given on the second line and a free translation is given on the third line. In the case of incorrect utterances, the free translation is given in a form intended to reflect the aberrance of the produced form. The actual utterance on

[3] My thanks to Pao-yuan Chen, Xiaoyu Chen, Shengli Feng. Thanks also to Sylvia Chen for help in clarifying some passages.

the first line is given in *pinyin* romanization (except for some phonemic paraphasias which are given in phonetic transcription; see below), with tone marks given only where necessary to facilitate comprehension. The number of the utterance in the Appendix is given below the example number in parentheses[4].

3. For aberrant utterances, the free translation on the third line is followed by the target or a non-aberrant version of the observed utterance (if determinable), preceded by 'c.f.', which is then glossed with morphemic and free translations.

4. The following conventions are adopted to describe abnormal speech:

   - Words in which phonological errors (termed *phonological paraphasias*) occur are normally presented within square brackets ([xxx]) in *pinyin* romanization. In cases where the precise phonetic form is crucially important, the error is given in broad phonetic transcription. Where necessary, target forms are presented in a footnote, and a translation of the target is given in the morphemic translation in the second line of the transcription. The free translation on the third line contains an incorrect English phonological form, in an attempt to give the reader an idea of the nature of the phonological error.
   - A wrong word which is not semantically related to the target is termed a *verbal paraphasia*. Verbal paraphasias are enclosed in angle brackets (<xxx>), with the target given in the text or a footnote.
   - A subtype of verbal paraphasia is a *semantic paraphasia*, an incorrect word which is semantically related to the target. Semantic paraphasias are enclosed in diamonds (◇xxx◇),and the target form is given either in the text or in a footnote.
   - A wrong word for which the target cannot plausibly be determined is termed *jargon* if it is a possible Mandarin word (i.e., if it is one of the possible Mandarin syllable shapes) and it occupies the form class slot appropriate to that word (e.g., a verb occurring in a verb slot). Jargon is enclosed in 'bowties' (⋈xxx⋈).
   - A nonexistent word coined by the speaker is a *neologism*. A neologism is defined as a form which either is not a Mandarin word (e.g., a non-occurring syllable shape in Mandarin such as

[4] Due to space limitations, the examples given in this chapter are sometimes edited versions of those which appear in full in the Appendix.

rēn or *puan*), or is a possible word but occupies a form class slot inappropriate for that word. Neologisms are enclosed in inverted triangles (∇xxx∇).

- Words or morphemes which are extraneous are enclosed in circled X's (⊗xxx⊗).
- Omitted words or morphemes are indicated by a null sign (ϕ) in the first line of the utterance, with a translation of the missing item given in parentheses in the second line.
- Improper word order is indicated by presenting the disordered words in small capitals (e.g., *TO EAT LIKE I CHINESE FOOD).
- Sentences or phrases which are deemed completely nonsensical are written in *italics*.

Although clearly defined, precise criteria have been given for the classification of speech errors, in practice it is often not clear which category an aberrant form should be assigned to. For example, if we know that the target is the word *chī* 'eat' and the observed form is **chū*, it is difficult to determine a priori whether the error is phonological (a substitution of *u* for *i*) or lexical (a substitution of the word *chū* 'exit' for the word *chī* 'eat').

As another example of the difficulty of categorizing disordered speech, consider the difference between neologism and jargon. Intuitively, neologism is a nonexistent word coined by the speaker, while jargon is the use of a bona fide word in an inappropriate context. However, jargon may sometimes be neologism 'in disguise', because a putative instance of jargon may only coincidentally take the shape of a Mandarin word (see discussion in 2.1.3). The result is that words labeled as neologisms in this study are unambiguously neologisms (because non-words are easy to identify), but words labeled as jargon might actually be neologisms.

To illustrate, in example 3.1 (from patient YXF), the word *kǎn* fits our criteria for jargon because it is an incorrect word given the context, and because it is a verb ('to chop') which occurs in a verbal syntactic slot and is suffixed with the verbal aspect marker *le*.

3.1 ⋈Kǎn⋈le yici.
chop-ASP 1-C:time
Chopped once.

However, the production of *kǎn* is not really an improper lexical selection: in actuality it is a phonological perseveration, based on a word in the previous sentence *kān* 'to watch over'[5], seen in 3.2 below. It is classified as jargon

[5] Which may itself be a spurious instance of jargon.

3.2	Zai	⋈kān⋈.	⋈Kǎn⋈le	yici.
	again	watch	chop-ASP	1-C:time
	Watch again. Chopped once.			

only because it fits the criteria we have established. This particular example is an obvious case, but in other cases it is often difficult to know when jargon is in fact a bona fide Mandarin word only by coïncidence. The reader is advised to survey the data with a critical eye, since aphasic speech errors are often subject to more than one possible analysis.

3.1 Subject #1: Li Xinzheng

3.1.1 Background

LXZ was a 23-year old female who suffered from left hemisphere damage as the result of cerebral trauma. Her speech may be described as non-fluent, with reduced phrase length and simplified grammatical structures. Her speech was replete with phonological, morphological, syntactic and semantic errors. LXZ's profile is seen in Table 3.1.

age	23	sex	female
lesion type	trauma	lesion location	fronto-temporal
diagnostic category	Broca's	fluency	poor
semantic content	poor-fair	speech effortful	yes
comprehension	fair	functor omission	yes
phrase length	reduced	complex syntax	no
distortions	yes	substitutions	yes
intonation	abnormal	anomia	yes
neologism	few	jargon	some
discourse structure	fair-poor	repetition	fair-poor

Table 3.1: Patient Profile: Li Xinzheng

LXZ's speech may be considered that of a 'typical' Broca's aphasic. Her speech is slow and deliberate, with simplified syntactic structure, omission and underemployment of function words (including total omission of the prenominal modification marker *de*), and some omission of verbs.

The most common parts of speech in LXZ's corpus are nouns, stative verbs (adjectives), verbs, and markers of negation. Conspicuously absent or underrepresented in her speech are function words such as the copula verb, determiner/classifier combinations, coverbs, the prenominal modification marker *de*, conjunctions (both sentence and discourse), adverbials, and sentence-final syntactic and discourse particles.

LXZ does not appear to have problems ordering the subject-verb-object constituents of the sentence per se, but at times she has problems with the *internal* ordering of noun and verb phrase constituents. Also, inappropriate repetition of some sentential elements sometimes gives the appearance of improper sentential word order.

Linguistic Background

LXZ was born and raised in Taiwan, acquiring principally Taiwanese (a dialect of the southern Min group), but also Taiwan Mandarin as her first languages, prior to age five[6]. The biggest difference between Taiwan Mandarin (and indeed most southern dialects of Mandarin) and standard Mandarin[7] is in the absence of retroflex consonants, which have generally merged with the apical consonant series (see Table 2.1 and accompanying discussion). This means that speakers of Taiwan Mandarin often produce *z, c* and *s* in place of *zh, ch* and *sh* respectively[8]. In all cases, I assume the production of an apical consonant by LXZ in place of a retroflex consonant *not* to be a phonological error.

3.1.2 Phonology

LXZ's phonological production was abnormal in several respects. First, her intonation was abnormal. The individual syllables in an utterance of Mandarin Chinese are normally produced with unequal stress (i.e., produced with variation in syllable length and amplitude, and in the amount of time separating the syllables). In this regard, Mandarin may be considered more a 'stress-timed' than 'syllable-timed' language (see discussion in section 2.1.2). LXZ's speech had none of these types of variation, but rather showed uniformity of syllable amplitude and length characteristic of a syllable-timed language (such as Japanese). Also, her rate of speech was slower than normal.

LXZ's speech was replete with errors in the production of consonants and vowels (phonemic paraphasias). 3.3 shows some examples of consonant and vowel error (represented in *pinyin* romanized Chinese).

3.3	shengri	→	*sanri[9]
	daojiang	→	*dejiang
	yigong	→	*yige
	qu	→	*zhi
	zuo shou	→	*zou zou

[6] Mandarin, the official language of Taiwan, is the language of instruction and is used for most public and official communications. Taiwanese is the native language of the majority (71%, Kubler 1985) of the inhabitants of Taiwan, but most residents of the larger cities have significant exposure to Mandarin before beginning formal education.

[7] For a detailed description of Taiwan Mandarin, see Kubler (1984).

[8] The retroflex *r* is more commonly retained in Taiwan Mandarin, perhaps because of the absence of its counterpart (viz., the phonetic [z]) in the apical series in standard Mandarin.

[9] The use of *s* in place of *sh* is normal in Taiwan Mandarin for this word, but the use of the apical nasal *n* in place of the velar nasal *ng* and the vowel *a* in place of *e* is not.

LXZ's production of individual tones was remarkably clear, and she made few tonal errors in spontaneous speech. However, she did make several tonal errors in a syllable repetition task as part of a different study (see subject #8 in Packard 1986). Since LXZ's speech had the abnormal syllable-timing quality discussed in the previous paragraph, the tone on each individual syllable was produced as though it occurred in isolation, i.e., in citation form. In this sense, her tonal production was abnormal, because the tones did not undergo the phonological conditioning (i.e., variations in length, amplitude and F_0) normally seen in connected Mandarin speech (see, e.g., Shen 1990; Kratochvil 1968). This abnormality in LXZ's tone production could be attributed to a deficit in monitoring the global, 'syntactic' phonological context, since the tones were produced as though in isolation, independent of that larger context (cf. Danly, Cooper and Shapiro 1983).

3.1.3 Lexical Selection

Verbal Paraphasias

A few instances of verbal paraphasia (improper word, not related to the target) were observed in LXZ's speech. As seen in 3.4, she substitutes *zùo* 'do' for *shŭ* 'to belong to (a sign of the zodiac)'. She substitutes *zùo*, a semantically broad, 'generic' verb for more specific verbs in other examples as well.

3.4	Ni	shŭ	zhu,	wo	<zùo>	niu.
(L8)	you	belong	pig	I	do	cow
	You're under the pig, I do the cow.					
cf.	Ni	shŭ	zhu,	wo	shŭ	niu.
	you	belong	pig	I	belong	cow
	You're under the pig, I'm under the cow.					

In 3.5, the incorrect word is a perseverative substitution of the word *shŏu* 'hand', which occurs earlier in the sentence, in place of the direct object *shì* 'thing'.

3.5	Wo	zuŏ	shŏu	dou	bu	hui	zuò	<shŏu>.
(L66)	I	left	hand	all	not	can	do	hand
cf.	Wo	zuŏ	shŏu	dou	bu	hui	zuò	shì.
	I	left	hand	all	not	can	do	thing
	I can't do anything with my left hand.							

In the following example (3.6), the subject uses the semantically broad

3.6	Ta	<zuò>	you	shou	wo	<zuò>	[zŏu]	[zŏu]
(L77)	he	do	right	hand	I	do	left	hand
	He does his right hand, I do my reft kand.							
cf.	Ta	yong	you	shou	wo	yong	zuo	shou
	he	use	right	hand	I	use	left	hand
	He uses his right hand, I use my left hand.							

verb *zuò* 'do' as a substitute for the verb *yòng* 'use'. In addition, *zŏu zŏu* is substituted for the phonologically similar *zŭo shŏu.*

Semantic Paraphasias

Many of the lexical selection errors committed by the patient are clear semantic paraphasias[10] (a wrong word semantically related to the target).

3.7	Zhan-ϕ	hao	◇duo◇.
(L151)	stand(-ASP)	very	much
	Stand a lot.		
cf.	Zhànle	háo	jiŭ.
	stand-ASP	very	long
	Has stood a long time.		

For example, in 3.7 the subject says *duō* 'a lot' instead of *jiŭ* 'a long time' (the deletion of *le* is discussed in the section on word formation). These two words are semantically related because they both refer to large amounts of something: *jiŭ* refers to the narrow category of time, while *duō* has a broader, more generic reference.

In example 3.8 'remember' and 'recognize' are semantically related, because they both refer to cognitive events involving the use of memory.

3.8	Wo	bu	◇renshi◇	ϕ[11]	le.
(L46)	I	not	recognize	(DO)	ASP
	I don't recognize.				
cf.	Wo	bu	jide		le.
	I	not	remember		ASP
	I don't remember.				

3.9 is a very interesting example of the substitution of an inappropriate question word. The patient produces the form *shenmo* 'what' instead of the proper form *ji* 'how many' in front of the word for 'years of age'. Strictly

[10] Note that this type of error is usually seen in Wernicke's rather than Broca's aphasia.
[11] Deletion of an obligatory direct object.

3.9	Ni	shi	◇shenmo◇	sui?	
(L6)	you	be	what	year	
	What years are you?				
cf.	Ni	ji		sui	
	you	how:many		year	
	How old are you?				

speaking, they might be considered more grammatically than semantically similar, since the characteristic they share is that they both function as question words. An interesting fact to point out is that LXZ correctly uses the copula *shi* with the question word *shenmo*, and in doing so avoids producing a structually incorrect sentence. This is because in that context the question word *ji* cannot be used with the copula, while the question word *shenmo* cannot be used without it.

3.10 shows the use of the incorrect but semantically related *dianliao*

3.10	Zhe	laoshi	zuo	pangbian	ϕ[12]	◇dianliao◇.
(L140)	This	teacher	sit	side	(do)	electric-cure
	This teacher is sitting on the side electrotherapy.					
cf.	Zhe	laoshi	zuo	pangbian	zhiliao.	
	This	teacher	sit	side	cure-cure	
	This teacher is sitting on the side treating me.					

'electrotherapy' in place of *zhiliao* 'therapy/to cure'. Although this error is a word substitution error, it is also an error in word formation, since what is erroneously substituted is a part of the larger complex word (i.e., *dian* is a substitute for *zhi*). This will be covered more fully in section 3.1.4.

Jargon

There are a couple of instances of jargon (i.e., the wrong word is used, but it is a possible word used in the correct form class category) in LXZ's speech.

3.11	⋈Gai⋈le	⋈dian⋈.
(L137)	cover-ASP	electricity
	He covered electricity.	

In the following example, she uses the word *gai* 'cover' as the verb of the sentence in a clearly inappropriate context. Note that the jargon form is inflected with the aspect marker *le*. Also in this example, the word *dian*

[12] An omission is posited here, and not in the following sentence with *zhiliao* because while *zhiliao* is a verb, the substituted word *dianliao* is a noun, and would require a preceding verb to make the sentence grammatical.

is anticipatory jargon which anticipates the incorrect substitution of *dian* 'electric' for *zhi-* 'cure' in the verb *zhiliao* 'cure' in the utterance which follows it (see example 3.10).

In the next example, LXZ produced the jargon form *diezhe* 'falling'. As

3.12	Wo	libairi...	wo	⋈die⋈zhe...
(L45)	I	Sunday	I	fall-ASP
	Sunday I was falling...			

in the previous example, *diezhe* is an example of an inflectional suffix (*-zhe* '-ing') suffixed to a jargon root *-zhe* verb.

Neologism

LXZ produced some neologistic speech (with neologism defined as a word nonexistent in Mandarin or a possible word used in the wrong form class

3.13	▽zùo	xiè	nǐ	ge▽...	Ni	◇zhan◇.	Ni	zuo.
(L157)	sit	thank	you	M	you	stand	you	sit
	??? You stand. You sit.							

category). In the following utterance, *zùo, xiè* and *nǐ* are all possible Mandarin words. What identifies them as neologistic 'word creations' is that the words do not make any sense in the form class slots they occupy.

3.1.4 Word Formation

LXZ's speech contained many irregularities in the formation of complex (i.e., multimorphemic) words. The first point to be observed is their relative paucity. LXZ's corpus contains a total of 243 words, of which 72 (or 29.6%) consist of two or more morphemes. Compare this percentage to the, e.g., more than 50% produced by the experimenter. Furthermore, 13.9% of LXZ's complex words contain errors (see Table 3.2). The fact that LXZ has a small proportion of complex words in her speech, and that 13.9% of these words contain errors, indicates that LXZ has difficulty building words with a complex morphological structure.

According to the theory of Mandarin word formation outlined in Chapter 2, words formed at lexical level IV are analogous to words which bear inflection in languages that have overtly observable inflectional processes (such as English), since regular inflection is posited to occur at lexical level IV. Since Broca's aphasics in other languages are known to have problems with inflection, the cross-linguistic prediction for our Chinese-speaking

Broca's aphasic is that lexical level IV would be especially subject to word formation deficit. Looking at Table 3.2 we see that there is indeed a great deal of error at level IV, with 36.4% of the words formed at this level produced incorrectly. This error rate is significantly greater than the combined error rate of the other three lexical levels (namely, 9.8%; versus 36.4%, using the population proportion significance test, $Z = 2.34$, $p < .02$, two- tailed). Furthermore, as seen in Table 3.2, the percentage of complex words which

	Level I	Level II	Level III	Level IV
number of tokens	5	35	21	11
number in error	0	1	5	4
percent in error	0%	2.9%	23.8%	36.4%

Table 3.2: Word Error at Various Lexical Levels: Li Xinzheng

are in error decreases in a stepwise manner as we move down the levels of the lexicon. The probability that the ordering of percentages which represents this stepwise 'grading' effect occurred by chance is less than .05 ($p <$ .05[13]). These findings suggest that not only is level IV most subject to morphological deficit in our non-fluent speaker, but also that complex words are less subject to deficit the 'deeper' in the lexicon they are formed[14].

The misuse of level IV elements in the speech of LXZ may be analogous to the inflection deficit seen in languages which have inflectional morphology. In the case of Mandarin, however, this level IV deficit occurs in the absence of syntactic agreement rules seen in other languages. This raises the question to what extent the observed level IV deficit is syntactic in origin. Either there is an as yet unspecified relationship in Mandarin between syntax and the formation of complex words, or the level IV deficit is caused by factors that do not involve syntax.

It is interesting to note that one grammatical marker that is categorized as level IV, the verbal aspect marker *le* (NB: this is the *le* with narrow scope, only over the verb), occurs with normal frequency in this subject (see Table 3.3), as it did in the speech of another Broca's aphasic analyzed in a previous Chinese aphasia case study (Packard 1990a). This fact is evidence that while *le* has many properties that make it appear inflectional in nature, it is nonetheless a rather unique grammatical entity, since it

[13] The probability of the four percentages randomly occurring in the observed order is 0.042. This is because the number of possible orderings of the four values is 4! (4 factorial), or 24, and one in 24 is 0.042.

[14] The proportion of level IV words in error (36.4%) is also greater than that of the fluent patient YXF (13.1%); see footnote 32.

is not omitted as often as one would expect on analogy with agrammatic inflection deficits in other languages.

There is, however, one instance of *le* omission as the following example

3.14	Zhan-φ	hao	◇duo◇.
(L151)	stand(-ASP)	very	much
	Stand a lot.		
cf.	Zhanle	hao	jiu.
	stand-ASP	very	long
	Has stood a long time.		

shows (the improper use of *duo* was discussed in section 3.1.3). In this example, the verbal *le* would have a meaning of perfectivity, or 'completed action'.

Moving on to other specific examples of aberrant word formation, an error referred to earlier is the substitution of *dian* 'electricity' for *zhi* 'to

3.15	Zhe	laoshi	zuo	pangbian	φ	<dian>liao.
(L140)	This	teacher	sit	side	(do)	electric-cure
	This teacher is sitting on the side electrotherapy.					
cf.	Zhe	laoshi	zuo	pangbian	zhiliao.	
	This	teacher	sit	side	cure-cure	
	This teacher is sitting on the side treating me.					

cure' in the complex word *zhiliao* 'to cure' (3.10). The error is repeated as 3.15, with the annotation reflecting the fact that it was a subpart of the word that was improperly substituted to yield the new word (it was accordingly termed a word substitution error in 3.10). Also note that in the formation of the word, the item that was improperly substituted is also of a different form class (i.e., the noun *dian* 'electricity' for the verb *zhi* 'to cure').

Another clear example of defective word formation is the omission of a

3.16	wu-φ	yue
(L102)	five(-C)	month
	May	
cf.	wuge	yue
	five-C	month
	five months	

level III element, the classifier *-ge*, seen in 3.16. This example will be discussed in greater detail in the section on classifiers.

The examples of jargon in 3.11 and 3.12 (*gaile* and *diezhe*) are affixed with the regular (level IV) word formation elements *-le* and *-zhe*. These are errors in the sense that improper morphemes ('jargon stems') are used in the word-building process. As such, they are considered errors for the purposes of our analysis. Strictly speaking, however, since the level IV affixation occurs properly, there is no deficit in the structure *per se* of the words.

3.1.5 Syntax

LXZ's syntactic production is abnormal by virtue of its reduced structural complexity, restricted length, and her omission and underemployment of grammatical function words.

Utterances produced by LXZ are abnormally short, with many abnormal utterances consisting simply of a subject plus a time adverbial expression. Mandarin does allow sentences of the form [subject-predicate], where the predicate contains no obvious verbal element (usually in cases where the copula 'is' would be used in English with predicate adjectives; see 2.3.3), but in most contexts, a verb is obligatory. In examples 3.17-3.21 below, the verb of the sentence is improperly omitted.

3.17	Wo	[sān]ri	ϕ	wuyue	shiyi	ri.
(L26)	I	birthday	(be)	May	11	day
	My barthday May 11th.					
cf.	Wo	shengri	shi	wuyue	shiyi	ri.
	I	birthday	be	May	11	day
	My birthday is May 11th.					

3.18	Wo	ϕ-ϕ	sige	yue.
(L88)	I	(know-ASP)	four-C	month
	I four months.			
cf.	Wo	renshile	sige	yue.
	I	know-ASP	four-C	month
	I knew (him) four months.			

3.19	Wo	wushi	nian	ϕ	ϕ.
(L30)	I	five-ten	year	(born)	(MOD)
	I was the year '50.				
cf.	Wo	wushi	nian	sheng	de.
	I	five-ten	year	born	MOD
	I was born in the year '50[15].				

3.20	Jintian	ϕ	siyue	ba	hao.	
(L92)	today	(be)	4-month	8	day	
	Today April 8th.					
cf.	Jintian	shi	siyue	ba	hao.	
	today	be	4-month	8	day	
	Today is April 8th.					

3.21	Jintian	ϕ	yige	yue	wu	tian.	
(L97)	today	(have)	1-C	month	5	day	
	Today one month five days.						
cf.	Jintian	you	yige	yue	wu	tian.	
	today	have	1-C	month	5	day	
	Today it has been one month five days.						

In terms of the basic syntactic structure of her utterances, LXZ seems to have trouble constructing sentences of the canonical full form [subject-mod-verb-object] (where 'mod' refers to preverbal sentential modifiers; see 2.3.1). LXZ appears to have trouble producing these modifiers in the context of an entire sentence. This may be because adverbial modifiers are usually

3.22	ϕ	DAOJIANG	WUYUE	SHIYI	RI	ϕ	ϕ
(L23)	(from)	name	5-month	ten-one	day	(grad.)	(MOD)
	Daojiang May 11th.						
cf.	Wuyue	shiyi	ri	cong	Daojiang	biye	de
	5-month	ten-one	day	from	Daojiang	grad.	MOD
	Graduated from Daojiang on May 11th.						

3.23	Wo	<èr>	[zhì]	gongzuo.
(L43)	I	two	go	work
	I gone to work togain.			
cf.	Wo	you	qu	gongzuo.
	I	again	go	work
	I went to work again.			

3.24	Wo	wushi	nian	ϕ	ϕ.
(L30)	I	five-ten	year	(born)	(MOD)
	I was the year '50.				
cf.	Wo	wushi	nian	sheng	de.
	I	five-ten	year	born	MOD
	I was born in the year '50.				

[15] The 50th year of the Chinese republic, i.e., 1961.

function words. As seen in examples 3.22-3.24, when LXZ succeeds in producing the adverbial element, the verb is omitted. In the same way, she often successfully produces the verb, only to omit or otherwise have problems with the adverb. In 3.25, LXZ succeeds in following a subject with a place modifier, and then subsequently follows the modifier with an

3.25	Wo	ϕ	Daojiang	⊗wo⊗	biyele.
(L21)	I	(from)	Daojiang	I	graduate-ASP
	I graduated I Daojiang.				
cf.	Wo	cong	Daojiang	biyele.	
	I	from	Daojiang	graduate-ASP	
	I graduated from Daojiang.				

improper repetition of the subject rather than with the verb. It is as though once she produces the adverbial, she must repeat the subject in order to properly 'license' production of the verb.

Word Order

In LXZ's speech corpus there are very few instances of aberration in the canonical [subject-mod-verb-object] sentence word order, with most apparent instances of bad sentential word order being explainable in other ways. For example, in 3.25, the subject (*wo* 'I') has apparently occurred in the wrong sentential position (following the adverb). It seems more likely, however, that the error is in fact an improper repetition of the subject. However, there are some instances of improper word order occurring *within sentential constituents*. The first is in example (3.26), in which

3.26	ϕ	DAOJIANG	WUYUE	SHIYI	RI	ϕ	ϕ
(L23)	(from)	name	5-month	ten-one	day	(grad.)	(MOD)
	Daojiang May 11th.						
cf.	Wuyue	shiyi	ri	cong	Daojiang	biye	de
	5-month	ten-one	day	from	Daojiang	graduate	MOD
	Graduated from Daojiang on May 11th.						

the time adverb (*wuyue shiyi ri*) and place (*Daojiang*; actually part of a coverbial phrase) occupying the adverbial slot have improperly reversed positions[16]. The second example of improper order within a sentential

[16] This example also demonstrates the general difficulty LXZ has with the pre-verbal modification slot.

3.27	Wo	YANJING	ZUOBIAN	ϕ[17]	tuchu	le.
(L117)	I	eye	left-side	MOD	protrude-out	ASP
	My eye left stuck out.					
cf.	Wo	zuobian	de	yanjing	tuchu	le.
	I	left-side	MOD	eye	protrude-out	ASP
	My left eye stuck out.					

constituent is shown in 3.27, in which the [modifier-head] order within the complex noun phrase that constitutes the subject is improperly reversed[18]. Note that these examples of improper word order within sentential constituents could be seen as instances of improper order *within maximal projections*, but for the fact that at least one 'sentential constituent' (viz., the preverbal modifier slot) is not usually analyzed as a maximal projection.

In Chapter 4 we will discuss the possibility that disordered elements *within* sentential constituents (or possibly maximal projections) constitutes a general characteristic of non-fluent aphasia, representing a potentially significant generalization about aphasia types.

Function Words

LXZ's use of function words is quite abnormal. Following are examples of functor omission, underemployment and misuse.

Copula The following three examples (3.28-3.30, repeated from previous examples) illustrate omission of the copula *shi*.

3.28	Wo	[sān]ri	ϕ	wuyue	shiyi	ri.
(L26)	I	birthday	(be)	May	11	day
	My barthday May 11th.					
cf.	Wo	shengri	shi	wuyue	shiyi	ri.
	I	birthday	be	May	11	day
	My birthday is May 11th.					

[17] The omission and underemployment of *de* by this patient is discussed in section 3.1.5.

[18] Richard Sproat has suggested the possibility of a topic-comment structure such as [*wo yanjing*]$_{topic}$ [*zuobian de tuchu le*]$_{comment}$ for this utterance. This possibility is discounted here because it assumes a structure such as [*wo* [*yanjing*]$_i$]$_{topic}$ [*zuobian de* [e]$_i$*tuchu le*]$_{comment}$ (where the [e]$_i$ marks an empty category resulting from the movement of the noun *yanjing* to a position within the topic), which would seem to involve complexity outside the capability of this patient. Furthermore, I followed the judgements of the interviewer and another Taiwan Mandarin informant for the interpretation offered here.

3.29	Jintian	ϕ	siyue	ba	hao.
(L92)	today	(be)	4-month	8	day
	Today April 8th.				
cf.	Jintian	shi	siyue	ba	hao.
	today	be	4-month	8	day
	Today is April 8th.				

3.30	Ta	zhi	ϕ	zhanϕ.
(L150)	he	only	(be)	stand(-ASP)
	He just stand.			
cf.	Ta	zhi	shi	zhanzhe.
	he	only	be	stand-ASP
	He's just standing.			

Copula omission is common in the speech of Broca's aphasics, and is a further indication of the agrammatic character of LXZ's speech.

Prenominal Modification Marker ***de*** It is significant to note that LXZ has not one instance in her speech (in over 60 utterances containing more than 240 words) of the most common word in Mandarin Chinese (Liu et al. 1975, Suen 1979), the prenominal modification marker *de*. This reflects LXZ's difficulty with function words, since *de* is a function word par excellence in Mandarin. This total absence of *de* corresponds to a case study of another Mandarin-speaking Broca's aphasic (Packard 1990a), in whose speech also were found no instances of this prototypical functor. This stands as rather convincing evidence that LXZ indeed fits the 'agrammatic' diagnostic category. An instance of the deletion of *de* from an obligatory context occurs in 3.27, repeated below as 3.31.

3.31	Wo	YANJING	ZUOBIAN	ϕ	tuchu	le.
(L117)	I	eye	left-side	(MOD)	protrude-out	ASP
	My eye left stuck out.					
cf.	Wo	zuobian	de	yanjing	tuchu	le.
	I	left-side	MOD	eye	protrude-out	ASP
	My left eye stuck out.					

Classifiers LXZ uses very few classifiers in her speech, even though classifiers are obligatory with nouns that are modified by numbers and determiners (see 2.16). In her corpus, LXZ produces a grand total of four classifiers, and has at least one instance of the omission of a classifier from an obligatory context, seen in 3.32[19].

3.32	Wo	ϕ	jiali	[yígè]	wu-ϕ	yue.
(L102)	I	(at)	home-in	altogether	five(-C)	month
	I home April altogeber.					
cf.	Wo	zai	jiali	yígòng	wuge	yue.
	I	at	home-in	altogether	five-C	month
	I was at home five months altogether.					

The finding of classifier underemployment and omission by LXZ agrees with the findings of Packard (1990a), who found underemployment and omission of classifiers by another agrammatic Chinese-speaking Broca's aphasic. The findings of Tzeng et al. (1991) are also confirmed by our results. Those investigators found omission of classifiers in obligatory contexts by their aphasic subjects, especially in their Broca's subjects.

LXZ uses very few noun phrase determiners which, in addition to numbers, would be the only appropriate contexts for the use of classifiers. The fact that there are relatively few obligatory contexts for classifiers suggests that LXZ may be employing the strategy of avoiding contexts where classifiers would be used (Tzeng et al. 1991 also suggest that their subjects employed such a strategy).

Coverbs LXZ has *no* instances of coverb (see 2.3.1) use in her speech corpus, and has several instances of the omission of coverbs from obligatory environments. In examples 3.33 and 3.32 (repeated as 3.34), the coverbs

3.33	Wo	ϕ	Daojiang	⊗wo⊗	biyele.
(L21)	I	(from)	Daojiang	I	graduate-ASP
	I graduated I Daojiang.				
cf.	Wo	cong	Daojiang	biyele.	
	I	from	Daojiang	graduate-ASP	
	I graduated from Daojiang.				

'from' and 'at' are omitted from obligatory contexts. In the first example the deleted coverb would occur in conjunction with the sentence main verb ('graduate'), while in the second example the 'coverb' (*zai*, 'at') is actually

3.34	Wo	ϕ	jiali	[yígè]	wu-ϕ	yue.
(L102)	I	(at)	home-in	altogether	five(-C)	month
	I home April altogether.					

[19] Richard Sproat points out that classifiers are the closest thing that Mandarin has to morphological agreement, and so the classifier deletion seen here may be considered parallel to the loss of agreement morphology in a language like Italian.

cf.	Wo	zai	jiali	yígòng	wuge	yue.
	I	at	home-in	altogether	five-C	month
	I was at home five months altogether.					

functioning as a sentence predicate. The absence of coverbs and their deletion from obligatory environments is explained by the underuse and omission of function words commonly seen in Broca's aphasia.

Auxiliary Verbs LXZ uses almost no auxiliary verbs in her speech. The one example of an auxiliary verb in her corpus is the verb *hui* 'can' in example 3.5. Interestingly, LXZ's correct use of the auxiliary verb in this utterance was followed by a phonemic paraphasia affecting the object of the main verb, possibly indicating a 'cost' associated with the production of the auxiliary verb.

Adverbs LXZ has problems using words which normally occupy the adverbial modification slot between the subject and the predicate, as noted in 3.1.5. Below are some examples of adverb misuse. In 3.35 LXZ omits the

3.35	Ta	ϕ	mei	zuo.
(L162)	he	(still)	not	sit
	He didn't sit.			
cf.	Ta	hai	mei	zuo.
	he	still	not	sit
	He hasn't sit yet.			

3.36	Wo	tou...	ϕ	hao	duo	le.
(L111)	I	head	(now)	good	much	ASP
	My head... much better.					
cf.	Wo	tou...	xianzai	hao	duo	le.
	I	head	now	good	much	ASP
	My head... is now much better.					

3.37	Huangshuiye	ϕ	hao	duo	le.
(L113)	yellow-water-liquid	(now)	good	much	ASP
	The pus much better.				
cf.	Huangshuiye	xianzai	hao	duo	le.
	yellow-water-liquid	now	good	much	ASP
	The pus is now much better.				

adverb *hai* 'still' which is highly preferred in this context. In 3.36 and 3.37, the adverb *xianzai* 'now', also preferred in the given context, is omitted.

In 3.38, the adverb *dou* is improperly inserted. This is noteworthy because the addition of extraneous elements, especially function words, is not generally seen in Broca's aphasia.

3.38 (L85)

3.38	Wo	⊗dou⊗	sange	yue	zhi
(L85)	I	all	three-C	month	MOD

All 3 months after I

hou	renshile	yige	ren.
after	know-ASP	one-C	person

knew a person.

cf.

Wo	sange	yue	zhi
I	three-C	month	MOD

After three months,

hou	renshile	yige	ren.
after	know-ASP	one-C	person

I knew a person.

Aspect Marker *le* In Table 3.3 we see that LXZ uses verbal and sentential *le* with about equal frequency. In general, LXZ's use of the aspect

verbal *le*	8
sentential *le*	7
Total *le*	15

Table 3.3: *le* Usage: Li Xinzheng

marker *le* appears quite normal. The same observation regarding a non-fluent aphasic speaker of Mandarin was made in Packard (1990a). If verbal *le* is considered in some sense analogous to verbal inflection which marks temporal aspect in other languages, then the frequency and accuracy with which non-fluent patients use this particle remains to be explained. One possible explanation is that aspect has a broader temporal scope than the punctive nature of tense. Huang (1982a, p. 165) considers verbal *le* to be different from other morphological markers of verb aspect in Mandarin in being generated in INFL, rather than being suffixed in the morphological component. See section 2.3.11 for further discussion.

Despite the relative resilience of the aspect marker *le*, there are a couple of instances of *le* misuse. In 3.39, verbal *le* is omitted from its position as a word suffix.

3.39	Zhan-ϕ	hao	◇duo◇.
(L151)	stand(-ASP)	very	much
	Stand a lot.		
cf.	Zhanle	hao	jiu.
	stand-ASP	very	long
	Has stood a long time.		

Example 3.40 shows the improper cooccurrence of sentential, 'wide-scope' *le*, a past time expression (*libairi*, 'Sunday'), and the negative marker

3.40	Wo	libairi	....	bu	◇renshi◇[20]	ϕ	le.
(L46)	I	Sunday	....	not	recognize	(DO)	ASP
	Sunday I .... don't recognize.						
cf.	Wo	libairi	....	bu	jide.		
	I	Sunday	....	not	remember		
	Sunday I .... didn't remember.						

bu. Since *libairi* ('Sunday') is a time expression being used to refer to a time in the past, and the predicate is negated by *bu*, it is incorrect to end the sentence with *le*. The past time expression and the negative marker may cooccur (meaning 'didn't VERB'), but the addition of *le* makes the sentence ungrammatical (see examples 2.40-2.41)[21].

Verbs

Although there are many verbs in LXZ's corpus, she actually omits several verbs in obligatory environments, or in environments in which omission must be considered only marginally acceptable. 3.41 is an example of the deletion of the verb 'to graduate'.

3.41		Daojiang	wuyue	shiyi	ri	ϕ	ϕ
(L23)		name	five-month	ten-one	day	(graduate)	(EMP)
	cf.	Daojiang	wuyue	shiyi	ri	biye	de.
		name	five-month	ten-one	day	graduate	EMP
		(I) graduated from Daojiang May 11th.					

3.42 is also an example of a sentence-final main verb deletion, with the verb in this case *sheng* 'to be born'.

[20] *renshi* is a semantic paraphasia for *jide*. Also, *renshi* takes an obligatory direct object in this context, which is omitted.

[21] This is a good example of how difficult it is to unambiguously determine which constituent is 'responsible' for the sentence being ungrammatical. For example, the sentence would also be acceptable if no past time expression were used (meaning 'I don't recognize (him) anymore'), or if it were not negated (meaning 'I recognized (him) on Sunday').

3.42 Wo wushi nian ϕ ϕ.
(L30) I five-ten year (born) (EMP)
cf. Wo wushi nian sheng de.
I five-ten year born EMP
I was born in '50.

The main verb *renshi* 'to be acquainted with' is omitted in example 3.43, along with the aspect marker *le* that would be obligatory in this position.

3.43 ...renshile yige ren.
(L88) ...know-ASP one-C person
'...knew a person.'
Wo ϕ-ϕ sige yue.
I (know-ASP) four-C month
I four months.
cf. Wo renshile sige yue.
I know-ASP four-C month
I knew (him) four months.

3.1.6 Discourse and Pragmatics

LXZ displays improper discourse structure in her speech, manifested primarily in the discontinuity of topic[22]. Her use of topics that seem out of place is seen in the following selection (3.44), in which she becomes confused in the discussion of dates.

3.44 Wo ⊗dou⊗ sange yue
(L85) I all three-C month
All 3 months after I
zhi hou renshile yige ren.
MOD after know-ASP one-C person
knew a person.
Wo ϕ-ϕ sige yue.
I (know-ASP) four-C month
I four months.
Wo... wo ϕ jiali siyue san er...
I I (at) home-in four-month three two
I... I home April three two...
sanyue er hao... siyue er hao.
3-month 2 day 4-month 2 day
March 2nd... April 2nd.

[22] These findings are similar to those of Ulatowska et al. (1990).

Jintian	siyue	ba	hao.
today	4-month	8	day

Today is April 8th.

LXZ employs virtually none of the words used to mark discourse continuity in Mandarin (see 2.3.7 and 2.4). Such 'discourse conjunctions' as *nemmo* ('then, so'), *hai you* ('also'), *erqie* ('furthermore') and *ranhou* ('then, afterward') are completly absent from her speech.

LXZ's introduction of entities into the discourse is sometimes irregular. In 3.45, the words *mama* 'mother' and *cai* 'dish, course' are used in the

3.45	Mama,	ta	jide	wo...	wo	zhu	fan.
(L56)	mom	she	recall	I	I	cook	food

Mom, she remembers I... I cook food.

Wo	jide	le.	Cai,	wo	dou	bu	jide.
I	recall	ASP	dishes	I	all	not	recall

I remember. The dishes, I don't remember.

appropriate position for a sentential topic, namely sentence-initial position. However, these nouns are being introduced into the discourse for the first time. Entities which are newly introduced generally do not occur in canonical topic position, since that position is generally reserved for 'old' or previously mentioned information (see 2.4). LXZ's inappropriate use of sentence-initial position for the introduction of a noun into the discourse is an indication of her problems with discourse structure.

Despite these flaws in LXZ's use of discourse, we should note that the overall structure of her discourse is nonetheless often good, as one gets the feeling in reading her corpus that she is often able to preserve a semblance of topic continuity. This is especially true when her discourse structure is compared to that of a Wernicke's aphasic (such as YXF), in which random shifts of topic are the norm.

Turning to linguistic pragmatics, a remarkable characteristic of LXZ's speech is the total absence of the sentence-final particles which serve pragmatic functions such as exclamation, rhetorical question, emphasis, suggestion and assertion (see 2.4). Also, when giving short, confirmation-type answers to questions, LXZ always uses the stative verb *dui* 'right', and never uses very common pragmatic affirmation particles such as *ei* and *hei*, or the copula *shi*, which is also commonly used for affirmation response. LXZ's failure to use pragmatic particles may be explained by the fact that they are semantically empty function words. Her use of *dui* in short responses is probably because *dui*, as a stative verb, is a bona fide content word. This finding illustrates the unsuitability of the 'least effort' or 'economy' theory of non-fluent aphasic speech (e.g., Salomon 1914), since if the content of LXZ's speech were determined by a 'least effort' principle, it would be difficult to explain her overwhelming preference for using the stative verb *dui* as a short affirmation response.

3.2 Subject #2: Guo Jiande

3.2.1 Background

GJD is a 57-year-old male who suffered from left hemisphere damage as a result of multiple parietal and occipital infarcts. His speech may be described as syntactically simple and often correct, but perseverative and void of referential meaning, with extreme overuse of semantically empty words (including function words) and a corresponding underemployment of referential content words. GJD experiences severe perseveration in the production of certain words and phrases. His listening comprehension may be characterized as very poor, since he has difficulty giving answers to even the simplest of questions. GJD's profile is seen in Table 3.4.

age	57	sex	male
lesion type	infarct	location	parietal/occipital
diagnostic category	Wernicke's	fluency	fair-poor
semantic content	poor	effortful speech	no
comprehension	poor	functor omission	no
phrase length	short	complex syntax	no
distortions	yes	substitutions	yes
intonation	'normal'	anomia	severe
neologism	yes	jargon	yes
discourse structure	poor	repetition	poor

Table 3.4: Patient Profile: Guo Jiande

The most salient characteristics of GJD's speech are its short, impoverished structure and its semantic vacuity. The syntactic structure of GJD's speech is overly simple, and the syntactic slots tend to be filled with words which have little referential content. The words he uses are either perseverations of words that he or the experimenter has previously produced, or else words that have little intrinsic semantic content. GJD's speech therefore is filled with function words such as the prenominal modifier *de*, the conjunctions *buguo* ('but') and *nemmo* ('then'), the copula *shi*, classifiers (usually with preceding determiners or numbers), auxiliary verbs (primarily *yao* 'will, want'), and the semantically broad verb *you* 'have'. In addition, he uses many deictic items such as pronouns and the determiners *zhei* 'this' and *nei* 'that'. GJD makes heavy use of adverbials with minimal semantic content such as *dou* ('all'), *jiu* ('then, only'), *zhi* ('only'), *xianzai* ('now'), *you* ('again'), *hai* ('still') and *yuanlai* ('originally'). GJD also uses a lot of sentence final particles and hestitation pauses, which have a pragmatic function but have little referential content.

The semantic vacuity and relatively preserved (albeit simplified) grammatical structure of GJD's speech have resulted in his being categorized as a 'Wernicke's' aphasic, but his speech is not 'fluent' in the conventional sense, i.e., it does not contain long, facile strings of incomprehensible jargon. Rather, it is fluent in the sense that the output is rapid and continuous, and not slow and labored (as with a Broca's aphasic). In addition, his speech is rather unlike a 'typical' fluent aphasic in the reduced complexity of its grammatical structure.

Linguistic Background

GJD was born in Rehe in Sichuan, making him a speaker of southern Mandarin. He came to Taiwan around 1949, at the age of 23. As a speaker of southern Mandarin, as in the case of LXZ, when he produces apical consonants in place of retroflexes, they are not considered to be in error.

3.2.2 Phonology

GJD's speech is phonologically dysfunctional, with the greatest problem being phoneme and syllable perseveration. There are also some instances of phonological paraphasia, as seen in 3.46.

3.46	dōu	→	*dōng
	dànshì	→	*duànshì

As with patient LXZ, the phonotactics of Mandarin syllable structure are largely preserved in GJD's speech, even when non-words and phonological substitutions are produced. One exception to this is seen in 3.47, in which GJD produces a non-word that is also an impermissible syllable shape in

3.47	∇diăng..diáng∇	zheizhi	a.
(G17)	???	this-C	EXC
	??? this one.		

Mandarin. The syllable **diang* violates Mandarin phonotactic rules, since the final [iang] may not be preceded by a non-sonorant stop consonant.

3.2.3 Lexical Selection

Verbal Paraphasias

GJD produced several instances of verbal paraphasia. The first few examples involve the use of classifiers. In 3.48, he improperly uses a number

3.48	Kuaizi	shi	bijiao	ϕ	<yi>zhi	shou	ma.
(G23)	chopsticks	be	compare	(use)	one-C	hand	AFF
	As for chopsticks, I more one hand.						
cf.	Kuaizi	shi	bijiao	yong	zheizhi	shou	ma.
	chopsticks	be	compare	use	this-C	hand	AFF
	As for chopsticks, I use this hand more.						

to accompany the classifier rather than the appropriate demonstrative, such as *zhei-* ('this'). This explanation presumes that the verb *yong* ('use') should have appeared in the sentence and was omitted.

3.49	Wo	XIANZAI	BUGUO	jiu	you	<yizhi	shou>.
(G42)	I	now	however	only	have	one-C	hand
	I now but have only one.. one hand.						
cf.	Buguo	wo	xianzai	jiu	you	yige	xiaohaizi.
	but	I	now	only	have	one-C	child
	But now I only have one child.						

In 3.49, GJD improperly uses the perseverative form *yizhi shou* ('one hand') instead of the target *yige haizi* ('one child'). In producing the erroneous form, the subject produces the classifier appropriate to the erroneous form *shou* and not the target form *haizi*. This is a phenomenon we have seen before in our data, and indicates that in noun substitution, it is the entire noun phrase that has been substituted, and not just the head noun.

In 3.50, the object of the sentence should be *bingyi* ('military service').

3.50	Yige	ta	fu	<yige>.
(G156)	one-C	he	serve	one-C
	One he served one.			
cf.	Yige	ta	fu	bingyi.
	one-C	he	serve	military
	One, he served in the military.			

GJD instead substitutes the perseverative and semantically vacuous number-classifier combination *yige*.

3.51	HAI	YOU	YUANLAI	nei<ge>	shu	a...
(G214)	also	have	original	that-C	book	EXC
	There was also originally that book...					
cf.	Yuanlai	hai	you	neiben	shu	a...
	original	also	have	that-C	book	EXC
	Originally, there was also that book...					

In 3.51, the generic classifier *-ge* is improperly used in place of proper classifier for book, i.e., *-ben*[23].

In 3.52, the improperly substituted verb *yǒu* 'have' is neither semantically nor phonologically related to the putative target 'ask', but seems to be

3.52	Nemmo	yao	<you>	zidian	zenmoyang?
(G236)	then	want	have	dictionary	what:about
	Then what do (you) want to have about the dictionary?				
cf.	Nemmo	yao	wen	zidian	zenmoyang?
	then	want	ask	dictionary	what:about
	Then what do (you) want to ask about the dictionary?				

once again the substitution of a generic verb which has a wide semantic field.

In the final example of verbal paraphasia (3.53), in asking the experimenter if she wants to have a child, GJD improperly substitutes the verb *yong* 'use' for the verb *sheng* 'give birth to'. Since the verb 'use' sometimes

3.53	Xianzai,	zheige	xiaohair,	ni	yao bu yao	<yong>?
(G168)	now	this-C	child	you	want not want	use
	Now, this child, do you want to use it?					
cf.	Xianzai,	zheige	xiaohair,	ni	yao bu yao	sheng?
	now	this-C	child	you	want not want	bear
	Now, this child, do you want to have it?					

refers to the bearing of offspring by animals, it could be analyzed as a semantic error. However, it is more likely the substitution of a more general verb (as in the preceding example), in conformity with the general character of GJD's speech.

Semantic Paraphasias

There were no instances of semantic paraphasia in GJD's speech. This fact may be explained by the absence of semantic content of his speech in

[23] Note, however, that use of the 'generic' classifier *-ge* is sometimes seen as marginally acceptable as a substitute for more specific classifiers.

general. The contrast to be noted here is semantic *content* versus semantic *control*. GJD's speech lacks semantic content, while the following subject YXF lacks control over the semantics of his speech as manifest in his random use of words. Therefore it is understandable that GJD would make few semantic substitutions, since his speech is intrinsically somewhat void of semantic content to begin with.

Jargon

There are two instances of jargon in the speech corpus of GJD. In the first example (3.54), he produces the verb *hua* 'spend' in a grammatical slot

3.54	Hai	you	yige	yòu	yao	⋈huā⋈zhe	ta...
(G112)	also	have	one-C	again	want	spend-ASP	it
	There's also one that we again wanted to spend it...						

appropriate for a verb, but the context is totally inappropriate (i.e., what is being 'spent' is a child). Note that in this example, the jargon form is inflected with the level IV suffix *-zhe* indicating continuation. In the second

3.55	⋈Diǎn..diǎn⋈	yizhi	shou.
(G26)	count..count	one-C	hand
	Count..count one hand.		

example of jargon (3.55), the verb *dian* 'count' also appears in a verb slot, but is inappropriate to the context.

Neologism

GJD produces one instance of neologism in his speech, seen in example 3.47, repeated as 3.56.

3.56	∇diǎng..diáng∇	zheizhi	a.
(G17)	???	this-C	EXC
	??? this one.		

The form **diang* is not a possible Mandarin word, as discussed in section 3.2.2.

3.2.4 Word Formation

GJD makes several errors in the formation of words. As seen in Table 3.5, word formation problems plague the subject across all levels of the lexicon.

	Level I	Level II	Level III	Level IV
number of tokens	69	33	109	7
number in error	3	8	14	1
percent in error	4.3%	24.2%	12.8%	14.3%

Table 3.5: Word Error at Various Lexical Levels: Guo Jiande

In 3.57 we see a most interesting example of word formation error, with the improper insertion of the classifier *-ge* inside of the word *nemmo* ('so'), yielding the nonexistent word **negemo*. One explanation for this word

3.57	Wo	meiyou	ne⊗ge⊗mo	duo	a.
(G66)	I	not-have	that-C-so	many	EMP
cf.	Wo	meiyou	nemme	duo	a.
	I	not-have	that-so	many	EMP
	I don't have that many.				

formation error is that, according to the LPM theory of Mandarin word formation outlined in 2.2.1, both *neige* and *nemmo* are formed at lexical level III (by the affixation of *-ge* and *-mo* respectively to *nei-*). It may be that the erroneous insertion of *-ge* is because *-ge* and *-mo* affixation occur at the same level, allowing *-ge* 'easier access' to the internal structure of *nemmo*. Another, more intuitive, explanation for the error is that the determiner *nei-* 'that' occurs so frequently with the classifier *-ge* in the form *neige* that the subject inappropriately attaches *-ge* to the *nei-* even though it is part of a larger word. The same type of error is seen in 3.58, where

3.58	You	sige	nei⊗ge⊗yang	ren.
(G90)	have	four-C	that-C-C:type	person
cf.	You	sige	neiyang	ren.
	have	four-C	that-type	person
	There are four of that type of person.			

instead of *nei-* attaching to *-yang* 'kind, type' (which is functioning as a classifier in this context) to yield *neiyang* 'that type', the classifier *-ge* once again is 'attracted' by the determiner and is inappropriately inserted into a word-internal position. Once again, the affixation both of classifiers and of *nei-* are level III morphological processes, and so the intrusion of *-ge* into the word *neiyang* may be understood as a breakdown in word formation processes *within* a given lexical word formation level.

In 3.59 we see the omission of the nominal suffix *-zi*. A possible explanation for the omission of *-zi* (even though its suffixation is a rather 'deep' level II process) is its almost total lack of semantic content and absence of grammatical function.

3.59	Buguo	liangge	qiao	bian-ϕ.
(G132)	but	two-C	stick:up	braid(-NOM)
cf.	Buguo	liangge	qiao	bianzi[24].
	but	two-C	stick:up	braid-NOM
	But two of them kicked the bucket.			

Furthermore, GJD technically has been classified as a 'fluent' (albeit not prototypical) aphasic, and fluent subjects may not exhibit the 'grading effect' which we saw in the non-fluent patient LXZ, whereby fewer word formation errors occur at 'deeper' lexical levels. This possibility is further indicated by example 3.60, in which part of the conjunction *buguo* 'however'

3.60		ϕ-guo	ta	sishi	ji	nian...
(G44)		(how-)ever	he	forty	few	year
	cf.	Buguo	ta	sishi	ji	nian...
		however	he	forty	few	year
		However for forty-odd years he...				

is deleted. Since this word is formed at lexical level I, its decomposition is relatively unexpected given the strength with which morphemes are bound in words formed at this level. The deletion may also be attributed to the severity of this subject's affliction.

In 3.61 are additional examples demonstrating the severity of GJD's word formation deficit. In this short dialogue, the subject is unable to

3.61	E:	Nadiao[25],	shi bu shi?			
(G116)		take-away	be not be			
		Taken away, right?				
	S:	Meiyou.	Na-ϕ	yige.		
		not-have	take(-away)	one-C		
		No. Take one.				
	E:	Na	yige	a.	Nadiao	yige.
		take	one-C	EMP	take-away	one-C
		Take one. Took away one.				

[24] *Qiào biànzi* 'Stick up the braids' is a slang expression referring to death in Mandarin.
[25] Slang for an aborted pregnancy.

S:	Ei.	Na-ϕ	yige.	Na-ϕ	yige	jiu...
	AFF	take(-away)	one-C	take(-away)	one-C	then
	Take one. Take one then...					

produce the resultative ending *-diao* 'to fall away' attached to the verb *ná* 'take'.

The final example of word formation deficit demonstrates the improper omission of the prototypical functor *de*, here used as a word-forming element. GJD realizes his error and self-corrects.

3.62	...hai	yige	nu-ϕ.	Nude	la.
(G128)	also	one-C	female(-MOD)	female-MOD	EMP
	...there's also a g-. Girl.				

3.2.5 Syntax

The syntactic structure of GJD's speech may be characterized as non-complex, with some disturbances in word order. GJD fills the syntactic slots of basic structures with words of little semantic weight. He also uses an overabundance of adverbs, often placing several within the same sentence adverbial slot.

The simple syntax GJD employs is often structurally correct, as seen in the two correct examples of (SUBJ-MOD-VERB-OBJ) in 3.63 and 3.64 below.

3.63	Wo	dou	yong..	yong	you	shou.
(G39)	I	all	use	use	right	hand
	I always use.. use my right hand.					

3.64	Ta	dou	you	liangge.
(G52)	she	all	have	two-C
	She has 2 in all.			

However GJD rarely produces utterances that are structurally more complex than this, and his utterances in general rarely represent any meaningful relation to a coherent discourse.

GJD uses many complex noun phrases (as seen in 3.65 and 3.66), but

3.65	Liang-ϕ	bijiao	pangde.
(G3)	two(-C)	compare	fat-MOD
	Couple relatively fat ones.		

3.66	Bijiao	neige..	neige..	neiϕ	pangde.
(G5)	compare	that-C	that-C	that(-C)	fat-MOD
	That.. that.. fat.. fatter that one.				

does not embed such structures in matrix sentences.

Word Order

There are several instances of improper word order in GJD's speech. Interestingly, these word order errors most often involve the ordering of whole sentential constituents (such as the subject noun phrase or the sentence adverbial rather than the ordering of items within constituents (cf. examples 3.26 and 3.27 for patient LXZ, and following discussion). By far the majority of errors involve the use of adverbial elements. Examples of bad word order in 3.67-3.72 below all involve the placement of adverbials. In

3.67	HAI	YOU	YUANLAI...
(G214)	also	have	original
	There was also originally..		
cf.	Yuanlai	hai	you...
	original	also	have
	Originally, there was also...		

3.67, *yuanlai* 'originally' should come before the verb and before the adverb *hai* 'also'. In 3.68, the subject of the second clause *ta* should occur before

3.68	Naϕ	yige	JIU	TA	ϕ	yige.
(G119)	take(-away)	one-C	then	he	(left)	one-C
cf.	Nadiao	yige	ta	jiu	shèngxia	yige.
	take-away	one-C	he	then	left	one-C
	(He) took away one. Then he was left with one.					

the adverb *jiu*. In 3.69, the use of the first *jiu* is redundant and also occurs

3.69	... ⊗JIU⊗	BUGUO	TA	jiu...
(G153)	only	but	he	only
	...only but only she...			

in the wrong syntactic position, namely, at the beginning of the sentence.

3.70	YE	ZHEIZHI	bijiao	pang.
(G15)	also	this-C	compare	fat
cf.	Zheizhi	ye	bijiao	pang.
	this-C	also	compare	fat
	...this one is also relatively fat.			

In 3.70, the subject *zheizhi* 'this hand' and adverb *ye* 'also' are improperly reversed. In 3.71, the positions of the two adverbials *xianzai* 'now' and

3.71	Ta	<SHI>	YIGONG	XIANZAI	sange.
(G79)	she	be	altogether	now	three-C
	She now is altogether three.				
cf.	Ta	xianzai	yigong	you	sange.
	she	now	altogether	have	three-C
	Altogether, she now has three.				

yigong 'altogether' should be reversed. In addition, both adverbials incorrectly occur after the verb (the verb *shi* 'is' is an incorrect substitution for the verb *you* 'have').

3.72 is an example of the improper ordering of elements *within* a form class constituent. In this example, the internal constituents of of a complex

3.72	BIJIAO	NEI<GE>[26]	pangde.
(G79)	compare	that-C	fat-MOD
cf.	Neizhi	bijiao	pangde.
	that-C	compare	fat-MOD
	That relatively fat (one).		

noun phrase are disordered, with the extent adverbial *bijiao* occurring before the determiner *neige*.

Mistakes in word order also occur with words other than adverbs. In 3.73, the conjunction *buguo* improperly occurs in a sentence internal

3.73	WO	XIANZAI	BUGUO	jiu	you...
(G42)	I	now	however	only	have
	I now but have only...				
cf.	Buguo	wo	xianzai	jiu	you...
	however	I	now	only	have
	But I now have only...				

position instead of in its proper place at the beginning of the sentence. In the second sentence of example 3.74, we see the subject of the sentence wrongly occurring at the end rather than at the beginning of the sentence.

3.74	Yige	ta	fu	<yige>.	FU	<YIGE>	TA.
(G156)	one-C	he	serve	one-C	serve	one-C	he

[26] The incorrect classifier is discussed in the section on classifiers.

cf.	Yige	ta	fu	bingyi.	Ta	fu	bingyi.
	one-C	he	serve	military	he	serve	military

One, he served in the military. He served in the military.

The same error occurs in 3.75. In describing a picture of a person washing

3.75	XI	WAN	ZHEIGE	ϕ
(G196)	wash	dish	this-C	(be)

Washing dishes th-.. this.

cf. (e.g.)	Zheige	shi	xi	wan.
	this-C	be	wash	dish

This is washing dishes.

dishes, GJD improperly puts the subject *zheige* ('this') at the end of the sentence.

Function Words

GJD uses an overabundance of semantically empty function words. The following speech segment (3.76) presents an example of the general overuse of function words and lack of content words which typifies his speech.

3.76	Nansheng	dou	si	yige	la	de.	Hai	you
(G142)	male-student	all	die	one-C	EXC	MOD	also	have

Of all the boys, one died. There's also...

yige	le.	Hai	you...	yige	le.	Hai	you
one-C	ASP	still	have	one-C	ASP	still	have

...another. There's also... another. There's also...

zheige...	xianzai...	buguo	tade...	dou	meiyou	le.
this-C	now	but	him-MOD	all	not-have	ASP

...this... now... but his... is all gone.

Copula There are several instances of the copula *shi* in GJD's speech corpus. In two cases, the use of *shi* may be considered aberrant. The first was the substitution of *you* 'have' for *shi* as seen in 3.71. The second was the deletion of *shi* as seen in 3.75 **xi wan zheige*.

Prenominal Modification Marker *de* GJD uses the prototypical functor *de* a good deal, but usually uses it with no modified nominal head. Of the 12 occurrences of *de* in GJD's corpus, 10 are these so-called 'headless' forms in which the modified nominal is a null element (see 2.3.2). The headless form of the *de* structure is used in Mandarin when referring to a noun which is understood from the context, or when the noun is not specific (e.g., *the one* who hit the ball). This usage of *de* by GJD is interesting especially when compared with the non-fluent Broca's subject LXZ, who used no *de* whatsoever. The non-use of the structure by LXZ is an indication of her problems with grammatical structure, while the overuse of the headless *de* form by GJD is an indication of the (relative) grammatical integrity but semantic vacuity of his speech.

Classifiers The most obvious characteristic regarding GJD's use of classifiers is their overuse, both with determiners as hesitation pauses and with numerals as non-specific fillers. In addition, there are several specific instances of error in his use of classifiers. First, the improper insertion of the classifier *-ge* inside of *nemmo*, giving the improper form **negemo*, as seen in examples 3.77 and 3.78 (which are 3.57 and 3.58 repeated; see discussion in section 3.2.4).

3.77	Wo	meiyou	ne⊗ge⊗mo	duo	a.
(G66)	I	not-have	that-C-so	many	EMP
cf.	Wo	meiyou	nemme	duo	a.
	I	not-have	that-so	many	EMP
	I don't have that many.				

3.78	You	sige	nei⊗ge⊗yang	ren.
(G90)	have	four-C	that-C-C:type	person
cf.	You	sige	neiyang	ren.
	have	four-C	that-type	person
	There are four of that type of person.			

Also, classifiers were improperly omitted in examples 3.79-3.80.

3.79		neiϕ	pangde
(G5)		that(-C)	fat-MOD
	cf.	neige	pangde
		that-C	fat-MOD
		that fat one	

3.80		Liangϕ	bijiao	pangde.
(G3)		two(-C)	compare	fat
	cf.	Liangge	bijiao	pangde.
		two-C	compare	fat
		Two relatively fat (ones).		

In 3.81 and 3.82 GJD uses the wrong classifier.

3.81		nei<ge>	shu
(G214)		that-C	book
	cf.	neiben	shu
		that book	

3.82	E:	Zheizhi	haishi	zheizhi?
(G4)		this-C	or	this-C
		This one or this one?		
	S:	Bijiao	nei<ge>[27]	pangde.
		compare	that-C	fat-MOD
	cf.	Neizhi	bijiao	pangde.
		that-C	compare	fat-MOD
		That relatively fat (one).		

Coverbs GJD's speech is remarkable for its near total absence of coverbs, especially given his technical classification as a 'fluent' aphasic. The only coverb GJD uses (used as a coverb rather than a verb) is *gen*, seen below in 3.83.

3.83	Mm...	Ni	shuo	yao	gen	shu
(G219)	HES	you	say	want	with	book
	How did you say you want to want the dictionary					
	zenmoyang	yao	zidian?			
	what:about	want	dictionary			
	with the book?					

Two remarks should be made about the use of the coverb *gen* here. First, it had been used by the experimenter in the previous utterance so the possibility of its use by GJD as a mere perseverative repetition cannot be ruled out. Second, the sentence in which it is used is total nonsense, suggesting a lack of control over the use of the word.

A possible explanation for the lack of coverbs in GJD's speech is the impoverished nature of his syntactic structure in general, in spite of the fact that he is a 'fluent' aphasic. Coverbial phrases are moderately complex grammatical structures in Mandarin, so GJD may be avoiding the use of coverbs since they add just that much more complexity to the syntactic structure of the sentence.

[27] Once again, the use of the 'generic' classifier *-ge* is often marginally acceptable as a substitute for a more specific classifier.

verbal *le*	2
sentential *le*	7
Total *le*	9

Table 3.6: *le* Usage: Guo Jiande

Auxiliary Verbs The only auxiliary verb used by GJD in conjunction with a main verb is *yao* 'want', which he uses several times in the corpus (e.g., Appendix entries G75, G112, G150, G168, G219, G226, G236). This is a reflection of the impoverished syntactic structure of GJD's speech and its lack of semantic content.

Adverbs As seen in numerous examples (e.g., 3.67, 3.68, 3.70), GJD misuses adverbials such as *hai*, *dou*, *jiu*, *ye* as well as time adverbials such as *yuanlai* and *xianzai*. GJD is prolific in his use of adverbs, often placing them in the wrong syntactic position, or misordering them within the adverb slot. In many instances it seems as though GJD is using the adverbs as a kind of filler or hesitation pause. The result of such usage is that they appear in improper syntactic positions.

GJD's misuse of adverbs is easily explained by the fact that adverbs are classified as function words. The overgeneration of function words, including their placement in inappropriate slots, is a salient characteristic of GJD's speech. His overuse of adverbs is especially evident when his speech is compared to that of the Broca's aphasic LXZ, who underuses and omits adverbials.

Aspect Marker ***le*** As seen in Table 3.6, nearly all instances of *le* used by GJD are sentential, with wide scope. There are only two instances (*chaile* G226, and *shuole* G200) of 'verbal' le.

Conjunctions GJD overuses the 'discourse conjunction' *buguo* ('however'), often as a kind of filler or hesitation pause, as seen in examples 3.84-3.87 below (some repeated).

3.84	⊗Jiu⊗	buguo	ta	jiu	hai	yige	la.
(G153)	just	however	he	just	still	one-C	EXC
	Just however he just has one.						

3.85	⊗Wo⊗	buguo	ta	neige	jiu...			
(G126)	I	however	she	that-C	only			
	I however she only...							

3.86	Wo	XIANZAI	BUGUO	jiu	you	<yizhi	shou>.	
(G42)	I	now	however	only	have	one-	one-C	hand
	I now but have only one.. one hand.							

3.87	xianzai...	buguo	tade...	dou	meiyou	le.	
(G144)	now	however	he-MOD	all	not-have	ASP	
	now...but his...is all gone.						

GJD's use of *buguo* 'however' as a semantic filler is comparable to his use of adverbs for the same purpose. Both adverbs and conjunctions like *buguo* are semantically empty function words, which GJD has a tendency to overuse.

Verbs

There are several examples of main verbs omitted from obligatory contexts. In 3.88, the verb (presumably something like *shèng* 'to be left over') is

3.88	Ei.	Na-ϕ	yige.	Na-ϕ	yige	jiu...
(G119)	AFF	take(-away)	one-C	take(-away)	one-C	then
	Take one. Take one then...					

JIU	TA..	TA	ϕ	yige..	yige.
then	he	he	(leave)	one-C	one-C
then she.. she one.. one.					

omitted in the second clause. In the next example, the sentence contains no verb at all, having been omitted from its position between the adverb

3.89	Nan..	nan..	nansheng	jiu	ϕ	sige.
(G97)	male-	male-	male-child	only	(have)	4-C
	Boy.. boy.. boys just 4.					

jiu and the object *sige*. In 3.90, GJD responds to a question containing *you* 'have' with a sentence containing a subject and an adverb, but is

3.90	E:	Shei?	Shei	you	liangge?
(G70)		who	who	have	2-C
		Who? Who has 2?			

S:	Eh..	Wo	xianzai	φ	a.
	HES	I	now	(have)	EMP
	Eh.. I now.				

missing the obligatory verb. The verb would not have been obligatory had the adverb not been used.

Example 3.91 contains no predicate at all. Minimally, the sentence should contain a main verb. Also, for the sentence to be pragmatically correct it should contain a coverbial phrase stating what he does with the chopsticks. In 3.92 as well, the main verb *yong* 'use' is omitted.

3.91	Wo..	de..	zh-..	φ	kuaizi.
(G27)	I	MOD	[zh-]	(use)	chopsticks
cf. (e.g.)	Wo	yong	kuaizi.		
	I	use	chopsticks		
	I use chopsticks.				

3.92	Kuaizi	shi	bijiao	φ	<yi>[28]zhi	shou	ma.
(G23)	chopsticks	be	compare	(use)	one-C	hand	AFF
	As for chopsticks, I more one hand.						
cf.	Kuaizi	shi	bijiao	yong	zheizhi	shou	ma.
	chopsticks	be	compare	use	this-C	hand	AFF
	As for chopsticks, I use this hand more.						

In 3.93, GJD omits the verb *you* 'have' in a couple of places.

3.93	Mm.	You	liuge	ta..	ta	jiu	φ	yige.	Ta..
(G62)	AFF	have	6-C	she	she	only	(have)	1-C	she
	Mm. I have 6 she.. she only 1. She..								
	ta..	ta	you	liangge.	Ta	φ	liangge	sange.	
	she	she	have	2-C	she	have	2-C	3-C	
	she.. she has 2. She two three.								

3.2.6 Discourse and Pragmatics

GJD is severely aphasic, and therefore produces almost no coherent discourse structure. The words and sentences GJD uses often are repetitions or modifications of things that were just said, rather than being related to any meaningful discourse. GJD seemed able to produce the topic in the appropriate sentence-initial position. However, sometimes the 'topic' is

[28] This verbal paraphasia is discussed in the section on paraphasias.

jargon-like, and even when successfully produced, the comment usually is either jargon or is not related to the topic.

In terms of pragmatics, in giving short, affirmative answers to questions, GJD usually uses referentially-empty pragmatic affirmation particles such as *ei*, *hei*, *hm*, *mm* and *ho*. This is in stark contrast with the non-fluent subject LXZ, who never uses the pragmatic affirmation markers and almost always uses the content word *dui* 'right' for this purpose.

3.3 Subject #3: Yang Xifeng

3.3.1 Background

YXF is a 52-year-old male from Sichuan province. His neurological etiology is that of a massive CVA (cardio-vascular accident, i.e., stroke) in the temporo-parietal area of the left hemisphere. His speech symptoms are those of a classic Wernicke's aphasia, manifested in abnormally fluent speech with little semantic control, excessive jargon and neologism, poor comprehension, fairly intact syntax, and multiple phonemic paraphasias. The most remarkable and obvious characteristic of this patient's speech is its extreme fluency and meaninglessness. YXF's profile is seen in Table 3.7.

age	52	sex	male
lesion type	CVA	lesion location	temporo-parietal
diagnostic category	Wernicke's	fluency	good
semantic content	poor	effortful speech	no
comprehension	poor	functor omission	no
phrase length	normal	complex syntax	yes
distortions	some	substitutions	yes
intonation	normal	anomia	yes
neologism	yes	jargon	yes
discourse structure	poor	repetition	poor

Table 3.7: Patient Profile: Yang Xifeng

YXF's speech may be compared with that of GJD (subject #2), who also produced speech that had little meaning. One clear difference between the two subjects is that YXF uses a varied assortment of both content and function words to fill syntactic slots, while GJD's speech contains a high proportion of function words. Furthermore, the function words used by GJD form a very restricted set, i.e., the ones that are semantically the most general and least meaningful. The meaninglessness of YXF's speech is therefore due to the lack of relevance between the words he uses and any perceptible discourse context (i.e., he produces a lot of verbal and semantic paraphasias), while the meaninglessness of GJD's speech results from his use of words which have little intrinsic semantic content. Another difference between the two subjects is that YXF produces utterances that are longer and structurally more complex.

yisheng	→	*yijin	zhen	→	*jian
shuăng	→	*săng	xiáojiĕ	→	*xiáojiān
	→	*shuăi	dou	→	*de
sùi	→	*dùi	zùo	→	*zŭ
	→	*hùi	yìjiàn	→	*yīzhēn
zhun	→	*ji		→	*yìzhèn
dà	→	*duăi	dŏng	→	*dōng
	→	*duài	zhēn	→	*zhèn
dă	→	*dà	sì	→	*sī
cì	→	*cī	dà	→	*dā
zùo	→	*zŭo			

Table 3.8: Phonological Paraphasias: Yang Xifeng

Linguistic Background

YXF's native dialect is Sichuan Mandarin, which differs from standard Mandarin primarily in pronunciation (mostly in the use of apical rather than retroflex consonants) and lexical items. As in the case of the other two patients with a southern Mandarin background (LXZ and GJD), the production of an apical consonant in place of a retroflex consonant is not considered a phonological error.

3.3.2 Phonology

YXF made many errors in pronunciation, all of which were phoneme substitutions rather than phonetic distortions. Table 3.8 gives examples of these errors. Due to the fact that YXF's speech is rife with neologistic jargon, it can sometimes be difficult to unambiguously identify phonological errors in his speech. For example, it is often unclear whether the erroneous form is the 'incorrect' pronunciation of a 'correct' lexical retrieval, or whether it is some other type of error, such as jargon or a word substitution error (see examples 3.1 and 3.2, and related discussion). The targets in Table 3.8 could be identified with a high degree of certainty because of the surrounding context. Also, because YXF is a speaker of Sichuan Mandarin, it can sometimes be difficult to tell whether an apparent 'error' in pronunciation is in fact acceptable in YXF's Sichuanese subdialect of Mandarin. In such cases it was necessary to rely on the judgements of a native speaker of

Sichuan Mandarin[29].

3.3.3 Lexical Selection

YXF's speech was full of errors in lexical selection, most of which were instances of jargon and neologism.

Verbal Paraphasias

YXF produced only one instance of what could be defined unambiguously as a verbal paraphasia. The relative absence of verbal paraphasias in the text may be partially a matter of how terms are defined. That is, the target must be identifiable for an error to be termed a verbal paraphasia, but it is often difficult to identify an intended target word. In example 3.94, YXF was describing the 'cookie theft' picture often used to elicit speech production in aphasia (Goodglass and Kaplan 1972). The target production

3.94		Jiào	tā	bú	yào	<bǎng>.
(Y316)		make	him	not	want	tie:up
		To keep him from getting tied up.				
	cf. (e.g.)	Jiào	tā	bú	yào	diàoxiàqù.
		make	him	not	want	fall-down-go
		To keep him from falling.				

here ostensibly involves the girl helping the boy to keep from falling off the stool. Instead of a word for 'fall' (such as *diaoxia*, *shuai* or *diedao*), YXF produces the word *bǎng* meaning 'tie up', which clearly has nothing to do with the depicted scene.

Semantic Paraphasias

Many of YXF's word selection errors are words which are semantically related to the target. 3.95 and 3.96 are examples of semantic paraphasias which occur in the formation of words. In 3.95, the coverb *cong* 'from' improperly occurs in the place of *qu* 'go' in the formation of the word *qunian* 'last year'.

3.95		◇cóngnián◇
(Y30)		from-year
	cf.	qùnián
		go-year
		last year

[29] My thanks to Chen Xiaoyu.

When used as a part of a compound word, *cong* sometimes is used to denote past time, as in the compounds *congqian* (from-before) 'in the past', *congxiao* (from-small) 'since childhood', and *zicong* (from-from) 'ever since'. However, the word **congnian* does not exist. This therefore is an error of word formation, in which the substituted word component is semantically related to the target word component.

In 3.96, YXF uses the improper form of a number in forming a word. In Mandarin, the number 'two' occurs in two variant forms: *liang* and *er*. When 'two' modifies a noun, *liang* is used with an accompanying classifier, as in: *liangge ren* (two-C people) 'two people' (cf. **erge ren*). In all other cases, *er* is used (as in: *yi, er, san* 'one, two, three', *shier* 'twelve' or *ershi*

3.96	Wǒ...	◇liǎngshí◇	èr	◇nián◇	a.
(Y37)	I	couple-ten	two	year	EMP
cf.	Wǒ...	èrshí	èr	sùi	a.
	I	two-ten	two	year	EMP
	I'm twenty-two years old.				

'twenty'). In 3.96, YXF used *liang* in place of *er* in constructing the word *ershi*. These two errors involving **congnian* and **liangshi* resemble errors which involve grammatical case alternation in languages which use morphological case. This is because the errors in question involve alternate word forms which are nearly synonymous but differ in grammatical function, and alternate within a (albeit restricted) grammatical paradigm.

Note that utterance 3.96 also contains an additional semantic paraphasia. The word *nian* 'year' is improperly used in place of the semantically related *sui* 'year of age'.

The following error substitutes a word that is both semantically and grammatically related to the target. In 3.97, *duo* 'a lot' is incorrectly used in place of *ji* 'how many'. They are related because *duo* is also a question word meaning 'how much' (e.g., *duo gao* 'how tall?') or 'how many' (e.g., *duoshao ren* 'how many people?'). The subject's utterance is incorrect in

3.97	Dōu	bù	xiǎode	wǒ	zìjǐ	hǎo	◇dūo◇	sùi
(Y101)	all	not	know	I	self	very	much	year
	I don't even know that I myself am a lot of years.							
cf.	Dōu	bù	xiǎode	wǒ	zìjǐ	jǐ		sùi
	all	not	know	I	self	how:many		year
	I don't even know how old I myself am.							

another sense as well: the noun *sui* ('years of age'), unlike most nouns, cannot be modified by *duo*. YXF thus properly follows the form class selectional restriction by allowing *duo* to be followed by a noun, but errs in allowing the idiosyncratic **duo sui*. This mistake probably stems from the fact that *sui* can be preceded by other noun phrase quantifiers (such as numerals), and so the subject may be improperly generalizing from those permissible examples.

In the final example of semantic paraphasia, YXF substitutes his actual name for the noun 'name', *mingzi*. This is a form of semantic substitution,

3.98	E:	Zhe	shi	nide	mingzi.
(Y120)		this	be	you-MOD	name
		This is your name.			
	S:	Zhe	shi	wode	◇Yang Xifeng◇.
		this	be	I-MOD	Yang Xifeng
		This is my Yang Xifeng.			

because he uses a concrete member of a set in place of the abstract label which identifies the members of that set.

Jargon

One of the most distinguishing characteristics of YXF's speech is his extensive use of jargon, several examples of which are given below. What characterizes all of these examples is the use of apparently real Mandarin words in what appear to be proper form class slots, but in totally inappropriate semantic contexts.

In the first example (3.99), *liu* 'to leave' is a bona fide verb, and is identifiable as such by the fact that it takes the aspect marker *le* as a suffix.

3.99	*Nèige*	⋈*liú*⋈*le*	*neige*	*shenmo*	⋈*fēng xiá yǒu sè*⋈
(Y5)	that-C	left-ASP	that-C	what	wind canyon have color
	That left that whatever wind canyon has color?				

3.100	*Dāng*	*gė*	*bàngė*	*duō*	⋈*cèsuǒ*⋈	∇*sēn*	hǒ∇.
(Y49)	become	M	half-C	more	toilet	forest	???
	Became a more than half a toilet forest ??? .						

In 3.100, the noun *cesuo* 'toilet' occurs in a slot appropriate for a noun, i.e., in a position following *bange duo* 'more than half'.

In example 3.101, the word *gongsi* 'company' appears as the object of the sentence. Not only is it inappropriate for a person to refer to himself

3.101	*Wo*	*shi*	*da*	⋈*gongsi*⋈.
(Y86)	I	be	big	company
	I'm a big company.			

as a company, but also the context contained absolutely nothing related to a discussion of companies. Likewise in 3.102, in which the noun *shenjing*

3.102	*Lian*	*neige*	*shihou*	⋈*shenjing*⋈	*neige*
(Y88)	even	that-C	time	nerve	that-C
	Even at that time, that nerve				

dongxi	*a,*	*shi*	*ershier*	*[hùi].*
thing	EXC	be	twenty-two	years
thing was 22 cheers old.				

'nerve' occupies a syntactically appropriate slot, but the usage is manifestly inappropriate, since he attributes age to 'nerves', and the discussion had nothing to do with nerves.

The exchange in 3.103 is a good example of jargon which occurs in very simple responses by the subject.

3.103	E:	...gaosu	wo	ni	jiao	shenmo	mingzi.
(Y245)		tell	me	you	call	what	name
		...tell me what your name is.					
	S:	Wǒ	⋈tǔ⋈.	Wǒ	Yang	Xifeng.	
		I	spit	I	Yang	Xifeng	
		I spit. I'm Yang Xifeng.					
	E:	Hao,	dui.				
		good	right				
		Good, right.					
	S:	⋈Zhuàn⋈,	dùi	bù	dùi?		
		spin	right	not	right		
		Spin, right?					

In the preceding example the sentences are syntactically simple and the articulation is clear, so it is easy to observe the lack of relevance of the jargon forms to the linguistic context. This is true also in 3.104, in which a

3.104	Dou	bu	hui	⋈xiè⋈	ma.
(Y387)	all	not	able	diarrhea	EXC
	I can't have diarrhea.				

syntactically simple sentence contains an instance of jargon.

In the final example of jargon, the subject uses the syntactic structure *[VERB$_1$-bu-qilai VERB$_2$]* (meaning 'can't VERB$_1$ it up to VERB$_2$ it', e.g., *nabuqilai chi* 'can't pick it up to eat it'), using the generic, semantically

3.105	Yǒudė	dōu	bú	hùi	jiǎng,	nòngbùqǐlái	nòng.
(Y478)	some	all	not	able	speak	do-not-up-come	do
cf.	Yǒudė	dōu	bú	hùi	jiǎng,	jiǎngbùqǐlái	shūo.
	some	all	not	able	speak	speak-not-up-come	talk
	Some things I can't say at all, I can't get (speak) them out.						

broad verb *nong* 'to do' for both $VERB_1$ and $VERB_2$. Note that the problem is not the use per se of the semantically empty verb *nong* (cf. *nongbuqilai chi* 'can't get it up to eat it', or *nabuqilai nong* 'can't pick it up to do it'), but rather that the same verb is repeated in both positions. The verb has the added anomaly of being semantically broad in meaning.

Neologism

Neologism, like jargon, is present throughout YXF's speech corpus. In providing glosses for examples of neologism, I must give contrived rather than real translations, since by definition a non-word has no real translation equivalent. I try to provide a feel for the general nonsensical character of the neologistic speech in the translation by using real morphemes that happen to correspond to the phonetic form of the observed neologism.

The neologistic utterances vary in the amount of sense that they make, with most making no sense at all. In 3.106, only the determiner-classifier

3.106	∇*diān*∇	*nèige*	∇*xiǎn fēn*∇	*a.*	*Nèige*	⋈*líu*⋈*le* ...
(Y4)	insane	that-C	danger part	EXC	that-C	left-ASP
	insane that danger part. That left...					

combination is 'real Mandarin', and the rest is neologistic nonsense. The utterance in 3.107 is perfectly normal until the subject produces the

3.107	*Wèishénmȯ*	*wǒ*	*qítā*	*dė*	*shíhȯu*	∇*fǔ dīn*∇	*ȧ?*
(Y9)	why	I	other	MOD	time	???	Q
	Why did I ??? at other times?						

neologism **fǔ dīn*[30]. In analyzing speech of this sort it is tempting to impute meaning to the utterance. For example, in 3.108 we might be lured into

3.108	*Na*	∇*bù qióng*∇	*wo*	*dou*	*meiyou*	*ma.*
(Y10)	that	not poor	I	all	not-have	EXC
	That unpoor, I didn't have any.					

---

[30] Note that the syllable *dīn* does not exist in Mandarin.

believing that since the neologism *bù qióng* happens to correspond to the Mandarin morphemes which mean 'not poor', the subject might actually have been saying something about poverty. Such meaning, however, is illusory. In 3.109, the neologism *xiǎn xián jīn fù* has nothing whatever to

3.109	⋈Dǎ⋈	gė	∇xiǎn xián jīn fù∇.
(Y23)	hit	M	danger salty gold father
	Hit a danger salty gold father.		

do with gold, salt, danger or any of the other potential meanings which happen to correspond to the neologistic syllables produced by the subject. In reality, '*xiǎn xián jīn fù*' is a phonological perseveration which approximates the subject's (actual) name, which he had produced in the previous utterance. The same may be said for 3.110, which had nothing to do with

3.110	*Dāng*	*gė*	*bàngė*	*duō*	⋈*cèsuǒ*⋈	∇*sēn*	hǒ∇.
(Y49)	become	M	half-C	more	toilet	forest	???
	Became a more than half a toilet forest ??? .						

toilets or forests, even though the subject produced those syllables in his utterance.

Example 3.111 was a uttered by YXF toward the beginning of a recording session, when asked how he was on that particular day. He correctly

3.111	Wǒ	∇hóu∇	nǐ	∇sān dēn∇	hěn	hǎo.
(Y216)	I	monkey	you	three ???	very	good
	I monkey you three ??? very well.					

starts his response with *wo* 'I' and ends it with *hen hao* 'very good', but the intermediate portion of the utterance is filled with neologistic nonsense. In 3.112, it is difficult to determine just how much syntactic structure, if any,

3.112	∇Lǎo shēng, lǎo shēng∇.	Ta	you	∇yān shēng∇.
(Y275)	old sound old sound	he	have	smoke sound
	Old noises, old noises. He has smoke noises.			

there is in the utterance. The second half of the utterance seems to contain a subject and a verb (*ta you*, 'he has'), but the rest is strictly nonsense.

In 3.113, the first neologistic form is a reduplication (*zī zì*) occupying a verbal slot, properly preceded by a subject and adverb.

3.113	Wo	dou	∇zī zī∇	na	∇shǎo gēn∇	a.
(Y279)	I	all	???	that	few root	EXC
	I always ??? those few roots.					

The object position is occupied by what appears to be a neologistic nominal

3.114	∇Yīn nǐ tē dǐ∇
(Y326)	sound you ??? low
	To sound you ??? low.

form (*shǎo gēn*). 3.114 contains no words which give us the slightest clue to the presence of syntactic structure.

In 3.115, the words *yě* and *yè* are neologistic verb forms, the second of which is used to construct a complex potential resultative verb (see 2.2) by adding the suffix *-qilai*. Note that YXF is apparently in command of this

3.115	Dou	bu	neng	∇yè∇,	∇yě∇bùqǐlái	a.
(Y388)	all	not	able	page	wild-not-rise-come	EMP
	I can't page, I can't wild.					

complex word structure. This is apparent because the meaning of the word structure and the syntactic structure which precedes it are synonymous. That is, *bu neng* $VERB_i$ and $VERB_i$*buqilai* both mean (loosely) 'to be unable to $VERB_i$'[31].

3.3.4 Word Formation

YXF's primary word formation deficit is not in the inability to build word structures per se, but in his inability to use real, semantically appropriate morphemes within those word structures. YXF does have a great deal of difficulty producing real words, but he seems to have relatively little problem using the rules of word structure. There are many complex words (such as compounds, resultative phrases, potential resultatives, and so forth) in YXF's speech which are completely normal. Furthermore, he performs Level IV affixation (e.g., *-le, -guo*) with little apparent difficulty. We may conclude provisionally that YXF has little problem utilizing morphological structure to build words.

The mistakes that YXF commits in making words almost exclusively involve the selection of improper morphemes. In 3.116 (previously given as

[31] See Caplan et al. (1972), and Panzeri et al. (1990) for discussion of jargon roots used in proper word formation.

3.116 ◇cóngnián◇
(Y30) from-year
cf. qùnián
go-year
last year

3.95), the target is the word *qunian* 'last year'. YXF produces the nonexistent word **congnian*, substituting the semantically related *cong* 'from' for the target *qu* 'go' in forming the word. 3.117 (also repeated) is similar, where once again a semantically related but incorrect morpheme is substituted in the formation of a word.

3.117	Wǒ...	◇liǎngshí◇	èr	◇nián◇	a.
(Y37)	I	couple-ten	two	year	EMP
cf.	Wǒ...	èrshí	èr	sùi	a.
	I	two-ten	two	year	EMP
	I'm twenty-two years old.				

In this example (also seen previously in the section on semantic paraphasias), YXF uses the wrong word for 'two' in forming the word for 'twenty', improperly selecting the form that is used with classifiers (i.e., *liang*) rather than the one that is used to form larger numbers (i.e., *er*). The semantic relation between the target and observed morphemes for these two examples is discussed in greater detail in section 3.3.3.

In 3.115 (repeated as 3.118), once again there is no problem with the structure per se, but rather in the selection of morphemes used to fill the slots. The word structure *VERB-bùqǐlái* in Mandarin means 'to be unable to VERB'.

3.118	Dou	bu	neng	∇yè∇,	∇yě∇bùqǐlái	a.
(Y388)	all	not	able	page	wild-not-rise-come	EMP
	I can't page, I can't wild.					

Since the verb in this word structure must be an active (rather than stative) verb, the word **yěbùqǐlái* is incorrect because *yě* 'wild' is a stative verb (i.e., an adjective).

In Table 3.9 we see some noteworthy aspects of YXF's word formation. His proportion of word formation errors is rather small (6.6% of his complex words contain errors), and his word formation errors are distributed fairly evenly among the four lexical levels. This suggests that in fluent Wernicke's aphasic speech, no one lexical level of word formation is subject to deficit more than any other. This is in stark contrast to what we observed in the Broca's subject LXZ, who made her greatest percentage of lexical errors

	Level I	Level II	Level III	Level IV
number of tokens	106	175	191	61
number in error	4	17	6	8
percent in error	3.8%	9.7%	3.1%	13.1%

Table 3.9: Word Error at Various Lexical Levels: Yang Xifeng

at level IV[32], and successively smaller percentages at levels III, II and I. In addition, the percentage of complex words in error for YXF (6.6%) is significantly smaller than that of LXZ (13.9%; population proportion significance test, $Z = 2.22$, $p < .03$, two-tailed).

3.3.5 Syntax

YXF's syntactic difficulties are manifest in bad word order, redundant word insertion, and improper conjoining of structures. His use of syntactic structure appears analogous to his use of word structure in the sense that while he makes some errors in building the structure itself, he makes many more errors in selecting the elements that fill the slots in the structure. This is common in Wernicke's aphasia, and may be thought of as a problem with lexical insertion rather than with syntactic structure per se[33].

YXF's speech contains a good deal of syntactic complexity. Some examples of this are embedded sentences and questions (Y101, Y438), the *shi...de* focus construction (Y138, Y201 to Y202), the *ba* construction (Y163, Y204, Y300), object topicalization (Y461 to Y462), relative clauses used as time adverbials (many examples), reported speech (Y193, Y200 to Y202), and the *lian...dou* discontinuous construction (Y190).

One very interesting fact to note about the syntactic structure of YXF's utterances is that they often seem *locally* correct (ignoring for a moment his semantic problems), but *globally* incorrect. That is, if we view portions of his utterances through a 'window'[34] only two to three words in length, the part of the sentence seen through that window seems grammatical, and the utterance is ungrammatical only when the larger syntactic context is

[32] Viz., 36.4%. The difference between LXZ's 36.4% and YXF's 13.1% just misses statistical significance at the .05 level using a conservative two-tailed test: using the population proportion significance test, $Z = 1.90$, $p < .06$, two-tailed.

[33] Edgar Zurif points out that this is no doubt an oversimplified view of the way such processing actually takes place. For example, syntactic structure building and lexical insertion may not be so easily dissociated.

[34] My thanks to Bob Frank for this characterization of the phenomenon.

viewed. To illustrate, in 3.119 below the time adverbial *wo lai de shihou*

3.119	Wo	lai	de	shihou	wo	shi	tongji	de
(Y39)	I	come	MOD	time	I	be	register	MOD
	When I came it was when I registered							

shihou	wo	shi	a...	Ei?
time	I	be	EXC	EXC
I was uh... huh?				

may properly be followed by *wo shi*, and *wo shi* may be followed by *tongji de shihou*, with no local violations of grammaticality. When we look at the global structure however, we see that *wo lai de shihou* may not be followed by the larger constituent *wo shi tongji de shihou*. To give another example, in 3.120 *zheyang chide* makes no sense when the overall meaning of the

3.120	Shì	xianzai	nongde	dou	zheyang	chide...
(Y167)	matter	now	do-ADV	all	this-way	eat-MOD
	The matter is now done and eaten in this way...					

sentence is taken into account. However from a local perspective, *dou* may be followed by *zheyang*, and *zheyang* may be followed by *chide*. These examples demonstrate that YXF seems to have preserved knowledge of *local* grammaticality, but that he has restricted knowledge of *global* grammatical structure. An approach toward understanding this deficit will be offered in section 4.5.2.

Word Order

Several instances of improper word order occur in YXF's speech. Interestingly, most of the word order problems involve the disordering of sentential constituents (as opposed to the disordering of elements that occur within form class constituents (see examples and discussion in 3.1.5 and 3.2.5). Also, most errors involve constituents that normally occur between the subject and the verb (such as adverbs). In 3.121, the adverb *ye* is misplaced,

3.121	YE	NI	zuoguo	de	a.
(Y137)	also	you	do-ASP	EMP	EMP
	You've done also it before.				
cf.	Ni	ye	zuoguo	de	a.
	you	also	do-ASP	EMP	EMP
	You've also done it before.				

improperly occurring in pre-subject position. The same is true in 3.122,

3.122		DOU	XIANZAI	DE	SHIHOU...
(Y66)		all	now	MOD	time
		Always at the time of now,			
	c.f.	Xianzai	dou...		

in which the adverb *dou* improperly precedes the time adverbial. In example 3.123, both the adverbs *ye* and *dou* improperly precede the subject.

3.123		YE	DOU	XIAOHAIZI...
(Y424)		also	all	child
		All also the children...		
	cf.	Xiaohaizi ye dou...		
		The children also all...		

In 3.124, the subject *women* appears in the wrong position with respect to the adverbial slot. The proper position for the subject is either before or

3.124	XIANZAI	MASHANG	YAO	WOMEN	huiqu	le.
(Y448)	now	immediate	want	I-PL	return-go	ASP
cf.	Xianzai	women	mashang	yao	huiqu	le
	now	I-PL	immediate	want	return-go	ASP
	Now we're about to go back.					

after the moveable time adverb *xianzai*, and before the non-moveable time adverb *mashang*. In this sentence, *women* 'we' improperly follows the adverbs and the auxiliary verb.

In 3.125 the coverbial ('prepositional') phrase *dui xiaohaizi* 'to children' precedes the adverbs and auxiliary verb instead of following them and

3.125		Wo	DUI	XIAOHAIZI	DOU	BU	NENG	jiang
(Y 458)		I	to	child	all	not	able	speak
		I can't even to children talk.						
	cf.	Wo	dou	bu	neng	dui	xiaohaizi	jiang.
		I	all	not	able	to	child	speak
		I can't even talk to children.						

occurring adjacent to the main verb *jiang*.

In the final example, the object of the relative clause (albeit a jargon word) *liangge dian*, occurs outside of the relative clause, to the right of

3.126	[CHÈN]XIALAI	DE	SHIHOU	LIANGGE	⋈DIÀN⋈ ...		
(Y56)	left-down-come	MOD	time	2-C	store		
	When was reft over two stores...						
c.f.	Shengxialai	liangge	⋈diàn⋈	de	shihou...		
	left-down-come	2-C	store	MOD	time		
	When two stores were left over...						

the head noun *shihou* ('time' or 'when').

Function Words

As with many fluent aphasics, YXF's misuse of function words lies in his overuse of these elements, examples of which are seen below.

Copula YXF's use of the copula is largely intact. In the following example, however, the subject inserts the copula *shi* where it does not belong,

3.127	Wo	⊗shi⊗	sishi...	yinggai	shi...	ershier	sui.
(Y26)	I	be	forty	should	be	twenty-two	year
cf.	Wo	sishi...	yinggai	shi	ershier	sui	
	I	forty	should	be	twenty-two	year	
	I'm forty... make that twenty-two years old.						

since (unlike in English) the copula is not used in age expressions in Mandarin.

Prenominal Modification Marker ***de*** YXF's use of the prototypical functor *de* is characteristic of his speech deficit in general. That is, although he uses *de* in a grammatically correct manner, he often either uses the *de* structure without the modified head, or uses the noun *shihou* 'time' as the stereotypic head. This usage is typical of the overall semantic vacuity of YXF's speech, because the 'headless' *de* structure is semantically empty, relying on context for its meaning, and the *shihou* form is a vacuous, stereotypic production.

There are a couple of examples in which YXF uses an inappropriate word in the head position of the *de* structure. In 3.128, he fills the head

3.128	E:	Zhe	shi	nide	mingzi.
(Y120)		this	be	you-MOD	name
		This is your name.			

S:	Zhe	shi	wode	◇Yang Xifeng◇.
	this	be	I-MOD	Yang Xifeng
	This is my Yang Xifeng.			

position with his name 'Yang Xifeng' rather than with the noun 'name' (*mingzi*)[35]. In 3.129, a neologism occurs in head position. There is no

3.129	S:	Wo	dou	shi	wo	Yang Xifeng	de	∇guai wei∇.
(Y228)		I	all	be	I	Yang Xifeng	MOD	???
		I'm all my Yang Xifeng's ???.						

possible word **guai wei* in Mandarin. This is especially true given that each of the syllables carries a mid-level tone, a tonal value which does not occur contrastively in Mandarin.

Classifiers YXF uses a lot of classifiers, partly because of the role of the structure [*determiner-classifier*] in hesitation pauses (usually *zheige* 'this' or *neige* 'that'), which are common in fluent aphasia. Nonetheless he uses a varied assortment of classifiers in his speech, and uses them in a grammatically correct manner. Some examples are: *neiju hua* (that-C:sentence speech) 'that sentence', *zhexie dongxi* (this-C:PL thing) 'these things', *siguan* (four-C:bottle) 'four bottles', *zheici* (this-C:time) 'this time', *bange duo* (half-C more) 'more than half', and *naxie shiqing* (that-C:PL matter) 'those matters'.

Coverbs YXF uses many coverbs in his speech (e.g., Appendix utterances Y2, Y265, Y269, Y314, Y391, Y397, Y429, Y439 and Y458). The only instance of misuse of the structure involves the coverb *dui*, 'to/toward'. In that example (3.125), the coverbial phrase appears adjacent to the subject rather than directly to the left of the main verb (* *Wo dui xiaohaizi dou bu neng jiang*).

Adverbs It is interesting to note that most of YXF's word order difficulties involve the use of adverbials, as seen in many of the examples in section 3.3.5. The misuse of adverbials and the post-subject adverbial slot was also seen in the speech of GJD, although GJD's instances of overgeneration and misplacement of adverbs are more severe. Nonetheless, we arrive at a preliminary generalization: fluent aphasic speakers of Mandarin have problems in restricting and controlling the output of adverbial elements. This is especially evident when the speech of GJD and YXF is contrasted with that of LXZ, who severely undergenerated adverbial elements.

[35] See section 3.3.3 for a discussion of the nature of this substitution error.

Aspect Marker ***le*** YXF's use of the aspect marker *le* appears fairly normal. The breakdown of the types of *le* used is seen in Table 3.10. One

verbal *le*	25
sentential *le*	32
Total *le*	57

Table 3.10: *le* Usage: Yang Xifeng

instance of *le* deletion does occur, however, as seen in example 3.130.

3.130	Shenmo	shi	wo	dou	wangϕ.
(Y102)	what	matter	I	all	forget(-ASP)
	I've forget everything.				
cf.	Shenmo	shi	wo	dou	wangle
	what	matter	I	all	forget-ASP
	I've forgotten everything.				

Adverbial Modifier ***de*** There is an instance of the improper use of the postverbal adverbial modification structure by YXF, seen in 3.131. The

3.131	Shì	xianzai	nongde	dou	zheyang	chide.
(Y167)	matter	now	do-ADV	all	this-way	eat-ADV
	The matter has now gotten to eat this way.					
c.f. (e.g.)	Shì	xianzai	nongde	bu	hao.	
	matter	now	do-ADV	not	good	
	The matter is now being done poorly.					

verb-adverb combination *nongde* ('make/do') should be followed by an stative verb (adjectival) or sentential modifier, but instead is followed by another adverbial phrase. This is another example of the 'local structure good, global structure bad' phenomenon discussed on page 91, since *xianzai nongde dou* is grammatically acceptable, as is *dou zheyang chide*, but the string in its entirety is ungrammatical.

Markers of Negation In 3.132, YXF improperly uses negation by redundantly placing the marker *bu* in preverbal position to negate the complex resultative verb *kanqilaile*, which has already been negated word-internally

3.132	Aiya,	⊗bu⊗	kan*bu*qilaile.
(Y422)	EXC	not	see-not-up-come-ASP
	Darn, I can't not see.		

cf. Aiya, kanbuqilaile.
EXC see-not-up-come-ASP
Darn, I can't see.

(see section 2.2). The use of the negative marker *bu* in this way is structurally incorrect as well as redundant, since a resultative verb such as *kanqilaile* may not be negated by placing *bu* in the normal preverbal slot.

Conjunctions There is nothing particularly unusual about YXF's use of conjunctions within sentences. Also, although the structure and content of his discourse are abnormal (see next section), he uses conjunctions as discourse connectives at a normal rate and in a largely appropriate manner.

3.3.6 Discourse and Pragmatics

YXF's discourse structure is highly fragmented, replete with nonsensical, random shifts of topic. This parallels his problem with syntactic structure, which (as discussed in section 3.3.5) is often locally grammatical but globally ungrammatical. Applying this concept to discourse, the topic of YXF's conversation often seems appropriate or meaningful when sampled at any given 'local' point (i.e., when viewed through a 'window' of limited size), but the individual 'local' topics are unrelated, and do not cohere into a meaningful whole.

However, YXF does show evidence of control over certain aspects of discourse, namely the use of appropriate sentential positions for introducing and then making continued reference to a discourse entity. In the sentences given in 3.133, the discourse entity *xiaojie* 'young lady' is introduced by

3.133	Neige	hai	you	yige	xiaojie.	Xiaojie	zai	zheli...
(Y312)	that-C	also	have	one-C	girl.	girl	at	here
	There's also a girl. The girl is here...							

YXF in sentence final position, which is the appropriate sentence position for introducing a 'new' entity into the discourse. YXF then continues to speak of the young lady in the second sentence, properly placing *xiaojie* in sentence initial position, appropriate for its status as an 'old' or 'given' discourse entity.

Concerning his knowledge of linguistic pragmatics, YXF generally has little idea of what he or his interlocutor are saying, much less have a feel for appropriate contexts and shades of pragmatic meaning. However, he does use many pragmatic sentence-final particles, and uses them correctly.

3.134	Xianzai	wo	yanjing	hen	cha	lei!
(Y67)	now	I	eye	very	bad	EXC
	Now my eyes are very bad!					

For example, in 3.134, the sentence final particle *lei* is used as a marker of exclamation.

3.4 Subject #4: Zheng Youjuan

3.4.1 Background

Mrs. Zheng is a 57-year old female who was hospitalized following a left hemisphere CVA (stroke), with a complaint of 'difficulty in speech'. Her auditory comprehension was fully intact, and her speech production deficit was characterized by word-finding difficulty, phonemic paraphasias, neologism, and by omission and improper substitution of words. ZYJ is the least severely aphasic of the four patients in this study. Her profile is seen in Table 3.11.

age	57	sex	female
lesion type	CVA	lesion location	?
diagnostic category	Broca's (?)	fluency	good
semantic content	good	effortful speech	yes
comprehension	good	functor omission	some
phrase length	'normal'	complex syntax	yes
distortions	yes	substitutions	yes
intonation	normal	anomia	yes
neologism	yes	jargon	no
discourse structure	good	repetition	?

Table 3.11: Patient Profile: Zheng Youjuan

ZYJ performed fairly well at giving short answers to questions, but had considerable difficulty providing longer answers and maintaining a narrative. She suffered from a self-reported inability to produce utterances. At those times when ZYJ reported subjective difficulty, when encouraged to speak she often produced manifestly inappropriate and incomprehensible language. Part of ZYJ's problem is undoubtedly simple anomia (inability to name), in which case she is experiencing a problem in lexical retrieval. But the nonsense produced by ZYJ when she is encouraged to produce longer stretches of speech suggests a output processing deficit in addition to simple anomia. ZYJ thus seems best diagnosed as having a mild form of Broca's aphasia with moderate anomia.

Linguistic Background

ZYJ was a housewife born and raised in the city of Beijing. The dialect of Mandarin spoken in Beijing is the basis for standard Mandarin as the national language of China. However, the Mandarin spoken in Beijing nonetheless has a large number of colloquial words that do not occur in standard Mandarin. Also, speakers of colloquial Beijing Mandarin put the level II nominalizing suffix *-r* on many more words than in standard Mandarin.

3.4.2 Phonology

In her attempt to pronounce words, ZYJ often missed the target completely, rather than producing a distorted version of the target. Therefore her phonological errors are considered mostly phonemic substitutions. Some examples of ZYJ's non-tonal phonological errors are seen in Table 3.12. ZYJ produces one very clear tonal error, a substitution of a rising tone for

jì	→	*yì
dōu	→	*tū
dài	→	*dùi
xiǎng	→	*dǎng
shì	→	*zhì

Table 3.12: Nontonal Phonological Errors: Zheng Youjuan

a falling tone in the word *zùi* 'most', as seen in example 3.135. The error

3.135 (Z318)	zùi	→	*zúi

was produced twice in succession. The reason this tone error is so clear is that the subject goes on to produce the same word, this time with the proper tone, in the sentence which follows it in the corpus (see Z318 in the Appendix).

3.136 gives examples of phonological errors which involve syllable structure. In these cases, either two syllables are blended into one, or one syllable

3.136	zhīdào	→	*zhào	(Z47)
	shuō huà	→	*shuā	(Z221)
	dōu	→	*tū wū	(Z98)

is split into two. The first blend (**zhào*) does not violate the phonotactic rules of Mandarin and observes syllable structure constraints. The produced syllable contains the initial of the first syllable and the rime and tone of the second syllable[36].

The second blend error, however, appears to violate the stipulation that lexical tone remain associated with the nuclear vowel of the syllable (see section 2.1.3). In this blend (**shuā*), the nuclear vowel [a] of the second word *huà* is taken without its tone [ˋ]. The tone of the blend (high level tone [ˉ]) is contributed by *shuō*, which does not contribute its nuclear vowel [o] to the blend. This example demonstrates the independence of segment (i.e., consonant and vowel) and tone in a tone language, because in the blend error, the tone comes from one rime while the nuclear vowel comes from the other (see also Figure 4.3 and accompanying discussion).

Another example of a phonological paraphasia involving tone-segment dissociation is seen in 3.137, in the form of an anticipatory phonological error. The target is the word *lǎo* 'old' as in *lǎo dà* 'the oldest'.

3.137 [dǎ]dà.. [dǎ]dà
(Z315) old-big old-big
cf. lǎodà.. lǎodà

ZYJ produces the target fall-rise tone (ˇ) correctly, but improperly produces the consonant-vowel sequence *da* in place of *lao*, anticipating the syllable *dà* 'big'.

These examples of tone-segment dissociation in 3.136 and 3.137 may be considered evidence that segments and tones constitute independent 'tiers' in the phonological systems of tone language speakers (see, e.g., Goldsmith 1990, Bao 1990, Yip 1980). The examples also constitute evidence that phonological system breakdown can damage the processes that result in the association of these independent tiers.

3.4.3 Lexical Selection

Verbal Paraphasias

ZYJ produced no errors which may be clearly classified as verbal paraphasias.

Semantic Paraphasias

ZYJ produces two errors which may be classified as semantic paraphasias. In 3.138, the subject improperly substitutes the adverb *ye* for the adverb *hai*. The meaning of the two words is nearly identical (i.e., 'also'), with

[36]Just as in the *fǎn qiè* system of spelling. See the analysis of Mandarin syllable structure in 2.1.3.

3.138	Zhe	◇ye◇	you	shenmo?
(Z415)	here	also	have	what
cf.	Zhe	hai	you	shenmo?
	here	also	have	what
	What else is here?			

the only difference between the two being one of grammatical function. *ye* is used to mean 'also' when what is being 'added' is part of the grammatical subject (e.g., I want a pen. He *also* wants a pen.). *hai* is used when what is being 'added' is part of the object (e.g., I want a pen. I *also* want a book.).

In 3.139, in speaking of distance from home ZYJ gives the number of a bus route rather than the number of miles. Both the general context and the presence of the word (coverb) *lí* ('distant from') indicate that what

3.139	...lí	nahar[37]	jiu	shi	◇sanshiwu	lu◇.
(Z527)	from	there	only	be	thirty-five	road
	...route 35 from there.					

should appear here is a number of miles. It is possible to analyze this error as an omission of the word 'miles' (*lǐ*) from the structure which gives the number of miles of distance (i.e., *sanshiwu lǐ lu* thirty-five mile road, 'thirty-five miles'), which would also yield *sanshi wu lu*. Although this seems like a simple and reasonable explanation, we may discount it for two reasons. First, it was indeed the 'route 35 bus' that ran to ZYJ's home, and second because the distance to her house was much less than 35 miles.

Jargon

There are no identifiable instances of jargon in ZYJ's speech. Most jargon-like utterances in her speech are actually neologisms, so classified because there is not enough valid context in those utterances to properly establish the form class identity of the spoken forms.

Neologism

Many examples of *apparent* jargon in ZYJ's speech are actually neologisms, because it is not possible to determine with reasonable certainty that they are real words occurring in appropriate form class slots. Example 3.140 is just such a case, in which the subject produced the phonetic string [*chéng aì rén*] with no apparent context. It is possible to analyze the syllables into the words *chéng* 'become' and *aìrén* 'spouse'.

[37] Colloquial Beijing Mandarin for *nar* 'that place'.

3.140 ∇Chéng aìreń∇.
(Z29) become spouse
Become a spouse.

Furthermore, the linear order of these words happens to correspond to that of verb and direct object. However, the meaning attributed to the syllables is arbitrary (because of the total lack of context involving 'becoming a spouse'), and therefore the form class is a fiction, since there are in reality no identifiable lexical items upon which to base a form class analysis.

In 3.141, although I have glossed *dìshí* as 'earth rock', in fact the meaning of the two syllables is unclear. The neologism in 3.142, *jié zhào*, has no

3.141	Zhe	shenmode..	shenmo..	shenmo	∇dì shí∇
(Z160)	this	something	what	what	earth rock
	This whatever..what..what earth rock				

3.142	Shuo	ya.	Hai..	hai	mei...	∇jié.. jié zhào∇
(Z163)	speak	EXC	still	still	not	???
	Talk. I still..still haven't... ???.					

discernable meaning either in isolation or in the context in which it occurs. ZYJ produced the exchange in 3.143, which is full of neologisms, in trying to relate the name of a television program she had been watching.

3.143	Zhe	dianshi	shi	shenmo	ya?	∇Gé gē bìng∇..
(Z192)	this	television	be	what	EXC	revolution song sick..
	What was on the TV? Revolution song sick..					

∇Gé gē bìng∇.. ∇gé gē bìng jiā∇.. ..∇jiāshàng∇.
revolution song sick revolution song sick home home-on
Revolution song sick.. revolution song sick home.. on home.

E: Shi 'Gémìng Jīatíng' ma?
be revolution family Q
Was it 'Revolutionary Family'?

S: Bú shì. ∇Fù lù hù∇ ∇gémìng jiàshǐ∇..
not be ??? revolution pilot
No. ??? revolutionary pilot..

∇bié jiā zhài zhǎ dė hòu∇. Ss!
don't home debt fry MOD thick EXC
Don't house debt fried thick. Ss!

In 3.144, it is impossible to establish either the identity of the neologistic

3.144	Zhào	zheige...	∇jīng...jīng shī∇
(Z529)	according	this-C	startle teacher
	According to this... startle.. startle teacher		

zhe	∇jīng shī∇...	uh...
this	startle teacher	HES
this startle teacher... uh...		

spoken forms, or the form class identity of the slots occupied by them.

3.4.4 Word Formation

ZYJ makes several errors in the formation of complex words. In 3.145, she omits the second half of the verbal compound *jìdé* 'to remember', in addition to dropping the initial consonant *j* (phonetically, [tφ]) from the first syllable.

3.145		Na	wo	jiu	bu	[yì]-φ	le.
(Z14)		that	I	just	not	rem(ember)	ASP
	cf.	Na	wo	jiu	bu	jìdé	le.
		that	I	just	not	remember	ASP
		That I just don't remember.					

In 3.146 (3.137 repeated) we see a word formation error caused by an anticipatory phonological paraphasia. Instead of *lǎodà* 'the oldest', ZYJ says **[dǎ]dà*, anticipating the production of the second syllable in producing the first. The subject retains the proper tone of the target morpheme (third tone) on the first syllable of the word, but for the consonant-vowel sequence

3.146		*[dǎ]dà
(Z315)		[dǎ]-big
	cf.	lǎodà
		old-big
		'the oldest'

uses the *da* of the second syllable[38]. Technically, *lǎodà* is a noun which is composed of two adjectives, and would therefore ordinarily be considered an exocentric word, formed at level I of the lexicon. But the word *lao* is a productive prefix in Mandarin, routinely placed before names or other nouns as a term of endearment or address (cf. *lao-Wang* 'old Wang', *lao-er* 'old number two'; see Chao 1968). Because this method of noun derivation

[38] The possibility that the lexical item *dǎ* 'to hit' is what is substituted in the first syllable is remote, because there is no semantic or structural relation between this form and the target. Also, it would entail the substitution of an active verb for a stative verb in the formation of a complex noun, which is unlikely.

is moderately productive, the process occurs at level II of the lexicon (along with other derived nouns), and therefore may be seen as more susceptible to error or decomposition than an exocentric word formed at level I.

Many of the errors in word formation committed by ZYJ involve the use of resultative verbs. Recall from section 2.2 that resultative verbs are the class of complex verbs which may insert a positive or negative 'potential' morpheme in between the morphemes that make up the complex verb. These verbs generally take the basic form *VERB-RESULT*, and become *VERB-CAN(NOT)-RESULT (come/go)* with the insertion of the potential

3.147	Wo	jiu	shuobu-ϕ-lai...	shuobuchulai.
(Z39)	I	just	speak-not-(out)-come	speak-not-out-come
	I just can't speak it... speak it out.			

3.148		Kanbu-ϕ-lai	shi	shenmo.
(Z387)		see-not-(out)-come	be	what
	cf.	Kanbuchulai	shi	shenmo
		see-not-out-come	be	what
		(I) can't tell what it is.		

3.149		Shuobu-ϕ-ϕ
(Z143)		speak-not-(out)-(come)
	cf.	shuobuchulai
		speak-not-out-come
		(I) can't speak it out.

infix and the optional addition of the words for 'come' or 'go' (*lai* and *qu*). As seen in 3.147-3.149, the misuse of the resultatives usually leaves the first verb and the potential infix intact, and what is generally omitted is the result morpheme (a verb), or some combination of the result morpheme and the word for 'come' or 'go'. Note that in all cases it is the canonically-defined head of the word (i.e., the first verb; see Packard 1990a) that is retained in the production of the resultative verb compound.

A summary of ZYJ's word formation errors broken down by lexical level is seen in Table 3.13. Note that the highest percentage of errors is at Level IV (20.0%). This error rate is significantly greater than the combined error rate of the other three levels (i.e., 8.4%; population proportion significance test: 20.0% versus 8.4%, $Z = 2.20$, $p < .03$, two-tailed). This is further evidence that level IV morphological elements are particularly susceptible to misuse in non-fluent speakers. ZYJ does not, however, show as obvious a 'grading effect' as was observed in the prototypical Broca's patient LXZ, where the percentage of forms in error increases at succesively deeper levels in the lexicon. This may be because ZYJ is not a prototypical Broca's

	Level I	Level II	Level III	Level IV
number of tokens	73	135	112	35
number in error	7	10	10	7
percent in error	9.6%	7.4%	8.9%	20.0%

Table 3.13: Word Error at Various Lexical Levels: Zheng Youjuan

patient, as evidenced by other aspects of her speech which do not comport with the 'Broca's' diagnosis (e.g., her general retention of function words and near-normal fluency).

In the final example of word formation error, ZYJ incorrectly adds the *-r* suffix (see section 3.4.1) to the word for 'thirty-four', *sanshisi*.

3.150 sānshí[sèr]
(Z290) three-ten-four
cf. sānshísì
three-ten-four
'thirty-four'

Note that in producing this incorrect form, the subject properly implements a phonological rule that occurs upon the addition of the *-r* suffix, namely the rule that changes the sound represented orthographically in *pinyin* as *i* (phonetic [ɪ]; see Chapter 2) into *e* (phonetic [ɣ]; see Cheng 1973). This means that the morphological error, improper *-r* addition, appropriately triggered the operation of the phonological rule which changes the shape of the vowel. According to the theory of Lexical Phonology and Morphology (e.g., Kiparsky 1982), this morphological error should be considered a *lexical* (vs. *post-lexical*) error, since it occurred at a point early enough in the derivation where it still properly triggered the operation of the phonological rule.

3.4.5 Syntax

ZYJ's syntax is fairly normal for short responses, but problems arise in longer responses and in narrative utterances. A general characterization of her syntactic difficulty is that the sentences are of minimal length, with some disturbances in word order. Although ZYJ uses some words that are optional, for the most part she omits a word when that option is available. There are also several instances of ZYJ omitting words from obligatory environments, examples of which follow.

In 3.151, ZYJ uses backward anaphoric reduction, which is ungrammatical in Mandarin without the use of the coordinating conjunction *gēn* (the following experimenter and subject utterances confirm the target utterance).

3.151 E: Ou, zùo chē a.
(Z570) EXC ride car EXC
Oh, (they) take the bus.

S: Zùo ϕ qí chē a.
ride (car) straddle car EXC

(cf.) Zùo chē qí chē a.
ride car straddle car EXC
Ride the bus and ride bikes.

E: Ou, qí chē a.
EXC straddle car EXC
Oh, ride bikes.

S: Yǒu qí chē dė yǒu zùo chē dė.
have straddle car MOD have ride car MOD
Some ride bikes and some take the bus.

This is not considered an omission of a coordinating conjunction such as *gēn*, because the juxtaposition coordination structure without the conjunction is much more common than the structure with the conjunction (see 2.3.3). In 3.152 ZYJ omits the noun ('home') which serves as the object of the preposition (i.e., the noun in the coverbial phrase; see 2.3.1).

3.152 You yige xiaohaizi a, you yige
(Z114) have one-C child EXC have one-C
erxifer, zai wo ϕ.
son-wife at I (home)

cf. You yige xiaohaizi a, you yige
have one-C child EXC have one-C
There's a child, and a
erxifer, zai wo jia.
son-wife at I home
daughter-in-law at my home.

In 3.153, ZYJ omits the noun *bing* 'sickness' which is the direct object in *fa bing* 'get a sickness'.

3.153 E: Zenmo fa bing de? Naxie bu shufu?
(Z168) how start sick EMP which-C:PL not good
How did you get sick? Where did you feel bad?

S:	Wo	fa	*ϕ*..	fale	*ϕ*..	fa	*ϕ*..
	I	start	(sick)	start-ASP	(sick)	start	(sick)
	fa	*ϕ*	de	shihou...			
	start	(sick)	MOD	time			
cf.	Wo	fa	bing	de	shihou...		
	I	start	sick	MOD	time		
	When I got sick...						

The verb *sheng* 'to give birth' is omitted in 3.154 (in addition to the noun *sui* 'years').

3.154		Ershi	*ϕ*	*ϕ*	tou	da	erzi.
(Z288)		two-ten	(year)	(bear)	first	big	son
	cf.	Ershi	sui	sheng	tou	da	erzi.
		twenty	years	bear	first	big	son
		I had my first child when I was twenty.					

In 3.155 the subject omits the main verb of the sentence, *zuo* 'ride'. It is especially clear in this example that the word is not being deleted as the

3.155	E:	Tamen	ye	zuo	gonggong	qiche,	shi	ba?
(Z575)		he-PL	also	ride	public	car	be	SUG
		They also ride the bus, right?						
S:	Ye	*ϕ*	gonggong	qiche,	ye...			
	also	(ride)	public	car	also			
cf.	Ye	zuo	gonggong	qiche,	ye...			
	also	ride	public	car	also			
	They also ride the bus, and...							

result of (e.g.,) shortness of breath or the loss of a phonologically reduced final element, because the slot for the omitted verb occupies a sentence internal position, directly following the adverb *ye*.

Despite the problems outlined above, ZYJ does successfully produce several long sentences with fairly complex syntax. Some examples of these are seen in the Appendix, in utterances Z51 to Z52, Z65 to Z66, Z78 to Z79, Z153 to Z154, Z347 to Z348, Z406 to Z407, Z482 to Z483, Z493 to Z494, and Z573 to Z574.

Embedding

ZYJ produces many examples of both complex nominals (Z51 to Z52) and sentences (Z74, Z153, Z251) which are embedded in matrix sentences. When compared with the other three subjects, therefore, ZYJ's ability to embed into matrix sentences is good. However, although she is successful in several instances of embedding, she still generally has problems with complex syntactic structures of that type. For example, in 3.156 ZYJ omits the question word *zenmo* which would be used to introduce an embedded question.

3.156	E:	Ni	xianzai	zhidao	gai	shuo	shenmo	ma?
(Z230)		you	now	know	should	say	what	Q
		Do you know what you should say now?						
S:	Zhidao	ϕ	jiang	a.				
	know	(how)	speak	EXC				
cf.	Zhidao	zenmo	jiang	a.				
	know	how	speak	EXC				
	I know what to say.							

Word Order

ZYJ makes several errors in word order. In 3.157 she misplaces the adverb *yòu*, placing it before instead of after the subject.

3.157		Na	ker[39]	YÒU	WO	yao	shuo	ya...
(Z44)		then	but	again	I	want	speak	EXC
	cf.	Na	ker	wo	yòu	yao	shuo	ya...
		then	but	I	again	want	speak	EXC
		But (if) I want to talk again...						

In 3.158, the subject makes the same type of mistake in a relative clause as was seen in example 3.126 uttered by YXF, by placing what should be the object of the modifying clause to the right of the modified head, totally outside the modifying clause.

3.158		qiáo[40]	de	shihou	zheige...
(Z129)		watch	MOD	time	that-C
	cf.	qiao	zheige	de	shihou...
		watch	that-C	MOD	time
		when I was watching that...			

In 3.159 the subject takes the common idiomatic phrase *húshūobādào* (also, *húshuō*) 'to talk nonsense' and changes it to *_húdào shuō_. In this example,

3.159	Yi	shuo	hua	jiu	hú-ϕ-dàoshuō	le.
(Z227)	once	say	talk	just	confuse-ϕ-talk-speak	ASP

[39] Beijing dialect for *keshi* 'but'.

[40] Beijing dialect for 'watch'.

cf.	Yi	shuo	hua	jiu	húshūobādào	le.
	once	say	talk	just	confuse-speak-eight-talk	ASP
	As soon as I talk it's nonsense.					

not only did she reverse the order of the words *shuo* 'speak' and *dao* 'talk' (archaic), she also deleted the word *ba* 'eight'.

In 3.160, ZYJ misplaces the head noun within the direct object NP, placing it directly after the verb instead of having it follow the modifiers.

3.160	ZHUAN	CHE	NEIGE	SANSHI...LIU
(Z555)	change	car	that-C	36
	They change bus onto that thirty...six.			
cf.	Zhuan	neige	sanshiliu	che.
	change	that-C	36	car
	They change onto that thirty-six bus.			

In the final example of improper word order, ZYJ makes an interesting error and then corrects herself. The syntactic structure [*VERB* $NOUN_1$ GIVE $NOUN_2$], with the word 'give' in post-verbal position, is often semantically interchangeable with [GIVE $NOUN_2$ *VERB* $NOUN_1$] (cf. example 2.10). In the first structure, the post-verbal 'give' normally causes NOUN_2 to have a more 'dative' reading (e.g., '*to* NOUN_2'), while the pre-verbal 'give' in the second structure gives NOUN_2 a more 'benefactive' reading (e.g., '*for* NOUN_2'). However, as example 3.161 shows, the

3.161	Ting	yige	gei	xiao..	gei	xiaohar	ting	yige.
(Z614)	listen	one-C	give	child	give	child	listen	one-C
	Listen to one and give it to the kid... let the kids listen to one.							

subcategorization of the the verb *tīng* 'listen' disallows the dative reading (see A. Li 1990, pp. 100-103, Teng 1975), and so that verb cannot take a dative object. The subject first produces the incorrect form, presumably following the generalization of verbs which subcategorize for dative objects, then realizes her error and self-corrects.

Function Words

ZYJ makes some errors in the use of function words, as outlined below.

Copula ZYJ's use of the copula *shi* seems completely normal. There are no instances of *shi* omission, nor is there any apparent underemployment of *shi* in ZYJ's speech corpus.

Prenominal Modification Marker *de* ZYJ produces several instances of *de*, but her overall frequency of use of the particle is less than normal. Often the instances of *de* that she produces follow experimenter utterances which contain *de*, and often they appear without a lexical head. The fact that she uses *de* less than normal is, as we have seen, a potential diagnostic for Broca's aphasia.

In 3.162 ZYJ deletes a *de* in the partial repetition of an utterance by the experimenter. While the omission of the *de* does not strictly speaking

3.162 (Z607)
E: Jiang chang pian de bu xing.
talk long version MOD not good
Talking a long piece she doesn't do so well.
S: Chang..chang..chang pian ϕ shuobuliao.
long version (MOD) speak-not-able
A long..long..long piece I can't say.

make the utterance ungrammatical, nonetheless it is more acceptable with the *de*, and its omission in this context is an indication of her difficulty with functors.

Classifiers ZYJ uses classifiers with no apparent difficulty. In her speech corpus there are no instances of classifier deletion, use of the wrong classifier, or any other types of classifier misuse.

Coverbs ZYJ uses a lot of coverbs and coverbial phrases in her speech (e.g., Appendix utterances Z81, Z433, Z542, and Z618,) and uses them incorrectly a fair number of times (e.g., Z115, Z205 and Z595), including at least two omissions, seen in examples 3.163 and 3.164.

3.163 (Z237)
Jiu ϕ zanmen neihuir shuo hua yiyang...
just (with) we-PL that-C:time speak talk same
Just we were saying that time...
cf. Jiu gen zanmen neihuir shuo hua yiyang...
just like we-PL that-C:time speak talk same
Just like we were saying that time...

3.164 (Z404)
ϕ dengzi gòudezháo ye hao.
(with) stool-NOM grab-can-get also good
A stool it's easy to get it.
cf. Yong dengzi gòudezháo ye hao.
with stool-NOM grab-can-get also good
With a stool it's easy to get it.

verbal *le*	15
sentential *le*	59
Total *le*	74

Table 3.14: *le* Usage: Zheng Youjuan

Auxiliary Verbs ZYJ uses auxiliary verbs with little apparent difficulty, producing them with normal frequency, and good variety.

Adverbs In general, ZYJ's use of adverbs is correct, especially when her speech is compared to that of the other three patients. There is, however, one example of adverb misuse. In 3.157 (repeated below as 3.165),

3.165		Na	ker	YÒU	WO	yao	shuo	ya...
(Z44)		then	but	again	I	want	speak	EXC
	cf.	Na	ker	wo	yòu	yao	shuo	ya...
		then	but	I	again	want	speak	EXC
		But (if) I want to talk again...						

ZYJ puts the adverb *yòu* in the wrong position in the sentence.

Aspect Marker *le* In Table 3.14 we see a summary of the use of *le* by ZYJ. As seen in this table, most instances of *le* produced by ZYJ are sentential rather than verbal.

Adverbial Modifier *de* ZYJ uses the adverbial modification (with adverbial *de*, see 2.3.6) more than the other subjects (e.g., Appendix utterances Z42, Z70 and Z71), and uses it correctly each time.

Conjunctions There is no evidence of underuse or misuse of conjunctions in ZYJ's speech. She uses the conjunction *keshi* (or the Beijing dialect variants *her* and *ker*) a lot in her speech, always using it in a correct manner. She also uses 'discourse conjunctions' (such as *nemmo* and *ranhou*) correctly, and with normal frequency.

3.4.6 Discourse and Pragmatics

ZYJ has very little problem with the structure of her discourse. This is apparent in the way she achieves proper topic continuity in her conversation with the experimenter (even though there are often times when she has trouble producing proper speech output). Furthermore, ZYJ introduces entities into the discourse in a normal manner, by placing them in sentence-final object position.

ZYJ's control of linguistic pragmatics also appears good, as indicated by her frequent and appropriate use of pragmatic attitude markers such as *ya*, *a*, *ei*, *aiya*, *hei*, *hm*, *mm* and *ou*.

3.5 Patient Summary

Of our four patients, two may be considered to fit the pattern of the traditional major syndromes. One is a moderate to severe Broca's aphasic (LXZ), and one is a severe Wernicke's aphasic (YXF). The other two do not fall neatly into traditional categories, but provisionally may be characterized as a mild anomic who displays some of the characteristics of Broca's aphasia (ZYJ), and a severe Wernicke's aphasic (GJD).

3.5.1 Li Xinzheng

LXZ's speech is that of a classic moderate to severe Broca's aphasic. Her output is effortful with a notable lack of fluency, and a dearth of function words, including no instances in her speech corpus of the prototypical functor *de* (including three omissions of *de* from obligatory contexts). She also shows a reduced length and complexity of syntactic structures, a reduced number of complex words, and an intonation deficit manifest in abnormal uniformity of syllable amplitude and length. LXZ's many errors in lexical selection tend to be phonologically rather than semantically based. She has problems forming complex words, especially at the 'shallowest' level of the lexicon (level IV). LXZ's word formation errors appear to show a 'grading' effect, whereby she makes fewer word formation errors the more deeply in the lexicon the words are formed.

3.5.2 Guo Jiande

The character of GJD's speech is somewhat anomalous, because of its almost total lack of semantic content in the context of reduced fluency. He generally overuses function words and underuses content words, with the result being strings of semantically vacuous but often well-formed speech. This subject, unlike YXF, does not show variety in his production of content words. He overproduces the same stereotypic ones, connected by stereotyped function words such as the deictic determiner/classifier combinations *zheige* and *neige*, the copula *shi*, the conjunction *buguo*, and the adverbs *dou*, *hai*, *bijiao*, *xianzai* and *jiu*. Once he produces content words he tends to use them perseveratively, putting them into slots appropriate to their form class but using them with inappropriate semantic reference. Like many fluent speakers, GJD overuses pronouns. He uses the prototypical functor *de* a lot, but usually with a lexically empty head. GJD often uses the combination of number/classifier (e.g., *yige*) or determiner/classifier (e.g., *neige*) as a semantically non-specific element in a nominal slot.

3.5.3 Yang Xifeng

YXF's speech is that of a classic Wernicke's aphasic. YXF displays the 'press of speech' and neologistic jargon characteristic of Wernicke's subjects, in the context of poor auditory comprehension. He rambles on and on, creating words and syntactic structures of considerable length and complexity while making very little sense. YXF produces grammatical structures that are locally grammatical but globally ungrammatical. He shows characteristic overuse of grammatical function words, especially deictic determiner/classifier function word combination. He also overuses the semantically neutral word *shihou* ('time') as the nominal head of his noun modification structures with *de*, or leaves the head completely empty to form a semantically vacuous 'headless relative'. YXF contrasts with GJD in his extreme fluency, use of neologism in nearly every utterance, and in the length, complexity and variety of his utterances. YXF has a word formation deficit manifest in the substitution of inappropriate or neologistic morphemes within largely intact word structures. Unlike the Broca's patients LXZ and ZYJ, YXF's word formation errors are not mostly located at level IV of the lexicon, but instead are rather evenly spread across the four lexical word formation levels.

3.5.4 Zheng Youjuan

The traits that best characterize the dysfunctional speech output of ZYJ are her obvious and self-reported inability to initiate speech (often with the production of neologistic jargon when she is encouraged to speak at those times), the presence of phonemic paraphasias (including the tone-segment dissociation described in section 3.4.2), the omission of morphemes within words, disordered syntax (mainly improper word or constituent order), noun omission, and some verb omission. The syndrome that most closely fits ZYJ's symptoms is a mild version of Broca's aphasia, with significant anomia. The designation 'mild' is intended to account for the fact that she is somewhat fluent, produces grammatical structures of moderate length, and approaches normal levels in her use of functors.

Chapter 4

Discussion

In this final chapter, I will list findings which are especially noteworthy, and give a brief summary of linguistic symptoms which may serve as diagnostics for the two major aphasia syndromes in Chinese. Then I provide a description of agrammatism in Chinese, and discuss the contribution the Chinese data make to our understanding of the nature of agrammatism. I also address other issues raised in Chapter 1. Finally, I offer an explanation for the two major aphasia syndromes, suggested by our findings, which not merely suggests but *entails* the existence of autonomous linguistic components.

4.1 Significant Findings

4.1.1 Lexical Tone Production Deficits

It is very clear from the speech of the aphasic Chinese patients in this study that errors in the production of lexical tone are quite common in Chinese aphasia (see especially the tonal errors of YXF in Table 3.8). This finding supports previous findings of tone deficits in aphasic Chinese speakers (e.g., Packard 1986, Yiu 1989; c.f., Gandour 1987).

4.1.2 Intonation Deficit in Non-fluent Speech

The syllables produced by the non-fluent patient LXZ were remarkably uniform in their amplitude, length and intersyllabic intervals. This is not normal for Mandarin, since differences in syllable length, amplitude and interval are triggered by sentence intonation and lexical stress factors. This is apparently the first report of an *intonation* deficit (versus a *lexical tone* deficit; see 4.1.1) in a tone language speaker. Our finding of abnormal intonation supports the notion that lexical tone and intonation are dissociable in Chinese (Kratochvil 1968, Shen 1990), and that they may independently suffer differing degrees of deficit. This intonation deficit is discussed further in section 4.5.1.

4.1.3 The Independence of Phonological Tiers

The examples of tone-segment dissociation seen in our data (e.g., examples 3.136 and 3.137 by ZYJ) may be considered neurolinguistic evidence of independent phonological 'tiers' for segments and tones in tone languages (see, e.g., Goldsmith 1990, Bao 1990, and Yip 1980 for discussions of tonal and segmental tiers in tone languages; see also Dogil 1984 for discussion of selective impairment of different levels). These examples demonstrate how tier association may be compromised as a result of damage to the phonological system, providing neurolinguistic evidence of the 'psychological reality' of proposals which posit a stratified phonological component as part of a model of phonological processing.

4.1.4 Fluent versus Non-fluent Word Order Deficits

According to the speech data examined in this study, non-fluent and fluent patients may differ in the nature of their word order errors. Our non-fluent patient LXZ made ordering errors *within* form class categories (e.g., within noun phrases), but not in the order of words which are themselves constituents of a sentence (i.e., LXZ shows no aberrance in the basic order [S-mod-V-O]). The word order errors by the fluent subjects on the other hand usually involved sentential constituents. An example is seen in 3.27

4.1	Wo	YANJING	ZUOBIAN	ϕ	tuchu	le.
	I	eye	left-side	MOD	protrude-out	ASP
	My eye left stuck out.					
cf.	Wo	zuobian	de	yanjing	tuchu	le.
	I	left-side	MOD	eye	protrude-out	ASP
	My left eye stuck out.					

(repeated as 4.1; see also 3.160), in which the elements within the NP (i.e., the modifier and head noun) are reversed. The word order errors by fluent subjects on the other hand usually involve sentential constituents, as seen in example 3.70 from patient GJD (repeated as 4.2 below), and example 3.121 from patient YXF (repeated as 4.3).

4.2		YE	ZHEIZHI	bijiao	pang.	
		also	this-C	compare	fat	
		...this also one is relatively fat.				
	cf.	Zheizhi	ye	bijiao	pang.	
		this-C	also	compare	fat	
		...this one is also relatively fat.				

4.3		YE	NI	zuoguo	de	a.
		also	you	do-ASP	EMP	EMP
		You've done also it before.				
	cf.	Ni	ye	zuoguo	de	a.
		you	also	do-ASP	EMP	EMP
		You've also done it before.				

In both of these examples, the adverb *ye* is misplaced, improperly occurring before the subject.

The potential universal nature of this phenomenon, including possible explanations, will be discussed in 4.2.4.

4.1.5 'Graded' Morphological Deficit

The non-fluent patient LXZ displayed a word formation deficit that is 'graded' in nature. Complex words produced by LXZ were more subject to deficit at lexical level IV (as defined by the theory of LPM applied to Mandarin; Packard 1990b), and least subject to deficit at lexical level I (see Table 3.2 and accompanying discussion). This result and its far-reaching implications will be discussed in much greater detail, beginning in section 4.3.

The observed 'grading' effect in our Broca's patient provides an alternative explanation for the experimental results of Bates et al. (1991). These investigators used Chinese to test the hypothesis that the problem with verbs commonly seen in Broca's aphasics is due to complexity introduced by verb inflection paradigms (which they term a 'morphological' grammatical explanation of the phenomenon). The investigators used Chinese to test the hypothesis because of the well-known absence of such paradigms in Chinese. Their results indicated that Broca's subjects performed worse than Wernicke's subjects in lexical verb naming. The authors interpret their results as evidence that semantic or conceptual factors (independent of language-specific grammatical facts, such as presence or absence of verb inflection), rather than grammatical or lexical factors, account for the generally poor performance of Broca's speakers with verbs.

The alternative explanation suggested by the present study is that since complex verbs[1] in Chinese are mostly composed at lexical levels III and IV (see 2.2.1), they are more subject to deficit in Chinese Broca's aphasics than other types of complex words (see Table 3.2 and accompanying discussion). Therefore it seems clear that the results of the Bates et al. study do not necessarily rule out grammatical or lexical explanations for the problems in the use of verbs often seen in Broca's aphasia.

4.1.6 Lack of Sentence Embedding in Non-fluent Speech

The non-fluent speaker LXZ used no embedded sentences in her speech, in spite of the fact that in Mandarin, such sentences are not introduced by overt complementizers (see section 2.3.3). We may therefore conclude that the embedding itself, independent of whether it is overtly marked with complementizers on the surface, is difficult for non-fluent aphasic speakers.

4.2 Aphasia Syndrome Diagnostics for Chinese

This investigation has uncovered several speech characteristics that may serve as diagnostics for aphasia type in Chinese, which I will summarize briefly. For the most part I will not mention speech characteristics not specific to Chinese (e.g., fluency, phrase length, etc.; see Table 1.2 on p. 2) unless the manifestation in Chinese is different enough to warrant comment.

Although a diagnostic such as 'misuse of function words' is not specific to Chinese, I include it here for ease of reference, to provide a summary of function words and their misuse in Chinese aphasia. Other diagnostics (e.g., use of the nominal modification marker *de*) are included, even though they may redundantly fall under the more general category 'function word', because of their unusually high diagnostic value for aphasia in Chinese.

4.2.1 Function Words

Aphasia type is distinguished in Mandarin Chinese, as in other languages, by the abnormal use of function words. The common function words in Mandarin are the marker of nominal modification *de* (more on *de* below), determiner-classifier combinations that modify nouns (example 2.24; more on this below), auxiliary verbs (examples 2.12-2.13), coverbs (section 2.3.1),

[1] The majority by far of the responses elicited in the Bates et al. (1991) experiment were *complex* words.

$$[[\text{MODIFIER}] \quad [\text{de}] \quad [\text{NOUN}]]_{\bar{N}}$$

Figure 4.1: *de* Prenominal Modification Structure

conjunctions (section 2.3.7) and pragmatic 'mood' particles (more on these below). Predictably, non-fluent patients underuse these words and omit them from obligatory environments, while fluent patients have no difficulty producing these words and even tend to overuse them.

The Particle *de*

Of the Mandarin function words, the prenominal modification marker *de* appears to be an especially good diagnostic for aphasia type. Recall from section 2.3.2 that the general structure of a complex nominal with *de* is $[[X]$ *de* $[N]]_{\bar{N}}$, where N is a lexical noun and X is a modifier (seen in Figure 4.1). The modifier may be a noun phrase, a stative verbal (i.e., adjectival) phrase, a coverbial (i.e., 'prepositional') phrase, a regular verb phrase or a 'sentence' (as seen in examples 2.19-2.23).

In this and a previous study (Packard 1990a), it was found that the use of *de* by non-fluent aphasics is quite rare. Since *de* is the most common word in Mandarin (see, e.g., Liu et al. 1975, Suen 1979), its absence suggests a speech abnormality, and may be considered a clear sign of non-fluent aphasia.

Fluent patients on the other hand overuse the *de* structure, often with perseverative or semantically empty elements in both modifying and head (modified) positions. In head position, fluent subjects often use no lexical item at all (i.e., a lexically null head). Recall from the discussion in section 2.3.2 that the lexically null head in the *de* structure is often used for non-specific reference. This fact accounts for its frequency in fluent speech, because non-specific reference is often equated with reduced semantic content[2], which is a characteristic feature of the speech of these patients.

[2] It is interesting to note that in the first-language acquisition of Mandarin, children acquire the less specific, lexically headless form of the *de* modification structure before the lexically headed form (see Packard, 1988).

Classifiers

Classifiers are not function words per se, but are grammatical morphemes which are bound to a preceding quantifier to modify a following noun. The quantifier-classifier combination is, however, considered a function word, since it is grammatical in function and is not a member of a major class category (see section 2.2.1).

Our non-fluent patient LXZ underused classifiers and quantifier/classifier combinations, and omitted classifiers from obligatory environments. In contrast, the fluent patient YXF used many classifiers and quantifier/classifier combinations in his speech, usually in a grammatically correct manner. The finding of classifier underemployment and omission by LXZ confirms the findings of Packard (1990a), who observed the same treatment of classifiers in another agrammatic Chinese-speaking Broca's aphasic. These observations also comport with the findings of Tzeng et al. (1991), who found omission of classifiers in obligatory contexts by their aphasic subjects, especially the Broca's subjects.

4.2.2 Preverbal Modifiers

The use of words which usually occupy the preverbal modifier position (such as adverbs in examples 2.1-2.6, coverbs in examples 2.7-2.11 and auxiliary verbs in examples 2.12 and 2.13; see also example 2.14) appears to be a good diagnostic for aphasia type in Chinese. The non-fluent patient LXZ underused and omitted the words that occupy this position, while the fluent patients overused them, often misplacing them or putting them in more than one optional slot[3]. In general, the fluent speakers seem to experience great difficulty restricting and controlling the output of elements that occupy the preverbal modification slot.

The reason for the misuse of words that occupy this position may simply be that they are usually function words, with the only exceptions being time, frequency and manner adverbials. Regardless, they are all either adverbial or INFL phrase structure nodes (see discussion in section 2.3.11). Thus, the omission of these items in non-fluent speech may be explained by the fact that they are all non-lexical terminal elements as defined by Grodzinsky (1990), and thus fall under his proposed syntactic explanation for function word omission.

[3] Recall from section 2.3.1 that adverbials may occur in different orders *within* the sentential modifier slot, and some may occur either before or after the subject of the sentence.

Pragmatic Mood Particles

Pragmatic particles perform an important function in Mandarin (see 2.4), and appear to be diagnostic of aphasia type in Chinese. These particles are totally absent in the speech of the non-fluent patient LXZ. She used none of these particles in sentence-final position, and when giving simple affirmative responses to questions she always used the content word *dui* 'right' instead of a common pragmatic response word such as *hei*, *ei* or *hm*. The fluent speakers GJD and YXF on the other hand used these particles with great frequency, even to the extent that they are used as 'discourse fillers' or hesitation pauses.

4.2.3 Complex Words

Our non-fluent patient LXZ used fewer multisyllabic words than normal, and often omitted morphemes from complex words. Fluent patients produce complex words of normal length and complexity at a normal rate. However, they often improperly substitute morphemes within those complex words.

The non-fluent patient LXZ erred in forming complex words in a principled, 'graded' manner, according to their 'depth' of composition within the lexical component of the grammar, as defined by the theory of LPM applied to Mandarin (Packard 1990b). The 'shallower' in the lexicon these words are formed (i.e., the closer to level IV), the more likely LXZ was to make errors in their construction (see Table 3.2 and accompanying discussion). Fluent patients such as YXF on the other hand evidenced no such 'grading' effect in the incorrect formation of words. YXF made a significantly smaller percentage of total errors than the non-fluent patient LXZ in the construction of complex words (see Chapter 3, footnote 32), and those errors were randomly distributed across the levels of the lexicon (see Table 3.9).

I will argue in section 4.4.1 that word formation problems such as these are not unique to Chinese, but are in fact a universal attribute of agrammatism.

4.2.4 Word Order

As seen in sections 3.1.5, 3.2.5 and 3.3.5, non-fluent and fluent patients appear to make different kinds of word order errors. Our non-fluent patient made mistakes in the order of words *within* syntactic constituents (e.g., within noun phrases), but not in the order of words which are themselves acting as *sentential* constituents (i.e., LXZ apparently has no problem with the basic S-mod-V-O sentence order).

If this provisional generalization regarding the word order of fluent versus non-fluent speakers turns out to be correct, at least two explanations may be offered. One is that non-fluent speakers retain a basically intact functional sentence structure but suffer a loss of structure below the level of the sentence (this possibility is mentioned in Zurif 1984, p. 162). A second possibility is that the internal structure of more complex constituents often requires the use of function words (such as the prenominal modification marker *de* misused in example 4.1), which are known to be dysfunctional in non-fluent speech. In any event, this observation must be considered preliminary, and requires further study.

4.3 Agrammatism in Chinese

In Chapter 1, we considered what characteristics we might expect to find in Chinese agrammatic speech, since misuse of inflectional morphology—a grammatical feature presumed to be absent in Chinese—has been a criterial feature of agrammatism (see discussion in 1.1). We speculated that the symptom of inflection misuse either would not appear in Mandarin, or would appear in a different guise.

Our investigation found that agrammatism in Chinese is characterized by the simplification of syntactic structure, the omission and underemployment of free grammatical morphemes, and the omission and otherwise improper use of morphemes used in forming complex words. The complex words most subject to deficit were those formed at lexical level IV (as defined by the theory of LPM).

The simplification of syntactic structure and the omission of free grammatical morphemes are symptoms of agrammatism which have been found in virtually all languages studied to date, and so their appearance in Chinese is not surprising. However, whereas in other languages we find improper use of inflectional morphology, in Mandarin we find problems in complex word formation. Assuming that agrammatism is a fairly circumscribed, unitary phenomenon across languages (see 4.5.1), a reasonable investigative strategy is to equate these two seemingly disparate symptoms. Accordingly, I hypothesize that the word formation deficit in Mandarin is analogous to the inflection deficit seen in other languages.

Therefore my response to the question posed above is that *the 'inflection misuse' symptom of agrammatism does appear in Mandarin, albeit in a different guise: namely, as a problem in properly forming words, especially words formed at lexical level IV.* In section 4.4.1, I argue that this manifestation of agrammatism in Chinese may generalize to other languages, and that it provides a novel perspective on agrammatism and the aphasia syndromes.

4.4 The Nature of Agrammatism

Let us now attempt to reconcile the Chinese agrammatic data, with previous findings, beginning with the hypothesis that the symptoms outlined for Chinese agrammatism in 4.3 may be accounted for by positing a purely syntactic deficit.

The omission and underemployment of function words found in the speech of LXZ clearly are consonant with traditional notions of functor deletion in agrammatism, and may be explained by assuming a purely syntactic deficit. These findings comport with, e.g., Grodzinsky's (1990, p. 59) syntactic deficit hypothesis, which predicts the deletion of non-lexical syntactic terminal nodes (i.e., determiners, complementizers, adverbs, inflection, auxiliaries and case markers; according to to his definition 1). A syntactic deficit hypothesis thus is well able to account for the misuse of function words by the Chinese agrammatic speaker LXZ.

Problems in the formation of complex words by LXZ also provide prima facie evidence of a syntactic deficit. This is implied by the preponderance of morphological errors at the 'shallowest' or 'last' lexical level (level IV, in Chinese) in LXZ's speech, since the 'last' level of the lexicon is posited to be closely allied with the syntax according to the theory of LPM (see, e.g., Anderson 1992, Mohanan 1986, and Kiparsky 1982). Improper construction of level IV words in Chinese would therefore a priori suggest the involvement of a dysfunctional syntactic component.

However, in order to explain aberrant word formation in Chinese *solely* in terms of a syntactic deficit, a specific relationship must be posited between syntax and word formation. In current Chinese syntactic theory, such a relationship is only posited via the abstract syntactic phrase structure node INFL. Specifically, according to Huang (1982, p. 165) the verb suffix *le* originates in the syntactic INFL node and forms a complex word with the verb it suffixes to (see discussion on page 34). This treatment of INFL by Huang corresponds nicely with Grodzinsky's (1990) syntactic deficit hypothesis, since the INFL node is specifically mentioned by Grodzinsky as a non-lexical terminal node whose content is subject to deletion in agrammatic speech production. The theories of Huang and Grodzinsky therefore converge to yield the prediction that the verb suffix *le* will be omitted or otherwise misused in agrammatic Chinese speech.

Now, one instance of verbal *le* omission is indeed observed in LXZ's speech as seen in 3.39, repeated as 4.4 below.

4.4	Zhan-ϕ	hao	◇duo◇[4].
	stand(-ASP)	very	much
	(He) stand a lot.		
cf.	Zhanle	hao	jiu.
	stand-ASP	very	long
	(He) has stood a long time.		

In 4.4, verbal *le* is omitted from an obligatory context.

However, before we rush to accept this example of *le* omission as evidence of syntactic deficit, let us consider the following points. First, although this instance of *le* omission contributes to the total percentage of level IV word formation error, the overall use of verbal *le* actually is remarkably intact in LXZ's speech (see Table 3.3). Second, the use of *le* was also found to be remarkably intact in a previous Chinese agrammatic speaker (Packard 1990a). Third, there are several instances of the word *meiyou* in LXZ's speech corpus. According to Huang (1982, p. 165; see also Wang 1965), *meiyou* and *le* are allomorphs of the same abstract INFL element (see discussion on page 34), and so the misuse and low occurrence frequency of *meiyou* is predicted but is not observed in our data. Fourth, the word formation deficit in LXZ's speech is not confined to the word formation elements in non-lexical nodes such as INFL (i.e., *le*), but is reflected in the miscomposition of many other types of complex words as well. The miscomposition of other types of complex words is not expected according to Grodzinsky's theory. He explicitly states (1990, p. 60) that his model does not predict problems for morphology that are not syntactic in origin. Finally, the word formation problems in LXZ's speech are not confined to lexical level IV, but also occur in the remaining three levels of the lexicon, even though a syntactic connection to complex words formed at those lexical levels is not posited.

The idea of a linguistic disorder affecting primarily syntax (as opposed to lexical or semantic factors) has characterized most theories of agrammatism over the past several years (see summary in 1.2.1). These proposals, however, fail to account for the aberrant Chinese word formation data because none posits a mechanism whereby a dysfunctional syntax could be the cause of the observed word formation problems. Without such a mechanism explicitly attributing word formation problems to dysfunctional syntax, a syntactic account will not fully explain the range of problems seen in Chinese agrammatic speech.

---

[4] *duo* 'a lot' is a semantic paraphasia for *jiu* 'a long time', and is discussed in section 3.1.3. Also, the omission of the subject pronoun *ta* ('he') is acceptable in this context.

Other proposals positing defective word formation have been proposed[5] to explain agrammatic output, but these proposals also fail to account for the Chinese data. As discussed in 1.2.1, Lapointe (1983) proposed that the distinction between elements omitted and spared in agrammatism is morphological, and that a morphosyntactic account based on this morphological distinction can explain agrammatic deficits.

One problem with Lapointe's theory vis-à-vis the data presented here is that it crucially involves the syntax at all stages (viz., the retained elements in agrammatism are stem-level items that are inserted into morphosyntactic structures during lexical insertion). As I have argued above, a theory that does not allow for a portion of the explanation to be non-syntactic cannot fully account for the range of Chinese aberrant word formation data.

A second shortcoming of Lapointe's proposal is his explanation of function word omission. Lapointe considers function words not to be 'minimal stems' (hence subject to omission) because they are *inert*, i.e., because they do not participate in productive derivational processes. This 'morphological' analysis of function words is somewhat idiosyncratic and ad hoc, and in any event does not apply to function words in Chinese.

Finally, since Lapointe's proposal explains agrammatic data in terms of stem-level word formation units (crucially relying on his concept of 'minimal stem'), his theory does not address the Chinese data because the structural concepts he proposes for word formation do not apply in any straightforward manner to Chinese words.

4.4.1 An Independent Word Formation Deficit in Agrammatism

As we have seen, the agrammatic Chinese word formation data are not fully explained by assuming a purely syntactic or even morphosyntactic deficit. These data are, however, explained if we posit a deficit in the lexicon which specifically affects the construction of words.

The first indication that there is an independent deficit which affects word building in the lexicon is the occurrence of word formation errors in Chinese which cannot be explained with a syntactic account (as argued in 4.4 above). The second indication is the 'graded' nature of the word formation errors, i.e., the fact that the proportion of word formation errors in LXZ's speech increases from level I to level IV (see Table 3.2). There are no proposals in current syntactic theory which would explain such a grading

[5] As noted in Chapter 1, Miceli et al. (1982) and Saffran et al. (1980a) posit independent morphological effects in agrammatism, but define the term 'morphological' somewhat broadly to include free grammatical morphemes (i.e., function words) in addition to grammatical inflection.

effect. However, a word formation theory based on a stratified lexicon (as proposed by LPM) offers a number of plausible explanations (see 4.5.1).

Since a word formation deficit is independently needed to account for the Chinese data, we should consider the possibility that such a deficit is present in agrammatic speakers of other languages as well. Such an assumption may advance our understanding of agrammatism by enabling us to view the ubiquitous inflection deficit in a different light. Specifically, it would suggest that the inflection problem in agrammatism is partially due to a deficit in word construction. Given that inflection in any language *necessarily* involves the formation of complex words, the possibility that some portion of the inflection deficit is attributable to defective word formation seems quite plausible.

I therefore offer the following characterization of agrammatism, based on the presumption of a word formation deficit which is independently needed to explain the Chinese data: *Agrammatism is characterized by independent deficits in word formation and syntax.* The syntactic deficit explains the simplification of syntactic structure, function word deletion, and that portion of inflection error attributable to improper specification by the syntax. The word formation deficit explains complex word construction deficits in general, and also a portion of inflection error attributable to dysfunctional word construction. Thus, I am suggesting that *the misuse of inflection in agrammatism is caused by two independent sources of deficit: one affecting the syntax and one affecting word formation.*

In section 1.2.1 we speculated that syntax and word formation might be two independent sources of inflection error in agrammatism, and that some of the inflection error could in principle be accounted for by positing a morphological deficit. Researchers have presumed the syntactic component to be one source of inflection error because of the unequivocal existence of syntactic deficit in agrammatism. Now evidence from Chinese indicates that some of the inflection problem may be due to a deficit in word formation.

The Word Formation Deficit as a Universal in Agrammatism

The proposal that a word formation deficit accounts for a portion of the inflection error in inflecting languages entails that such a deficit is a *universal* feature of agrammatism. This is not an unreasonable hypothesis, given that misuse of inflection in agrammatism is seen in *all* inflecting languages, and *all* grammatical inflection appears via the medium of the complex word.

In accord with the idea that a word formation deficit accounts for inflection error, it may be no coincidence that in the Chinese agrammatic speaker LXZ, the greatest proportion of incorrect complex words were formed at lexical level IV—the 'last' or 'outermost' level, where inflection is affixed in inflecting languages (according to the theory of LPM). This is an indication that the complex word formation deficit in Chinese and the inflection deficit in other languages are *different manifestations of the 'same' deficit.* The graded nature of LXZ's lexical errors constitutes further evidence that a word formation deficit is a universal characteristic of agrammatism—one that contributes to the occurrence of inflectional error in languages that have significant inflectional morphology.

Of course, the presence of inflection error in inflecting languages does not in itself constitute proof of a deficit in word construction, since the occurrence of inflection error could be due to a faulty syntactic component. For further proof of such a deficit, we need evidence of *non-inflectional* word formation problems in languages other than Chinese. In other words, there must be evidence from other languages that errors occur in the formation of complex words through derivational affixation.

As mentioned in Chapter 1, several studies have found abnormal derivational affixation in agrammatic speech. deBleser and Bayer (1985, 1988) found that German agrammatic speakers have non-inflectional word formation problems. Libben (1990) found that his agrammatic patient committed non- inflectional word formation errors, and that the errors are based on the structural properties of complex words. Badecker and Caramazza (1989) also found that their Italian agrammatic patient committed many derivational word formation errors.

An examination of the data in Menn (1990) reveals that English agrammatics produced few derivationally-complex words compared to control subjects. Since there is nothing in the grammar of English which requires that derivationally-complex words be produced (c.f. the requirement that inflectionally-complex words be produced because of syntactic agreement requirements), the small number of derived words may reflect a strategy of avoidance on the part of the agrammatic patient. In one patient's (Mr. Franklin) speech, the number of derivationally-complex words is especially small, and in another patient (Mr. Eastman) there are errors involving derivational morphology. For example, '*absently' is produced instead of 'absent-mindedly'.

Thus, when data from other languages are examined, we find that the hypothesis of a word formation deficit in agrammatism is not easily rejected. We therefore adopt the working hypothesis that in agrammatism there is a deficit specific to the word formation component of the lexicon which affects the formation of words, such a deficit being independent of the deficit known to exist in the syntax. We further assume that the posited word formation deficit is responsible for some of the inflection problems seen in agrammatic speakers of inflecting languages.

4.5 A Modular Explanation of Aphasia Syndromes

The following is an explanation of Broca's and Wernicke's aphasia that is based on the theory of linguistic modularity, that is, the theory that the language components are modular computational systems that are functionally independent but nonetheless rely on specialized input from one another (see 1.2.2).

I propose that not only do language deficits in aphasia provide evidence for the modularity of the linguistic system, as argued by Linebarger (1989, 1990) and Caramazza and Berndt (1985), but also that the form of the major syndromes is in fact a *direct consequence* of linguistic modularity. Specifically, in one aphasia syndrome, a deficit affects processes that occur *within components*, while in the other aphasia syndrome, a deficit affects information transfer which occurs at the the *interface between components*. The type of aphasia that is the result of the *intra-component* deficit is Broca's aphasia, while Wernicke's aphasia is the result of an *inter-component deficit*.

The finding of the present study which suggests this explanation for the aphasia syndromes is the existence of an independent deficit in the non-fluent speaker LXZ that affects the formation of words (see 4.4.1). This lexical deficit stands in a complementary relation to the well-known deficits that affect the syntactic and phonological systems in non-fluent speech. Given that the processes adversely affected in non-fluent speech (phonological, word formation, syntactic) are just those that are posited to be 'modular' (i.e., automatic, fast, encapsulated, task-specific, etc.; see 1.2.2), it follows that it is precisely the processes within the individual modules that suffer damage in this syndrome. By the same token, we may characterize what is relatively spared in fluent aphasic production as just those processes that are modular. Hence, aspects of syntactic (e.g., Butterworth 1979, Kertesz 1982, Lavorel 1982), morphological (e.g., Garrett 1984, p. 183 and references cited there; Panzeri et al. 1990), and phonological (e.g., Buckingham 1980, as cited in Garrett 1984; Dressler 1985, as cited in Stark and Stark 1990) processes have been argued to be preserved in fluent aphasic speech, and are all component-internal processes[6]. Likewise, many of the problems traditionally noted for fluent speakers (e.g., improper words within preserved syntax; a 'correct' word with the wrong phoneme; 'proper' intonation on semantically anomalous sentences) may be easily understood

[6] Garrett (1984, p. 191) specifically suggests that syntactic and phonological systems are preserved in paragrammatic (fluent) speech but destroyed in agrammatic (non-fluent) speech.

as due to the faulty transfer of information at the I/O modular interface stage.

This explanation I have proposed for the aphasia syndromes raises many questions, in particular a most natural one regarding causation: Why would the posited inter/intra-modular dysfunctions occur, and why would they be caused in particular by focal brain damage? These questions will be discussed in sections 4.5.1, 4.6.1 and especially 4.5.4. What directly follows is a specific outline of how the proposed modular explanation accounts for the classical manifestations of fluent and non-fluent aphasia.

4.5.1 Intra-Component Deficit - Broca's Aphasia

My explanation for the language problems experienced by agrammatic Broca's speakers is that such problems result from deficits which affect constructional processes *within* the phonological, lexical (i.e., word formation) and syntactic components, with the degree of deficit in each component subject to individual case variation[7].

Phonological Component Deficit

The manifestations of deficit within the phonological component in non-fluent speech are the distortion and improper substitution of consonant, vowel and tone phonemes, and the incorrect timing and structuring of syllables. These problems reflect defects in the representation of phonological features (consonantal, vocalic, tonal or syllabic), or in the processes which combine those features into larger phonological units. Separate, specific deficits may be posited which distinguish between phoneme distortions and substitutions.

For example, phoneme substitution errors may be explained as the *categorically incorrect* '+' or '–' specification of a phonological feature. An example from our Chinese data is ZYJ's production of *[t'] (*pinyin 't'*) in place of [t] (*pinyin 'd'*, see utterance Z100 in the Appendix, or Table 3.12), which reflects the incorrect specification of the feature category *[+aspirated] in the place of [–aspirated]. Likewise, the substitution of an incorrect tone may be seen as the wrong '+' or '–' value for a tonal distinctive feature (see Packard 1986).

Phonetic *distortions* on the other hand may be explained as the *degraded or absent* specification (versus the *categorically incorrect* specification) of a '+' or '–' value for a given phonological feature. As an example, consider

[7] Quite in accord with this characterization, Garrett (1984, p. 185) describes agrammatics as deficient in 'phrasal integration', with the types of phrase being different in the different linguistic components (ibid., p. 179).

an instance of the phoneme [p'] which is distorted in that it 'sounds a little like the phoneme [b]'. The '[b]-ness' of [p'] might be due to a voice-onset time (VOT) value which falls in the 'neutral zone' between the [b] and [p'] phoneme boundaries (i.e., between $^{+}15$ and $^{+}35$ milliseconds for English). If we posit an aberrant *[ϕvoiced] (versus the correct [–voiced]) specification for the distorted [p'], the absent, unspecified [ϕ] value for [voiced] would place the onset of voicing anywhere along the VOT continuum between [p'] and [b], with some instances falling in the 'neutral zone' and some falling within the [b] boundary (see Blumstein et al. 1980, in which Broca's aphasics produce many tokens within the 'neutral zone'). In those cases where the produced form occurs in the 'neutral zone', the result is perceived as a phonetic distortion[8]. Further discussion, including a contrast posited between substitution errors in non-fluent versus fluent aphasia, will be offered in section 4.5.2.

As for the intonation deficit seen in the speech of LXZ (see section 3.1.2), ostensibly the normal intonation of Mandarin speech is computed within the phonological component using metrical algorithms, along the lines suggested by Duanmu (1990) or Shih (1986). According to these investigators, Mandarin stress and intonation is determined by rhythmic metrical beat patterns derived via a hierarchical tree or grid. LXZ's intonation deficit, in which all syllables are improperly produced with equivalent prominence, may be seen as a breakdown in the metrical computation process, resulting in LXZ placing an equal prominence on each syllable by default.

LXZ's intonation deficit is noteworthy because non-fluent patients have been shown to have abnormal intonation, especially in contrast with fluent patients (see, e.g., Monrad-Krohn 1947, Botez and Wertheim 1959, Kent and Rosenbek 1982, Ryalls 1982; c.f., however, Danly et al. 1982, and Danly et al. 1983). To my knowledge, this is the first report of an *intonation* deficit (versus a *lexical tone* deficit) in a tone language speaker. This supports the notion that lexical tone and intonation are dissociable in Chinese (Kratochvil 1968, Shen 1990), and that they may independently suffer differing degrees of deficit.

The improper merging of syllable constituents as seen in the speech of ZYJ (see example 3.136) may be explained with reference to the principles of syllable structure for Mandarin suggested by Bao (1990) or Duanmu (1990). Using these works as a point of departure, ZYJ's disyllable collapse errors (such as zhīdào → *zhào) may be seen as the straightforward deletion and inappropriate reattachment of onsets and rimes. In this example, the rime of syllable 1 and the onset of syllable 2 are deleted, followed by the

[8] Purely articulatory errors (as in dysarthria, for example), in contrast, would be the incorrect *motoric* implementation of a correctly specified phonological representation.

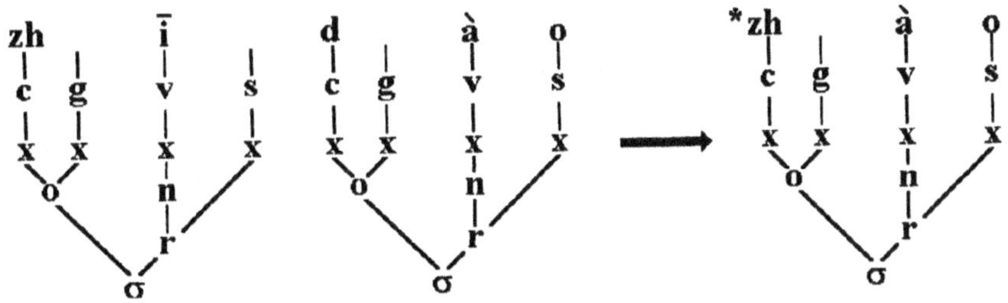

Figure 4.2: Hierarchical Representation of *zhào

misattachment of the syllable 1 onset to the rime of syllable 2, as seen in Figure 4.2.

Examples such as **shuā* in 3.136, however, cannot be understood in terms of a simple deletion and reattachment of syllable constituents. This

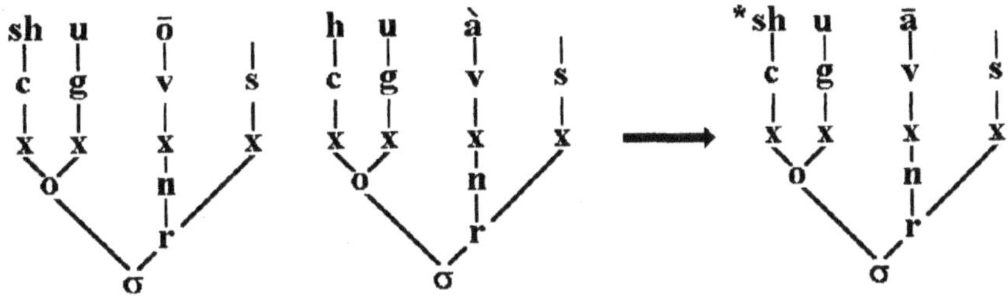

Figure 4.3: Hierarchical Representation of *shuā

is because, as seen in Figure 4.3, the rime which is retained contains the tone of the rime which was lost (see 3.4.2). Here, it is necessary to posit a separate tonal level in the phonological representation, since the tone improperly 'migrated' independent of the non-tonal constituent it was originally associated with.

Lexical Component Deficit

The component-internal deficit in the lexical component is manifest as a reduction in the number of complex words produced (see, e.g., the reference to Menn (1990) in 4.4.1), and the omission and otherwise misuse of morphemes within complex words. Thus, the lexical component deficit is posited to be a *constructional deficit specific to the formation of complex lexical items*. These findings confirm those of deBleser and Bayer (1985, 1988), who also posit an independent deficit in word formation to explain their data from German aphasia.

In the case of the Chinese agrammatic subject LXZ, the *graded* nature of lexical deficit is further evidence that it is restricted to the lexical component. This is because there is no factor outside of the lexicon (e.g., within the syntax) which is posited to affect the composition of Mandarin words in the observed graded manner. On the other hand, there are several possible explanations for the graded nature of the deficit if we assume a lexicon which is structured according to the theory of LPM presented in section 2.2.1.

For example, it is possible that the more levels a lexical representation must pass through, the more 'chances' there are for problems in the formation of a word, resulting in greater numbers of errors as representations move from level I to level IV. Or it is possible that the components of a word are inherently less stable the later in the derivation they are added, leading to an increased incidence of word formation error at later levels. Another possibility is that computational processing demands are greater for representations that must pass through a number of lexical levels, and that agrammatics have trouble producing computationally complex words (c.f. Libben 1990).

Positing a word formation deficit within the lexical component thus accounts for phenomena that otherwise resist parsimonious explanation, such as aberrant word formation data in Chinese and the occurrence of derivational complex word formation errors in other languages.

Syntactic Component Deficit

I suggest that the syntactic problems observed in non-fluent aphasia (functor deletion, word order problems, simplification of syntactic structure) result from a deficit within the syntactic component. Specific suggestions regarding the nature of this syntactic deficit have been offered by many investigators (see Chapter 1). Most of these are compatible with the notion of a deficit restricted to the syntactic component, because in general they do not posit problems which extend beyond the syntax. Other proposals, however, may not be compatible with the present hypothesis, depending upon how details of those theories are interpreted. Kean's (1977) explanation, for example, crucially relies on the interface between the phonological and syntactic components to explain agrammatic syntactic deficits, and so would appear to be incompatible with the proposed component-internal hypothesis. This is also true for Lapointe's (1983) morphosyntactic explanation, which crucially implicates the interface between morphology and syntax.

Explanations of syntactic deficit involving the properties of open- and closed-class vocabulary items (e.g., Bradley et al. 1980, Zurif 1980, Marcus 1982) may appear at first glance to be incompatible with the component-internal hypothesis, because they explain agrammatism in terms of a syntax/lexicon interface (viz., a problem in the lexical access of closed-class items for use in syntax). However, the closed-class retrieval hypothesis is compatible with the present proposal if we make one assumption regarding the membership of closed-class items: that closed-class vocabulary items—quite in line with with their non-referential nature and role in grammatical parsing—are an integral part of both the syntactic and lexical components. As suggested by Zurif (1982, p. 205; see also Zurif 1984), a closed-class vocabulary item may be

> "doubly-registered" – once in its specifically-accessed bin, which by hypothesis supports syntactic analysis, and again in the bin that also includes the open-class items.

Adopting this view, if the 'specifically-accessed closed-class bin' is an integral part of the syntactic component, then the closed-class retrieval hypothesis is consistent with the hypothesis presented here of a deficit restricted to the syntactic component[9].

Explaining 'Non-fluent'

The lack of fluency in Broca's aphasia is quite plausibly explained in the present model by assuming the disruption of 'fast' component-internal computational processes. Component-internal phonological, morphological and syntactic processes are posited to be 'automatic', rapid processes that are 'informationally encapsulated' and not subject to central control (see Fodor 1983, and Levelt 1989, pp. 20-22; see also section 1.2.2). This being the case, deficits which impair these component-internal processes will naturally cause a commensurate decrease in overall processing speed, leading to a substantial reduction of speech fluency.

Agrammatism: A Unitary Account

An important result that falls out of the present analysis is a unitary theoretical treatment of agrammatism. According to the present proposal, agrammatism is the manifestation of a deficit within the syntactic component (function word problems, shortened and aberrant syntactic structures)

[9] For more details regarding the differential properties of function words listed as open- versus closed-class items, see Marcus (1982) and Zurif (1982).

and a deficit within the lexical component (inflectional and other word formation problems). On the surface this may not appear like a unitary treatment, since the the two principal manifestations of the deficit (i.e., functor and inflection problems) appear dissimilar in nature. I suggest, however, that the two deficits appear different, despite their unified explanation, because *the computational processes which are disrupted within the syntactic and lexical components are quite different in nature.*

First, the lexical and syntactic components differ in the nature of the relationship that exists among the linguistic primitives they contain. In morphology, the primary means of relating primitives is *juxtaposition*. That is, the morphemes that make up words are combined with one another in linear fashion, without the presence of intermediate grammatical units which serve to connect them. In syntax on the other hand the relationship among primitives is hierarchical, with intermediate grammatical units (i.e., function words) that assist in marking the hierarchical relationships.

Second, the processes that we use to create and use words are fundamentally different from those we use to create syntactic structure. Intuitively speaking, the use of morphological rules to create new words is much more limited than our use of syntactic rules to create novel sentences. While we may possess underlying knowledge which represents the morphological rules we use to construct words, the words we form from these primitives are much more likely to be stored away in 'list' type format (as dictionary entries) than is the case with formed sentences. It seems unlikely (as syntacticians have argued) that language production taps a list of sentences stored away ready for use. On the other hand it does seem likely that we have a list of lexical items (some derived) stored away ready for insertion into syntactic structures.

Third, formally speaking the word formation component cannot consist of phrase structure rules such as those posited for syntax, because word structure fails to conform to basic tenets of the most widely accepted theory of syntactic phrase structure, namely, $\bar{X}$ (read: 'X-bar') theory. Briefly, the head of a phrase in syntax is considered to be that constituent in the phrase which is of the same form class as the immediately dominating node. In morphology, the head of a word cannot be configurationally defined in this way, but must be defined positionally, as that part of the tree structure which branches in a certain direction from the dominating node (Selkirk 1982, DiSciullo & Williams 1987). This reduces to vacuity the notion of an infinitely recursive generative system for word formation, making the constructional processes of the word formation component look very different from those of the syntactic component[10].

[10] For more and greater detailed arguments outlining differences between morphology

Thus, I argue that the apparently *different* manifestations of a *unitary* deficit in agrammatism are the result of *differences* in the nature of the processes which occur within the affected subsystems.

Finally, with regard to the posited component-internal deficit, it may seem counterintuitive that focal neurological damage could cause a deficit within several different components, when according to modularity theory the components are computationally independent. There are a couple of solutions to this apparent paradox. First, the components may very well share neurological hardware even though they are computationally independent (see discussions in 4.5.4 and 4.6.1). Under these conditions, focal damage to an area containing shared circuitry[11] would be expected to cause deficits within the different components. Second, while the processes within the separate linguistic components are generally different (as argued above), in fact they do employ many of the same types of structural operations. Some examples are the building of large structures from smaller ones, feature evaluation and matching, the evaluation of structural descriptions, and so forth. These commonalities shared by the different components suggest that they may *share certain processing algorithms* at a common source, while otherwise remaining *computationally independent*[12]. If the neural circuits supporting this common source are damaged, the effect on the shared algorithms might be manifest as comparable deficits within the different components.

4.5.2 Inter-Component Deficit - Wernicke's Aphasia

The syndrome that we call fluent or Wernicke's aphasia is due to a deficit involving interfaces among linguistic components. This deficit basically involves problems in modular I/O information transfer. The deficit is caused by damage to a command processor that somehow mediates the interface and I/O aspects of the language components. Such a command processor is posited to be 'located' at or near Wernicke's area.

In order to properly explain the component interface deficit in Wernicke's aphasia, I must first outline the speech production system that I am assuming, and the role of the linguistic components within that production system. The general framework is based on Garrett (1980, 1984), with some additional assumptions.

---

and syntax, see Zwicky (1992).

[11] Or as Richard Sproat (personal communication) puts it, what I am proposing is that damage occurs "...to an area that several different components use as their 'compute-engine'."

[12] As in the case of two computers sharing a program resident at a third location, or two separate programs sharing a common subroutine.

First, there is a *message level* which produces a prelinguistic message based upon information the speaker intends to communicate. By hypothesis, the message level itself neither constitutes a linguistic module nor contains specifically linguistic representations, since it responds to both linguistic and non-linguistic information (Garrett 1984, p. 173, citing Fodor et al. 1980). Next is the *functional level*, which contains both the syntactic and lexical components. The syntactic component is responsible for building syntactic structures, while the lexical component contains abstract lexical forms (concatenations of semantic, syntactic and phonological information), and is responsible for the construction of complex words. Next is the *positional level*, which includes the phonological lexicon containing phonological specifications of words in systematic phonemic form (see Garrett 1984, p. 180; see also Levelt 1989, p. 284).

The process of speech production is posited to occur as follows. When a prelinguistic 'message' is formed based on the speaker's intention to communicate, the message level sends a 'call' to the functional level which contains semantic and functional syntactic information. The call directly enters the syntactic module within the functional level and begins constructing a functional syntactic structure (or portion thereof). The syntactic component then sends a call to the lexical component for an abstract lexical item which possesses the appropriate functional and semantic specifications. This abstract lexical item in the lexical component, in addition to the specified functional and semantic values, also contains abstract phonological information in the form of an address specification. Concrete phonological (systematic phonemic) values corresponding to the address specification must be retrieved from another component, namely, the phonological component at the positional level[13].

The deficit in Wernicke's aphasia can now be understood as follows. By hypothesis, it is the transfer of information between components that is faulty. At the functional level, the call from the message level enters the syntactic component and properly constructs a syntactic functional structure appropriate to the message. When the syntactic component sends a call to the lexical component for the appropriate abstract lexical item, the semantic and functional information in that call may or may not survive the transit intact. If the transited semantic information is only minimally damaged, a semantically close but incorrect lexical item is selected, eventually resulting in a semantic paraphasia (assuming nothing goes wrong in the phonological specification further down the line). If the transited semantic form is more severely degraded, or if the transited functional information is

[13] Kean (1982, pp. 195-198) posits a deficit at this positional level of processing as the source of the problem in agrammatism.

degraded, the result is an incorrect, semantically inappropriate word, i.e., a verbal paraphasia. In both these instances, the result is a basically correct syntactic structure which contains inappropriate lexical items, a situation commonly observed in Wernicke's aphasia.

If the information in the call from the syntax to the lexical component survives the transition intact, the phonological address code in the abstract lexical item still risks becoming degraded or changed in transition to the phonological component. If the phonological code only minimally changes in transit, the result is a form that is phonologically similar to the target, i.e., a phonemic paraphasia. When the phonological code is severely degraded, to the extent that the retrieved form has the appearance of a non-word, a neologism (nonexistent word) results. Theoretically, signal degradation may occur at all component interface points. The result, in the worst cases, is severe neologistic jargon, a condition often seen in Wernicke's aphasia.

What follows is a detailed outline of how the posited component interface deficit results in the form of speech output seen in Wernicke's aphasia.

Phonological and Lexical Component Interface Deficit

The interface problem between the phonological and lexical components (described in general terms above) manifests itself in the form of the predominance of phonemic substitution errors versus other types of phonological errors in Wernicke's aphasia. These errors occur as the result of degradation of the phonological address code which occurs in the transition from the lexical to the phonological components. In the case of phonemic substitution errors, the degraded code results in an improper selection from the phoneme inventory. It is well documented that phonemic substitution errors occur more often than phonetic distortion errors in fluent aphasics, and furthermore that phonemic substitutions are more common in Wernicke's than in Broca's aphasics (e.g., Trost and Canter 1974, Klitch et al. 1979; Blumstein et al. 1980). The explanation of this overabundance of phonemic substitution errors is that it is the improper specification of a phoneme *in its entirety* (i.e., as a unitary bundle of distinctive features), that causes the error.

This is in contrast to the phonological deficit in Broca's aphasia, where both distortions and substitutions commonly occur. Recall from section 4.5.1 that phonological errors in patients with Broca's aphasia are posited to be due to an incorrect, degraded or absent specification for the value of a single phonological feature within a given phoneme. We can easily see the contrast between Broca's and Wernicke's phonological errors in the different origins of phonological substitution errors in the two groups.

A Wernicke's aphasic who produces *[p'a] rather than [ba] by hypothesis has, because of the degradation of the phonological code in transit from the lexical component, incorrectly targeted the unitary bundle of features corresponding to phoneme [p'] rather than the bundle for the target [b]. In contrast, the Broca's aphasic who produces *[p'a] in place of [ba] has, by hypothesis, a degraded or missing specification for the value of a feature such as [±aspirated] (see p. 131 for a discussion of the erroneous phoneme [p'] originating from *within* the damaged phonological component).

Concerning the potential existence of deficits *within* the lexical component in Wernicke's aphasia, I propose that in keeping with the theory presented here, such deficits do not occur in fluent aphasic speech[14].

Lexical and Syntactic Component Interface Deficit

The deficit in the interface between the lexical and syntactic components posited for fluent aphasia is clearly manifested in the improper selection of words from the lexicon for use in properly formed syntactic structures. As explained above, this deficit is the result of the degradation of the semantic or functional code specifying the appropriate lexical item in transit from the syntactic to the lexical component. The deficit is quite evident in fluent aphasic speech in the frequent use of inappropriate or nonexistent words within surprisingly intact syntactic structures. This is generally considered a prototypical characteristic of fluent aphasia, and is explained quite well by assuming a deficit in the exchange of information at the interface of the syntactic and lexical components.

Explaining 'Fluent'

Given the explanation for non-fluency in Broca's aphasia presented in section 4.5.1, it follows that the speech of a Wernicke's aphasic does not lose fluency because there is no disruption of the 'fast', automatic, structure-building processes that occur within the linguistic components. The *infor-*

[14] Since component-internal deficits are posited not to occur in fluent aphasia, the morphemic errors observed in construction of complex words by YXF and fluent aphasic speakers of other languages need to be explained. I suggest that what is commonly called the 'lexical' component is in fact composed of two separate subcomponents: the *'lexicon'* and the *'morphological'* or *'word formation' component*. The lexicon is the list of forms (called 'listemes' by DiSciullo and Williams 1987) that previously have been constructed or otherwise encountered by the speaker, consisting of both decomposed word formatives and whole words (c.f. Caramazza, Laudana and Romani 1988, who claim that words are retrieved in both full and morphologically decomposed form). The morphological component contains word formation rules organized according to the principles of LPM (see Chapter 2). A deficit in the interface of these two subcomponents is posited in fluent aphasia, resulting in the improper selection of morphemes for use in complex words.

mation that is transferred may be degraded in transit from component to component, but the transfer *process* itself proceeds at a normal pace. Since it is the encoded information that suffers disruption and not the process of its transfer per se, fluent speakers continue to produce speech at a normal rate.

Explaining 'Locally Grammatical Globally Ungrammatical'

In Wernicke's aphasia, sentences are often produced which are ungrammatical because of the global impropriety of word strings which seem locally correct (see section 3.3.5)[15]. It remains to be explained how global ungrammaticality could occur in the context of an intact syntactic component.

The acceptability of 2-3 word strings within larger ungrammatical contexts may be explained with reference to the 'n-gram' model of speech recognition and production (see, e.g., Miller and Chomsky 1963, Jelinek et al. 1991)[16]. In the case of a trigram production model, a given word to be produced by the model is selected according to the probability of its cooccurrence with the two words that immediately precede it, such probability having been computed over a large corpus of connected speech. When this process (also known as 'Markov chaining') is unconstrained by semantic or global context factors, the output looks surprisingly like the speech output of a Wernicke's aphasic speaker[17]. Since the n-gram 'chaining' is apparently being properly performed by the Wernicke's speaker, I suggest that this stochastic computational mechanism may be a very low-level process within the syntactic component, and that it is spared in Wernicke's aphasia by virtue of its status as a component-internal process.

The global ungrammaticality of such utterances, despite the putatively intact syntactic component, may be explained following Lavorel (1982). In his model, the global ungrammaticality of fluent speech is the result of lexicosemantic errors that cause the misselection of global phrasal nodes in the syntactic tree. On this account, the attachment of phrasal nodes to form larger sentential units is partially a function of the semantic subcategorization of lexical items for those phrasal nodes. According to the theory I have presented here, the lexicosemantic errors that cause the misselection of phrasal nodes is due to the lexical selection deficit which occurs at the

[15]This specific type of deficit has been termed *paragrammatism* (Goodglass 1976, p. 238), but different investigators have used this term in different ways (e.g., Kolk et al. 1985, Heeschen 1985, Butterworth and Howard 1987, Arbib et al. 1982).

[16]I am grateful to Bob Frank and Mitch Marcus for helpful discussions of this issue.

[17]The fact that n-gram production models produce output that makes local sense but is globally nonsensical was apparently first pointed out by Shannon and Weaver (1949). My thanks to Richard Sproat for this reference.

interface of the lexical and syntactic components[18].

The explanations for both the local grammaticality and the global ungrammaticality of word strings presented here are reasonable under the hypothesis that Wernicke's aphasia is caused by damage to a command processor that directs the interface (i.e., the I/O aspects) of the language modules. Improper lexical selection from the lexical component by the syntactic component causes the lexicosemantic misselection of phrasal nodes resulting in instances of global ungrammaticality, while the component-internal stochastic and syntactic processes remain intact.

4.5.3 Jakobson's Model Reconsidered

The model proposed here is reminiscent of Roman Jakobson's (1964, 1968, 1971) linguistic analyses of aphasic speech. Jakobson variously described Broca's aphasia as a 'combinatory', 'contiguity' or 'syntagmatic' disorder, because of the difficulty these patients have in stringing items together. Jakobson described Wernicke's aphasia as a 'similarity', 'selection' or 'paradigmatic' disorder, in which the patient has no problem in stringing together contiguous elements, but has problems selecting the proper items from paradigms for insertion into grammatical slots.

The proposed model lends support to Jakobson's framework because it confirms and further explains his characterizations of aphasic deficit. For example, the selection disorder which Jakobson posits for Wernicke's aphasia in the present framework is the result of a defective interface between linguistic components. Also, the combinatory disorder which Jakobson posits for Broca's aphasia is explained in the proposed framework as being due to a constructional deficit which occurs within the different linguistic components of these patients. While the theoretical framework I am proposing is based on a different premise, the results are similar, with the component-interface problem resulting in the improper selection of elements from one linguistic component for use in another, and the component-internal deficit causing problems in the combination of elements. A difference between Jakobson's framework and the one proposed here is that the present analysis frames the explanation in modular, cognitive science terms, assuming that the language faculty consists of a series of independent but interacting components.

---

[18] Eleanor Saffran (personal communication) has suggested that these globally ungrammatical sentences could be 'syntactic blends', analogous to phonological blends seen in speech errors and phonological paraphasias. I consider the hypothesis presented here to be a plausible explanation for the occurrence of such blends.

4.5.4 Excursus on Causation

Why does the posited inter/intra-modular deficit occur, and why in particular is it caused by focal brain damage? According to Caplan (1987, pp. 33-35), the aphasia syndromes can be explained with reference to anatomical, functional/psychological, or random factors. An anatomical explanation assumes that symptoms occur because of damage to a confluence of circuitry in a focal, circumscribed location[19]. Anatomical explanations implicitly deny a functional relation among the observed symptoms. A functional or psychological explanation is one in which the observed deficits are posited to occur due to damage which affects a part of a system which is functionally definable. An 'explanation' based on randomness simply means that the observed deficits are a chance occurrence. For Broca's and Wernicke's aphasia, I feel that we may exclude randomness in formulating our explanation, since these syndromes occur with enough frequency and consistency to warrant positing causality.

I suggest that the two major syndromes occur for anatomical and functional reasons: Broca's aphasia is due to *anatomical* factors, while Wernicke's aphasia is primarily a *functional* disorder.

On the view presented here, Broca's aphasia is an anatomically-based disorder because the linguistic components that suffer deficit in this syndrome are posited to be 'located' in Broca's area, and share a good deal of neural circuitry. In other words, the neural circuits used for computation by the phonological, lexical and syntactic components, while not wholly isomorphic, nonetheless overlap to a considerable degree.

In considering the possibility that the deficit in Broca's aphasia may be functional, given the theory presented here, one possibility comes to mind. If the linguistic components share certain computational algorithms (as discussed in section 4.5.1), the relationships among the components which rely on the shared algorithms could be considered functional relations. The deficits in the different components caused by damage to an area affecting the shared algorithms would therefore be considered functionally-related.

Wernicke's aphasia on the other hand is posited to be caused by damage to a command processor that mediates the I/O interface of language components (see 4.5.2). This being the case, the deficit is functional since the I/O interface among several disparate components would be a functional relation.

---

[19] *All* deficits are anatomical in the sense that they occur as a result of damage to neurological tissue.

4.6 Aphasia Theory Reconsidered

The theory I have proposed here takes a stand (explicitly or implicitly) on many of the issues that were raised in section 1.2. Let us now consider how some of those issues have been addressed by the present proposal.

4.6.1 Validity of The Notion 'Syndrome'

I would argue that Broca's and Wernicke's aphasia are valid as syndromes in a sense that extends beyond the clinical and anatomical implications of the term. Specifically, I suggest that both Broca's and Wernicke's aphasia are *theoretically significant* entities, and that Wernicke's aphasia is both a *theoretically and functionally significant* entity.

Regarding theoretical significance, the explanations of both syndromes are consistent with a modular theory of language, suggesting that there is indeed a theoretical basis for the syndromes. The building of structure is posited to take place *within* the linguistic components. A deficit occurring within a component will disrupt the buiding of structure that occurs there, yielding the symptoms seen in Broca's aphasia. Likewise, the transfer of paradigmatic data bundles is posited to occur *between* components, and the degradation of the information during transfer results in the manifestations of the Wernicke's syndrome. If this explanation of Broca's and Wernicke's aphasia is correct, then the patterns of symptoms that cooccur do so for theoretically relevant reasons. Therefore the occurrence of syndromes would not have only limited theoretical significance (contra Badecker and Caramazza 1989, and Marshall 1982).

Concerning functional significance, for Wernicke's aphasia I have proposed that a functional relationship exists between a command processor and the interface that takes place between the linguistic components, viz., that the command processor somehow has a role in mediating the exchange of information (e.g., phoneme, morpheme and lexical information) among linguistic components. Wernicke's area is posited to contain the neurological hardware that supports this command processor.

I suggest that the cooccurrence of phonological, lexical and syntactic deficits seen in the syndrome of Broca's aphasia does not have a functional basis, because there is no functional relationship posited among the distinct computational processes that occur within the phonological, lexical and syntactic components. That is, the linguistic components appear to be functionally independent[20]. Damage to a single, focal anatomical locus

[20] Of course, there is a functional relation posited among the components in that they transfer information amongst themselves. But it is precisely this functional relation that is posited to be compromised in Wernicke's aphasia.

(Broca's area) can be understood as potentially causing coincident deficits in three discrete linguistic components under the reasonable assumption that the phonological, lexical and syntactic components are distributed throughout Broca's area, and share a significant amount of neurological hardware. In other words, phonological, lexical and syntactic computation all are posited to take place independently within that same section of cortex. These three language components are 'located' at or near Broca's area, and they are *computationally, but not necessarily neurologically, distinct*[21].

I therefore agree with Badecker and Caramazza (1985) and Marshall (1982) that Broca's aphasia and agrammatism are not functionally definable syndromes. But contra Badecker and Caramazza, and Marshall, I *do* believe that there is a functional basis for the cooccurrence of symptoms seen in Wernicke's aphasia, and also believe that both Broca's and Wernicke's aphasia are theoretically significant entities.

4.6.2 Linguistic Modularity and Aphasia

In 1.2.2, we discussed the role that language components might play in accounting for the occurrence of syndromes in aphasia. The explanations offered for the occurrence and form of aphasia syndromes in 4.5 (as well as the explanations for the non-fluent and fluent character of speech output in the two major syndromes given in sections 4.5.1 and 4.5.2 respectively), not only comport with the hypothesis that the linguistic system is modularly organized (as argued by Linebarger 1989, 1990, and Caramazza and Berndt 1985), but actually *entail* that the occurrence and form of aphasia syndromes is a *direct consequence* of linguistic modularity.

4.6.3 Fractionation of Components

The theory of aphasia presented here offers a plausible explanation for why the idealized 'fractionation' of linguistic components so seldom occurs (see 1.2.2). Under the present proposal, the isolation of components does not often occur following focal brain damage because the components in all likelihood share neurological hardware, as discussed in 4.6.1. In such a situation, focal damage to the shared hardware is bound to cause deficits that cut across theoretical component boundaries, causing varying degrees of disturbance in the different linguistic abilities.

[21] As discussed in section 4.5.1 above, the components may share certain algorithms while still remaining computationally independent. If this is true and constitutes a functional relation, then it would be the only functional relation that I would posit (but see footnote 20) among the three separate components—one that might derive from their shared use of computational algorithms.

4.6.4 Representation versus Processing

Returning to the issue of dysfunctional processes versus representations discussed in 1.2.5, the evidence from this study indicates that aphasic performance may be attributed in most cases to problems in the *on-line processing* aspects of language production that occur within and between the linguistic components.

The abnormal syllable structures seen in 3.4.2 are explained in 4.5.1 by positing deficits in on-line syllable construction, resulting in the deletion and misattachment of syllable nodes. The abnormal speech timing seen 3.1.2 was analyzed in 4.5.1 as a breakdown in on-line metrical computation processing.

The lexical and syntactic deficits seen in Broca's aphasia are explained by positing deficits in on-line building of morphological and syntactic structure. For the lexical and syntactic problems seen in Wernicke's aphasia, the deficit is explained as a defect in the on-line exchange of modular information.

The one area where a representational deficit seems plausible following the theory proposed here is in the phonetic distortions and substitutions produced in non-fluent aphasia (discussed in 4.5.1). Recall that for both distortions and substitutions in non-fluent speech, it was posited that phoneme distortions and substitutions occur as the result of incorrect or degraded representation of phonological features. So it seems a 'degraded representation' hypothesis here is plausible. However, it is possible that here also, the deficit is in the constructional processes which combine phonological distinctive features into larger phonological units. At present, so little is known about feature concatenation versus feature representation that positing deficits in the construction of phonemes via feature concatenation seems premature.

4.6.5 The Distinctive Character of Syndromes

In 1.2.4 we considered the views of some investigators who have proposed that Broca's and Wernicke's aphasia may be explained by positing underlyingly similar deficits, and that therefore the two syndromes are not distinct. The explanation I have offered here outlines clearly-defined linguistic and functional differences between the two syndromes. If we consider these differences together with the well-known distinct anatomical loci that give rise to the syndromes, this must be considered good, converging, evidence that the syndromes of fluent and non-fluent aphasia are indeed different in kind.

4.7 Summary and Conclusion

In this investigation, I have shown many ways in which Chinese aphasia corresponds with aphasia in other languages. I have also pointed out where the Chinese data are different, causing us to reevaluate traditional assumptions. I have also identified several speech characteristics which are helpful in diagnosing aphasia type in Chinese.

In addition to the different perspective offered on language breakdown, this work has also provided a novel approach toward understanding Chinese grammatical structure, especially the structure of words. We found that complex Chinese words may be analyzed within a theory of word structure (Lexical Phonology and Morphology) which predicts their likelihood of misuse by non-fluent aphasics.

The finding that word formation deficits exist in non-fluent speech, and are not fully explained by syntax, suggests that the word formation component is an independent source of deficit in agrammatism. I have argued that this word formation deficit extends to other languages as well, making it a universal feature of agrammatism.

In syntax, we found that the functor omission and syntactic simplification seen in agrammatism in other languages is also a characteristic of Chinese agrammatism. Thus, the explanations proposed for syntactic deficit in other languages account for the Chinese data as well. We also observed that there may be qualitative differences between non-fluent and fluent aphasic speakers in the nature of their word order errors. This finding is preliminary, but alerts us to look for the phenomenon in other languages. We also found a lack of complex embeddings in non-fluent speech, despite the absence of overt complementizers in Chinese. This indicates that it is the embedding per se, and not the use of overt markers of such embedding, that causes problems for the non-fluent speaker. With regard to the identity of 'coverbs', these data provide neurolinguistic support for the view that the words that are called coverbs may be verb-like or preposition-like, depending on usage. The evidence is that in non-fluent speech, coverbs are generally retained when used as verbs (content words) and generally omitted when used as prepositions (function words).

Other tentative hypotheses may also be offered based on the syntactic phenomena observed in these data. For example, since topicalization remains surprisingly intact in non-fluent speakers, this may be considered evidence of the non-complex, base-generated nature of topic structures versus their derivation via syntactic movement rules in Chinese. Also, while the aspect marker *le* has many properties that cause it to appear inflectional in nature (and is even posited by some to be base-generated in the syntactic INFL node), since it is not omitted as expected on analogy with inflection in other languages, it must be considered different from inflection.

Finally, I have presented a theory of aphasia, based on the cognitive science modularity hypothesis, which accounts for the major syndromes in a theoretically coherent manner. In offering this modular explanation, I have defended the concept of *syndrome* in aphasia by imputing theoretically plausible linguistic functions to Broca's and Wernicke's areas, damage to which results in the two major syndromes. This modular account also explains the fluent and non-fluent character of aphasic speech in a way that has a theoretical basis and is intuitively plausible.

If we are to entertain a theory of language and cognition that posits the existence of modules having certain properties, then we must also entertain the hypothesis that when processing breaks down, it will do so in a way that in some way reflects the properties of the modules. This study has proposed that following neurological damage, breakdown may affect operations that occur either within or between linguistic modules, and that aphasia symptoms differ accordingly.

Virtually all investigators in the field of neurolinguistics recognize the contribution that linguistic theory has made to our understanding of the brain-language relationship. One of my goals in this work has been to show how evidence from aphasia makes a significant contribution to the linguistic enterprise. I hope this work encourages more cross-linguistic study of aphasia, and that it serves as an impetus for further investigation into the role of modularity in cognitive deficit.

Bibliography

[1] Anderson, S. (1992). *A-Morphous Morphology.* New York: Cambridge University Press.

[2] Arbib, M., Caplan, D. and Marshall, J. (1982). Neurolinguistics in historical perspective. In Arbib, Caplan and Marshall (Eds.).

[3] Arbib, M., Caplan, D. and Marshall, J. (Eds.) (1982). *Neural Models of Language Processes.* New York: Academic Press.

[4] Badecker, W. and Caramazza, A. (1989). A lexical distinction between inflection and derivation. *Linguistic Inquiry 20.1,* pp. 108-116.

[5] Badecker, W. and Caramazza, A. (1985).On considerations of method and theory governing the use of clinical categories in neurolinguistics and cognitive psychology: The case against agrammatism. *Cognition 20,* pp. 97-125

[6] Bao, Z. (1990). *Fanqie* languages and reduplication. *Linguistic Inquiry 21.3,* pp. 317-350.

[7] Bates, E., Frederici, A. and Wulfeck, B. (1987). Grammatical morphology in aphasia: evidence from three languages. *Cortex 23,* pp. 545-574.

[8] Bates, E. and Wulfeck, B. (1989a). Comparative aphasiology. *Aphasiology 3.2,* pp. 111-142.

[9] Bates, E. and Wulfeck, B. (1989b). Crosslinguistic studies of aphasia. In MacWhinney and Bates (Eds.).

[10] Bates, E., Chen, S., Tzeng, O., Li, P., and Opie, M. (1991). The noun-verb problem in Chinese aphasia. *Brain and Language 41,* pp. 203-233.

[11] Benson, D. F. and Geschwind, N. (1971). The aphasias and related disturbances. In Baker and Baker (Eds.), *Clinical Neurology.* New York: Harper and Row.

[12] Berndt, R. and Caramazza, A. (1980). A redefinition of Broca's aphasia: implications for a neuropsychological model of language. *Applied Psycholinguistics 1*, pp. 225-278.

[13] Biq, Y-O. (1990). Conversation, continuation, and connectives. *Text 10 (3)*, pp. 187-208.

[14] Blumstein, S, Cooper, W. Goodglass, H. Statlender and Gottlieb, J. (1980). Phonological production deficits in aphasia: a voice-onset time analysis. *Brain and Language 9*, pp. 153- 170.

[15] Blumstein, S. (1973). *A Phonological Investigation of Aphasic Speech.* The Hague: Mouton.

[16] Botez, M. and Wertheim, N. (1959). Expressive aphasia and amusia following right frontal lesion in a right-handed man. *Brain 82*, p. 186.

[17] Bradley, D., Garrett, M. and Zurif, E. (1980). Syntactic deficits in Broca's aphasia. In Caplan (1980).

[18] Buckingham, H. (1980). On correlating aphasic errors with slips of the tongue. *Applied Psycholinguistics 1*, pp. 199-220.

[19] Butterworth, B. (1979). Hesitation and the production of verbal paraphasias and neologisms in jargon aphasia. *Brain and Language 8*, pp. 133-161.

[20] Butterworth, B. (Ed.) (1980). *Language Production, Vol. 1.* New York: Academic Press.

[21] Butterworth, B. and Howard, D. (1987). Paragrammatisms. *Cognition 26*, pp. 1-37.

[22] Caplan, D. (Ed.), (1980). *Biological Studies of Mental Processes..* Cambridge, MA: MIT Press.

[23] Caplan, D. (1985). Syntactic and semantic structures in agrammatism. In Kean (Ed.).

[24] Caplan, D. (1987). *Neurolinguistics and Linguistic Aphasiology.* Cambridge, UK: Cambridge University Press.

[25] Caplan, D., Kellar, L. and Locke, S. (1972). Inflection of neologisms in aphasia. *Brain 95*, pp. 169-172.

[26] Caplan, D., Lecours, A.R., and Smith, A. (Eds.) (1984). *Biological Perspectives on Language.* Cambridge, MA: MIT Press.

[27] Caramazza, A. (Ed.), (1990). *Cognitive Neuropsychology and Neurolinguistics.* Hillsdale, NJ: Erlbaum.

[28] Caramazza, A., Laudana, A., and Romani, C. (1988). Lexical access and inflectional morphology. *Cognition 28*, pp. 297-332.

[29] Caramazza, A., and Berndt, R. (1978). Semantic and syntactic processes in aphasia: a review of the literature. *Psychological Bulletin 85.4*, pp. 898-918.

[30] Caramazza, A., and Berndt, R. (1985). A multicomponent view of agrammatic Broca's aphasia. In Kean (Ed.), pp. 27-63.

[31] Carlson, G. and Tanenhaus, M. (Eds.) (1989). *Linguistic Structure in Language Processing.* Dordrecht: Kluwer Academic Publishers.

[32] Chan, M. (1984). Word formation in Mandarin: a preliminary sketch. Paper presented to the West Coast Conference on Linguistics (WESCOL). Vancouver, Canada.

[33] Chao, Y-R. (1968). *A Grammar of Spoken Chinese.* Berkeley: University of California Press.

[34] Cheng, C.C. (1973). *A Synchronic Phonology of Mandarin Chinese.* The Hague: Mouton.

[35] Chomsky, N. (1981). *Lectures on Government and Binding.* Dordrecht: Foris.

[36] Cole, P. (1981). *Radical Pragmatics.* New York: Academic Press.

[37] Comrie, B. (1990). Word order in the Germanic languages— subject-verb or verb-second?: evidence from aphasia in Scandinavian languages. In Menn and Obler, (Eds.).

[38] Cutler, A. (1980). Errors of stress and intonation. In Fromkin (Ed.), pp. 67-80.

[39] Danly, M., Cooper, W. and Shapiro, B. (1983). Fundamental frequency, language processing and linguistic structure in Wernicke's aphasia. *Brain and Language 19*, pp. 1-24.

[40] Danly, M. and Shapiro, B. (1982). Speech prosody in Broca's aphasia. *Brain and Language 16*, pp. 171-190.

[41] deBleser, R. and Bayer, J. (1985). German word formation and aphasia. *The Linguistic Review 5*, pp. 1-40.

[42] deBleser, R. and Bayer, J. (1988). On the role of inflectional morphology in agrammatism. In Hammond and Noonan (Eds.).

[43] deBleser, R. and Bayer, J. (1990). Morphological reading errors in a German case of deep dyslexia. In Nespoulous and Villiard (Eds.).

[44] DeFrancis, J. (1984). *The Chinese Language: Fact and Fantasy.* Honolulu: University of Hawaii Press.

[45] Dell, G. (1984). Representation of serial order in speech: evidence from the repeated phoneme effect in speech errors. *Journal of Experimental Psychology: Learning, Memory and Cognition, 10*, pp. 222-233.

[46] DiSciullo, M. and Williams, E. (1987). *On the Definition of the Word.* Cambridge, MA: MIT Press.

[47] Dogil, G. (1984). Nonlinear phonology in the area of speech and grammar pathology. In van der Hulst, H, and N. Smith (Eds.), *Advances in Non-linear Phonology.* Dordrecht: Foris. Pp. 161-178.

[48] Dressler, W. (1985). *Morphonology.* Ann Arbor: Karoma Press.

[49] Duanmu, S. (1990). A Formal Study of Syllable, Tone, Stress and Domain in Chinese Languages. Ph.D. dissertation, MIT.

[50] Fromkin, V. (Ed.), (1973). *Speech Errors as Linguistic Evidence.* The Hague: Mouton.

[51] Fromkin, V. (Ed.), (1980). *Errors in Linguistic Performance: Slips of the Tongue, Ear, Pen and Hand.* New York: Academic Press.

[52] Futter, C. and Bub, D. (1986). A level-ordered theory of morphological paralexias. Presented at the Academy of Aphasia, Nashville, Tn.

[53] Gandour, J. (1987). Tone production in aphasia. In J. Ryalls (Ed.), pp. 45-57.

[54] Garrett, M. F. (1980). Levels of processing in sentence production. In Butterworth (Ed.).

[55] Garrett, M. F. (1984). The organization of processing structure for language production: applications to aphasic speech. In Caplan, Lecours and Smith (Eds.), pp. 172-193.

[56] Goldsmith, J. (1990). *Autosegmental and Metrical Phonology.* Oxford, UK: Basil Blackwell

[57] Goodglass, H. (1976). Agrammatism. In Whitaker (Ed.), *Studies in Neurolinguistics, Vol. I.* New York: Academic Press.

[58] Goodglass, H. (1990). Inferences form cross-modal comparisons of agrammatism. In Menn and Obler (Eds.).

[59] Goodglass, H. and Kaplan, E. (1972, 1982). *The Assessment of Aphasia and Related Disorders.* Philadelphia: Lea and Febiger.

[60] Grodzinsky, I. (1984). The syntactic characterization of agrammatism. *Cognition 16*, pp. 99-120.

[61] Grodzinsky, I. (1986). Language deficits and the theory of syntax. *Brain and Language 27*, pp. 135-159.

[62] Grodzinsky, I. (1990). *Theoretical Perspectives on Language Deficits.* Cambridge, MA: MIT Press.

[63] Hammond, M. and Noonan (Eds.) (1988). *Theoretical Morphology.* New York: Academic Press.

[64] Heeschen, C. (1985). Agrammatism versus paragrammatism: a fictitious opposition. In Kean (Ed.).

[65] Hoequist, J. (1983). Syllable duration in stress-, syllable- and mora-timed languages. *Phonetica 40*, pp. 203-237.

[66] Hoosain, R. (1991). *Psycholinguistic Implications for Linguistic Relativity: A Case Study of Chinese.* Hillsdale, N.J.: Lawrence Erlbaum Associates.

[67] Howie, J. (1976). *Acoustical Studies of Mandarin Vowels and Tones.* Cambridge: Cambridge University Press.

[68] Huang, J. C-T. (1982a). Logical Relations in Chinese and the Theory of Grammar. Ph.D. dissertation, MIT.

[69] Huang, J. C-T. (1982b). Move *wh* in a language without *wh* movement. *The Linguistic Review 1.4*, pp. 369-416.

[70] Huang, J. C-T. (1984). On the distribution and reference of empty pronouns. *Linguistic Inquiry 15.4*, pp. 531-574.

[71] Huang, J. C-T. (1989). *Wo paode kuai* and Chinese phrase structure. *Language 64.2*, pp. 274-311.

[72] Jackendoff, R. (1972). *Semantic Interpretation in Generative Grammar*. Cambridge, MA: MIT Press.

[73] Jakobson, R. (1956). Two aspects of language and two types of aphasic disturbances. In R. Jakobson and M. Halle (Eds.). *Fundamentals of Language*.

[74] Jakobson, R. (1968). *Child Language, Aphasia, and Phonological Universals*. The Hague: Mouton.

[75] Jakobson, R. (1971). *Studies on Child Language and Aphasia*. The Hague: Mouton.

[76] Jelinek, F., Merialdo, B., Roukos, S., and Straus, M. (1991). A dynamic model for speech recognition. In Price (Ed.).

[77] Joanette, Y. and Brownell, H. (1990). *Discourse Ability and Brain Damage*. New York: Springer-Verlag.

[78] Kean, M-L. (1977). The linguistic interpretation of aphasia syndromes: Agrammatism in Broca's aphasia, an example. *Cognition 5*, pp. 9-46.

[79] Kean, M-L. (1980). Grammatical representations and the description of language processing. In Caplan (Ed.).

[80] Kean, M-L. (1982). Three perspectives for the analysis of aphasic syndromes. In Arbib, Caplan and Marshall (Eds.), pp. 173-201.

[81] Kean, M-L. (Ed.), (1985). *Agrammatism*. New York: Academic Press.

[82] Kehayia, E. Caplan, D. and Piggott, G.L. (1984). On the repetition of derivational affixes by English agrammatics. *McGill Working Papers in Linguistics*, Vol. 2, No. 1.

[83] Kent, R. and Rosenbek, J. (1982). Prosodic disturbance and neurologic lesion. *Brain and Language 15*, p. 259.

[84] Kertesz, A. (1982). Two case studies: Wernicke's and Broca's aphasia. In In Arbib, Caplan and Marshall (Eds.), pp. 25- 44.

[85] Kiparsky, P. (1982). Lexical morphology and phonology. In I.-S. Yang (Ed.), *Linguistics in the Morning Calm*. Seoul: Hanshin. Pp. 3-91.

[86] Klitch, R., Ireland, J. and Weidner, W. (1979). Articulatory and phonological aspects of consonant substitutions in apraxia of speech. *Cortex 15*, p. 451.

[87] Kolk, H. (1978). Judgement of sentence structure in Broca's aphasia. *Neuropsychologia 16*, pp. 617-626.

[88] Kolk, H., Van Grunsven and Keyser (1985). On parallelism between production and comprehension in agrammatism. In Kean (Ed.), pp. 165-206.

[89] Kratochvíl, P. (1968). *The Chinese Language Today.* London: Hutchinson & Co.

[90] Kubler, C. (1984). *Varieties of Spoken Standard Chinese, Volume II: A Speaker from Taipei.* Dordrecht, Holland: Foris Publications.

[91] Kubler, C. (1985). *The Development of Mandarin in Taiwan: A Case Study of Language Contact.* Taipei, Taiwan: Student Book Co.

[92] Lapointe, S. (1983). Some issues in the linguistic description of agrammatism. *Cognition 14*, 1-41.

[93] Lapointe, S. (1985). A theory of verb form use in agrammatism. *Brain and Language 24*, 100-155.

[94] Lavorel, P. (1982). Production strategies: a systems approach to Wernicke's aphasia. In Arbib, Caplan and Marshall (Eds.), pp. 135-164.

[95] Levelt, W. (1989). *Speaking: From Intention to Articulation.* Cambridge, MA: Bradford Books/MIT Press.

[96] Levine, R. (Ed.), (1992). *Formal Grammar: Theory and Implementation.* New York: Oxford Univesity Press.

[97] Li, Y-H. Audrey (1991). *Word Order and Constituency.* Dordrecht: Kluwer.

[98] Li, Y-F. (1990). On V-V compounds in Chinese. *Natural Language and Linguistic Theory 8*, pp. 177-207.

[99] Li, C., and Thompson, S. (1981). *Mandarin Chinese: A Functional Reference Grammar.* Berkeley: University of California.

[100] Libben, G. (1990). Morphological representations and morphological deficits in aphasia. In Nespoulous and Villiard (Eds.), pp. 20-31.

[101] Linebarger, M. (1989). Neuropsychological evidence for linguistic modularity. In Carlson and Tanenhaus (Eds.), pp. 197- 238.

[102] Linebarger, M. (1990). Neuropsychology of sentence parsing. In A. Caramazza (Ed.), pp. 55-122.

[103] Liu, Y.M., Chung, C.Y. and Wang, S.C. (1975). *Frequency Table for Common Chinese Words.* Taipei: Liu-kou Press (in Chinese).

[104] Lu, Z-W. (1964). *Hanyu de Goucifa [Chinese Morphology].* Beijing: Scientific Publishing Co.

[105] Luce, R., Bush, R. and Galanter, E. (Eds.) (1963). *Handbook of Mathematical Psychology.* NY: Wiley and Sons.

[106] MacWhinney, B., and Bates, E. (Eds.) (1989). *The Crosslinguistic Study of Sentence Processing.* New York: Cambridge University Press.

[107] Marin, O., Saffran, E, and Schwartz, M. (1976). Dissociations of language in aphasia. *Annals of the New York Academy of Sciences, 280*, 868-884.

[108] Marcus, M. (1982). Consequences of functional deficits in a parsing model: Implications for Broca's aphasia. In Arbib, Caplan and Marshall (Eds.), pp. 115-133.

[109] Marshall, J. (1982). What is a symptom-complex? In Arbib, Caplan and Marshall (Eds.), pp. 389-409.

[110] Martin, A. and Rigrodsky, S. (1974). An investigation of phonological impairment in aphasia, Part II. *Cortex 10*, p. 329.

[111] McCawley, J.D. (1992). Justifying part-of-speech assignments in Mandarin. *Journal of Chinese Linguistics 20.2*, pp. 211-246.

[112] Menn, L. and Öbler, L. (Eds.) (1990). *Agrammatic Aphasia: A Cross-language Narrative Sourcebook.* Philadelphia and Amsterdam: John Benjamins.

[113] Miceli, G., Mazzucchi, A., Menn, L. and Goodglass, H. (1983). Contrasting cases of English and Italian agrammatic aphasics. *Brain and Language 19*, pp. 65-97.

[114] Miceli, G. and Caramazza, A. (1988). Dissociation of inflectional and derivational morphology. *Brain and Language 35*, pp. 24-65.

[115] Miller, G. and Chomsky, N. (1963). Finitary models of language users. In Luce, Bush and Galanter (Eds.).

[116] Mohanan, K. P. (1986). *The Theory of Lexical Phonology.* Dordrecht: Reidel.

[117] Monrad-Krohn, G.H. (1947). Dysprosody or altered 'melody' of language. *Brain 70*, p. 405.

[118] Nespoulous, J. and Villiard (Eds.) (1990). *Morphology, Phonology and Aphasia.* New York: Springer-Verlag.

[119] Norman, J. (1988). *Chinese.* Cambridge: Cambridge University Press.

[120] Packard, J. (1984). A Linguistic Investigation of Tone Laterality in Aphasic Chinese Speech. Cornell University Ph.D. Dissertation.

[121] Packard, J. (1986). Tone production deficits in nonfluent aphasic Chinese speech. *Brain and Language 29*, pp. 212- 223.

[122] Packard, J. (1988). The first-language acquisition of prenominal modification with *de* in Mandarin. *Journal of Chinese Linguistics 16.1*, pp. 31-53.

[123] Packard, J. (1990a). Agrammatism in Chinese: a case study. In Menn and Obler (Eds.), pp. 1191-1223.

[124] Packard, J. (1990b). A lexical morphology approach to word formation in Mandarin. *Yearbook of Morphology 3*, pp. 21-37.

[125] Packard, J. (1992). Why Mandarin morphology is stratum-ordered. Paper presented to the Fourth North American Conference on Chinese Linguistics. Ann Arbor, Michigan.

[126] Panzeri, M., Semenza, C., Ferreri, T. and Butterworth, B. (1990). Free use of derivational morphology in an Italian jargonaphasic. In Nespoulous and Villiard (Eds.), pp. 72-94.

[127] Paradis, M., Hagiwara, H., and Hildebrandt, N. (1985). *Neurolinguistic Aspects of the Japanese Writing System.* New York: Academic Press.

[128] Patterson, K. (1980). Derivational errors. In Coltheart, M., Patterson, K. and Marshall, J. *Deep Dyslexia.* London: Routledge and Kegan Paul.

[129] Price, P. (Ed.), (1991). *Readings from the Fourth DARPA Speech and Natural Language Workshop.* San Mateo, CA: Morgan Kaufmann.

[130] Prince, E. (1981). Toward a taxonomy of given–new information. In Cole (Ed.), pp. 223-255.

[131] Ramsey, S.R. (1987). *The Languages of China.* Princeton: Princeton University Press.

[132] Rizzi, L. (1985). Two notes on the linguistic interpretation of Broca's aphasia. In Kean (Ed.), pp. 153-164.

[133] Ross, C. (1991). Coverbs and category distinctions in Mandarin Chinese. *Journal of Chinese Linguistics 19.1*, pp. 79-114.

[134] Ryalls, J. (1982). Intonation in Broca's aphasia. *Neuropsychologia 19*, p. 335.

[135] Ryalls, J. (Ed.), (1987). *Phonetic Approaches to Speech Production in Aphasia and Related Disorders.* Boston: Beacon Hill Press.

[136] Saffran, E., Schwartz, M. and Marin, O. (1980a). Evidence from aphasia: isolating the components of a production model. In Butterworth, B. (Ed.).

[137] Saffran, E., Schwartz, M. and Marin, O. (1980b). The word order problem in agrammatism. II. Production. *Brain and Language 10*, pp. 263-280.

[138] Salomon, E. (1914). Motorische Aphasie mit Agrammatismus und sensorisch-agrammatischen Störungen. *Monatsschrift für Psychiatrie und Neurologie 35*, pp. 181-208, 216-275.

[139] Scholes, R. (1977). Syntactic and lexical components of sentence comprehension. In A. Caramazza and E. Zurif (Eds.), *Language Acquisition and Language Breakdown.*. Baltimore: Johns Hopkins Press.

[140] Schwartz, M., Linebarger, M. and Saffran E. (1985). The status of the syntactic deficit theory of agrammatism. In Kean (Ed.), pp. 83-124.

[141] Selkirk, E. (1984). *The Syntax of Words.* Cambridge, MA: MIT Press.

[142] Shannon, C. and Weaver, W. (1949). *The Mathematical Theory of Communication.* Urbana, IL: University of Illinois Press.

[143] Shen, Susan X. (1990). *The Prosody of Mandarin Chinese.* Berkeley: University of California Press.

[144] Shi, D-X. (1989). Topic chain as a syntactic category in Chinese. *Journal of Chinese Linguistics 17.2*, pp. 223-262.

[145] Shih, Chi-lin (1986). The Prosodic Domain of Tone Sandhi in Chinese. Ph.D. dissertation, University of California at San Diego.

[146] Sproat, R. (1985). On Deriving the Lexicon. Ph.D. dissertation, MIT.

[147] Sproat, R. (1986). Competence, performance and agrammatism: A Reply to Grodzinsky. *Brain and Language 27*, pp. 160-167.

[148] Stark, H. and Stark, J. (1990). Syllable structure in Wernicke's aphasia. In In Nespoulous and Villiard (Eds.), pp. 213- 234.

[149] Suen, C.Y. (1979). *Computational Analysis of Mandarin.* Basel: Birkhauser.

[150] Tai, J. and L. Wang (1990). A semantic study of the classifier *tiao. Journal of the Chinese Language Teachers Association 25.1*, pp. 35-56.

[151] Teng, S-H. (1975). *A Semantic Study of Transitivity Relations.* Taipei: Student Book Co.

[152] Thompson, S. (1973). Resultative verb compounds in Mandarin Chinese. *Language 49.2*, pp. 361-379.

[153] Travis, L. (1984). Parameters And Effects Of Word Order Variation. Ph.D. dissertation, MIT.

[154] Trost, J. E., and Canter, G. (1974). Apraxia of speech in patients with Broca's aphasia. *Brain and Language 1*, p. 63.

[155] Tsao, F-F. (1978). Subject and topic in Chinese. In Tang, Li and Cheng (Eds.) *Proceedings of the Symposium on Chinese Linguistics, 1977 Linguistic Institute.* Taipei: Student Book Co.

[156] Tzeng, O. J-L., Chen, S. and Hung, D. (1991). The classifier problem in Chinese aphasia. *Brain and Language 41*, pp. 184-202.

[157] Ulatowska, H., Allard, L., and Chapman, S. (1990). Narrative and procedural discourse in aphasia. In Joanette and Brownell (Eds.), pp. 180-198.

[158] Von Stockert, T. and Bader, L. (1976). Some relations of grammar and lexicon in aphasia. *Cortex 12*, pp. 49-60.

[159] Wang, W. S-Y. (1965). Two aspect markers in Mandarin. *Language 41*, pp. 457-470.

[160] Whitaker, H. (1970). Linguistic competence: evidence from aphasia. *Glossa 4*, 46-54.

[161] Yiu, E. M-L. (1989). Tonal Disruption in Chinese (Cantonese) Aphasics. Master's Thesis, Hong Kong University.

[162] Zurif, E. (1982). The use of data from aphasia in constructing a performance model of language. In Arbib, Caplan and Marshall (Eds.), pp. 203-208.

[163] Zurif, E. (1984). Psycholinguistic interpretations of the aphasias. In Caplan, Lecours and Smith (Eds.), pp. 158-171.

[164] Zurif and Caramazza (1976). Psycholinguistic structures in aphasia. In Whitaker and Whitaker (Eds.), *Studies in Neurolinguistics, Vol. 1.* New York: Academic Press.

[165] Zwicky, A. (1992). Some choices in the theory of morphology. In R. Levine (Ed.), pp. 327-371.

Appendix A

Subject Transcripts

This appendix consists of the interlinear translated transcripts of the speech samples of the four aphasic subjects Li Xinzheng, Guo Jiande, Yang Xifeng and Zheng Youjuan. For each line of speech spoken by either the experimenter or the subject, there follows a second line which is a direct morpheme-by-morpheme translation of the line spoken above, followed by a third line which is a free English translation of the utterance.

The following abbreviations are used in the appendix to designate the speaker:

E:	= Experimenter
E2:	= Experimenter #2
Fam:	= Member of Subject's Family
Obs:	= Observer
S:	= Subject

The following abbreviations are used for grammatical terms in the second line of the translation:

ADV	= Adverbial
AFF	= Utterance of Affirmation
ASP	= Aspect Marker
COMP	= Complement
DO	= Direct Object
EMP	= Particle indicating Emphasis
EXC	= Particle indicating Exclamation
HES	= Hesitation Filler
C	= Classifier
MOD	= Marker of Prenominal Modification
OBJ	= Direct Object Marker 'ba'
ORD	= Ordinal Prefix
PL	= Plural
Q	= Question Marker
SUG	= Particle of Suggestion

The aspect marker *le* is glossed as either sentential *le* (le_s) or verbal *le* (le_v).

The following conventions are used in the transcription and translation of speech data:

1. Utterances are divided into words using criteria outlined in Packard (1990b). Words consisting of more than one morpheme (complex words) are preceded with a subscript designating which lexical level they are formed at (e.g., $_{II}$WORD would be formed at level II).

2. For all utterances, the actual utterance is presented on the first line, a literal morphemic translation is given on the second line and a free translation is given on the third line. In the case of incorrect utterances, the free translation is given in a form intended to reflect the aberrance of the produced form. The actual utterance on the first line is given in *pinyin* romanization (except for some phonemic paraphasias which are given in phonetic transcription; see below), with tone marks given only where necessary to facilitate comprehension.

3. For aberrant utterances, the free translation on the third line is followed by the target or a non-aberrant version of the observed utterance (if determinable), preceded by 'cf.', which is then glossed with morphemic and free translations.

4. The following conventions are adopted to describe deficited speech:

- Words in which phonological errors (termed *phonological paraphasias*) occur are normally presented within square brackets ([xxx]) in *pinyin* romanization. In cases where the precise phonetic form is crucially important, the error is given in broad phonetic transcription. Where necessary, target forms are presented in a footnote, and a translation of the target is given in the morphemic translation in the second line of the transcription. The free translation on the third line contains an incorrect English phonological form, in an attempt to give the reader an idea of the nature of the phonological error.
- A wrong word which is not semantically related to the target is termed a *verbal paraphasia*. Verbal paraphasias are enclosed in angle brackets (<xxx>), with the target given in the text or a footnote.
- A subtype of verbal paraphasia is a *semantic paraphasia*, a wrong word which is semantically related to the target. Semantic paraphasias are enclosed in diamonds (◇xxx◇),and the target form is given either in the text or in a footnote.
- A wrong word for which the target cannot plausibly be determined is termed *jargon* if it is a possible Mandarin word and it occupies the form class slot appropriate to that word (e.g., a verb occurring in a verb slot). Jargon is enclosed in 'bowties' (⋈xxx⋈).
- A nonexistent word coined by the speaker is a *neologism*. A neologism is defined as a form which either is not a Mandarin word (e.g., *rēn* or *puan*), or is a possible word but occupies a form class slot inappropriate for that word. Neologisms are enclosed in inverted triangles (∇xxx∇).
- Words or morphemes which are extraneous are enclosed in circled X's (⊗xxx⊗).
- Omitted words or morphemes are indicated by a null sign (ϕ) in the first line of the utterance, with a translation of the missing item given in parentheses in the second line.
- Improper word order is indicated by presenting the disordered words in small capitals (e.g., *TO EAT LIKE I CHINESE FOOD).
- Sentences or phrases which are nonsensical are written in *italics*.

A.1 Interlinear Translation of Li Xinzheng

L 1	E:	Ni	gaosu	wo	ni	jinnian	ji	sui,	a.
		you	tell	I	you	this-year	many:Q	year	EMP
		Tell me how old you are this year.							

L 2	S:	Wo	$_{II}$ershisan	sui.
		I	23	year
		I'm 23.		

L 3	E:	Ershisan,	a.
		23	EMP
		23.	

L 4	S:	Dui.
		right
		Right.

L 5	E:	Na	ni	cai	wo	ji	sui.
		then	you	guess	I	how:many	year
		Now guess how old I am.					

L 6	S:	Ni	shi	◇$_I$shenmo◇[1]	sui?
		you	be	what	year
		What old are you?			

L 7	E:	Wo	shu	zhu.
		I	belong	pig
		I was born under the pig[2].		

L 8	S:	Ni	shŭ	zhu,	wo	<zùo>	niu.
		you	belong	pig	I	do	cow
		You're under the pig, and I do the cow.					

L 9	E:	Niu,	a.
		cow	EMP
		The cow.	

---

[1] The target is the question word *ji* 'how many' rather than the question word *shenmo* 'what'.

[2] A sign of the Chinese zodiac.

L 10 S: Dui.
right
Right.

L 11 E: A, na women cha liang sui, a.
EMP then we differ two year EMP
Then we're two years apart.

L 12 S: Dui.
right
Right.

L 13 E: Wo ershiwu sui.
I 25 years
I'm 25 years old.

L 14 S: Ni $_{II}$ershiwu sui, wo $_{II}$ershisan sui.
you 25 years I 23 years
You're 25, and I'm 23.

L 15 E: Ou, zhende, ni ershisan a.
EXC really you 23 EXC
Oh really, you're 23.

L 16 S: (laughs)

L 17 E: Bucuo ma, ni jide hen qingchu, ei.
not-bad EXC you recall very clear EXC
Hey, not bad, you remember pretty clearly.

L 18 S: Dui.
right
Right.

L 19 E: Na ni ershisan sui, ni shi bu shi
then you 23 year you be not be
So you're 23. Have you

L 20 gaozhong biyele?
high-middle graduate-ASP
graduated from high school?

L 21 S: Wo ϕ [de]... [jiang] Daojiang ⊗wo⊗ $_{III,IV}$biyele$_v$.
I (from) Dao jiang Daojiang I graduate-ASP
I graduated I De... jiang Daojiang.

L 22 E: Ou, ni biyele.
EXC you graduate-ASP
Oh, you graduated.

L 23 S: Dui. ϕ DAOJIANG $_{II}$WUYUE $_{II}$SHIYI
right (from) Daojiang 5-month ten-one
Right. Daojiang the 11th

L 24 RI[3] ϕ ϕ
day (graduate) (ASP)
of May.

L 25 E: Ou, ni xianzai wuyue shiyi ri yao biye.
EXC you now May 11 day want graduate
Oh, you're graduating on May 11th.

L 26 S: Bu shi. Wo *$_{II}$[sān][4]ri ϕ $_{II}$wuyue $_{II}$shiyi ri.
not be I birthday (be) May 11 day
No. My barthday May 11th.

L 27 E: Ou, zhende. Na, kuai dao la!
EXC really then fast arrive EXC
Oh really. That'll be here soon!

L 28 S: Dui.
right
Right.

L 29 E: A.
EXC
Ah.

L 30 S: Wo $_{II}$wushi nian ϕ ϕ.
I five-ten year (born) (MOD)
I was the year '50[5].

[3] The order should be *wuyue shiyi ri cong Daijiang biye le.*

[4] For *shēng.* The use of *s* in place of *sh* is normal in Taiwan Mandarin for this word, but the use of the apical nasal *n* in place of the velar nasal *ng* and the vowel *a* in place of *e* is not.

[5] I.e., the 50th year of the Chinese republic, 1961.

L 31	E:	Wushi	nian.
		50	year
		The year '50.	

L 32	S:	Dui.
		right
		Right.

L 33	E:	Ou,	na	ni	yiqian	nian	nayige	xuexiao?
		EXC	then	you	before	study	which-1-C	school
		Oh, so what school did you study at before?						

L 34	S:	Wo	ϕ	Daojiang	⊗wo⊗	$_{III,IV}$biyele$_v$.
		I	(from)	Daojiang	I	graduate-ASP
		I graduated I Daojiang.				

L 35	E:	Ou,	ni...	Danjiang?
		EXC	you	Danjiang
		Oh, you...Danjiang?		

L 36	Fam:	Daojiang.
		Daojiang
		Daojiang.

L 37	S:	Daojiang.	Wo	$_{III,IV}$biyele$_v$.
		Daojiang	I	graduate-ASP
		Daojiang. I graduated.		

L 38	E:	Ou,	Daojiang...
		EXC	Daojiang
		Oh Daojiang...	

L 39	S:	Hao	jiu,	hao	jiu.
		very	long	very	long
		A long, long time.			

L 40	E:	...jiazhi,	shi bu shi?
		home-vocational	be not be
		...home economics school, right?	

L 41	S:	Dui.	Wo	$_{III,IV}$biyele$_v$.
		right	I	graduate-ASP
		Right, I graduated.		

L 42 E: Na, biye yihou jiu zuo shi, shi bu shi?
then graduate after then do work be not be
Then after graduating you went to work, right?

L 43 S: Wo <èr>[6] [zhì] $_{I}$gongzuo.
I two go work
I gone to work togain.

L 44 E: Ou, ni you gongzuo.
EXC you again work
Oh, you went to work again.

L 45 S: Dui. Wo $_{II}$libairi... wo ⋈*$_{IV}$die⋈zhe[7]...
right. I Sunday I fall-ASP
Right. I Sunday I was falling...

L 46 wo *$_{III}$renϕ... bu $_{III}$◇renshi◇ ϕ[8] le,.
I recog(-nize) not recognize (DO) ASP
I recog... didn't recognize.

L 47 E: Ou, zhei yangzi.
EXC that way
Oh, is that right.

L 48 S: Dui.
right
Right.

L 49 E: Ou, hen hao. Na ni yiqian shao bu shao fan?
EXC very good then you before cook not cook food
Oh, good. Now, did you cook before?

L 50 Bu shao fan?
not cook food
You didn't cook?

---

[6] For *yòu* 'again'.
[7] This is an example of a neologism which has proper inflection. See Caplan et al. 1972.
[8] Deletion of an obligatory direct object.

L 51	S:	Wo	bu	shao	fan.					
		I	not	cook	food					
		I don't cook.								
L 52	E:	Na	ni	hui	na	zhen,	dui bu dui?			
		then	you	can	hold	needle	right not right			
		But you can use a needle, right?								
L 53		Hui	feng	yifu,	dui bu dui?					
		can	sew	clothes	right not right					
		You know how to sew, right?								
L 54	S:	Ta	$_{III}$jide	le,.						
		she	recall	ASP						
		She remembers.								
L 55	E:	Ou.								
		EXC								
		Oh.								
L 56	S:	$_{II}$Mama,	ta	$_{III}$jide	wo...	wo	zhu	fan.		
		mom	she	recall	I	I	cook	food		
		Mom, she remembers I... I cook food.								
L 57		Wo	$_{III}$jide	le,.	Cai,	wo	dou	bu	$_{III}$jide.	
		I	recall	ASP	dishes	I	all	not	recall	
		I remember. The dishes, I don't remember.								
L 58	E:	Ou.	Na	ni	yiqian	shao	fan	de	shihou,	
		EXC	then	you	before	cook	food	MOD	time	
		Oh. Then before when you cooked,								
L 59		na	neige	chanzi	a,	ni	yong	nayizhi		
		hold	that:M	spoon	EMP	you	use	which:1:M		
		to hold the spoon, which hand did								
L 60		shou	na?	Yong	zheyizhi	shou?				
		hand	hold	use	this-one-C	hand				
		you use? You used this hand?								
L 61	S:	Dui.								
		right								
		Right.								

L 62 E: Ou, ni yong you shou, shi bu shi?
EXC you use right hand be not be
Oh, you used the right hand, right?

L 63 S: Dui.
right
Right.

L 64 E: Na ni you meiyou shuo... yong zuo shou
then you have not-have say use left hand
Then do you have any... like... other things that

L 65 zuo biede shiqing de xiguan?
do other thing MOD habit
you're in the habit of doing with your left?

L 66 S: Wo zuǒ shǒu dou bu hui zuò <shǒu>[9].
I left hand all not can do thing
My left hand can't do anyding.

L 67 E: Ou, zhende.
EXC really
Oh, really.

L 68 S: Dui.
right
Right.

L 69 E: Na ni jia you meiyou ren yongguo
then you home have not-have person use-ASP
Then has anyone in your family used

L 70 zuo shou zuo shi? You ren shi
left hand do thing have people be
their left hand to do anything? Some people

L 71 bijiao xihuan yong zuo shou.
compare like use left hand
like to use the left hand more.

[9] This is a phonologically-related lexical selection error. The target is *shi* 'thing'.

L 72	S:	$_I$Meiyou.
		not-have
		No.

L 73	E:	Meiyou	a.
		not-have	EXC
		No, huh.	

L 74	S:	Dui.
		right
		Right.

L 75	E:	Ou,	suoyi	nimen	quan	jia	ren
		EXC	so	you-PL	whole	family	people
		Oh, so your whole family					

L 76	dou	yong	you	shou.
	all	use	right	hand
	uses their right hand.			

L 77	S:	*Ta*	*<zuò>*[10]	*you*	*shou*	*wo*	*<zuò>*	*[zŏu]*[11]	*[zŏu].*
		he	do	right	hand	I	do	left	hand
		He does his right hand, I do my reft kand.							

L 78	E:	Ou,	zhei	yangzi.
		EXC	this	way
		Oh, is that right.		

L 79	S:	Dui.
		right
		Right.

L 80	E:	Hao.	Na	ni	shuo	ni	libaitian	jiu	bu
		good	then	you	say	you	Sunday	then	not
		Ok. So you said that on Sunday you weren't							

L 81	qingchu	le.	Na	shi	nayitian,
	clear	ASP	that	be	which-1-day
	clear. What month and				

[10] The target was *yong* 'use', which can also act as a coverb.
[11] For *zŭo*.

L 82		jiyue	jihao?					
		many:Q-month	many:Q-day					
		what day was that?						
L 83	S:	$_{II}$Libairi.						
		Sunday						
		Sunday.						
L 84	E:	Hei.	Jiyue	jihao?				
		AFF	many:Q-month	many:Q-day				
		Uh-huh. What month and what day?						
L 85	S:	Wo	⊗dou⊗	$_{III}$sange	yue			
		I	all	three-C	month			
		All 3 months after I						
L 86	E:	...sange	yue...					
		three-C	month					
		...3 months...						
L 87	S:	zhi	hou	$_{III,IV}$renshile$_v$	$_{III}$yige	ren.		
		MOD	after	know-ASP	one-C	person		
		knew a person.						
L 88		Wo	ϕ-ϕ	$_{III}$sige	yue.			
		I	(know-ASP)	four-C	month			
		I four months.						
L 89	E:	Ou,	ni	sige	yue[12].			
		EXC	you	4-C	month			
		Oh, you 4 months.						
L 90	S:	*Wo...*	*wo*	ϕ	$_{III}$*jiali*	$_{II}$*siyue*	*san*	*er...*
		I	I	(at)	home-in	four-month	three	two
		I... I home April three two...						
L 91		$_{II}$*sanyue*	*er*	*hao...*	$_{II}$*siyue*	*er*	*hao.*	
		3-month	2	day	4-month	2	day	
		March 2nd... April 2nd.						

[12] The experimenter repeats the error.

L 92		$_{II}$*Jintian*	*ϕ*	$_{II}$*siyue*	*ba*	*hao.*
		today	(be)	4-month	8	day
		Today April 8th.				

L 93	E:	Ou,	suoyi	ni	bu	qingchu	yijing
		EXC	so	you	not	clear	already
		Oh, so you've been unclear					

L 94	you	liu	tian	a?
	have	6	day	Q
	for 6 days already?			

L 95	S:	*Bu*	*shi.*	$_{II}$*Siyue...*	$_{II}$*sanyue*	*er*	*hao.*
		not	be	4-month	3-month	2	day
		No. April...March 2nd.					

L 96	E:	Ou.
		EXC
		Oh.

L 97	S:	$_{II}$*Jintian*	*ϕ*	$_{III}$*yige*	*yue*	*wu*	*tian.*
		today	(have)	1-C	month	5	day
		Today one month five days.					

L 98	E:	Ou	zhei	yangzi,	a.
		EXC	this	way	EXC
		Oh, is that right.			

L 99	S:	Dui.
		right
		Right.

L 100	E:	Ou,	ni	yijing	bu	qingchu	yige	yue
		EXC	you	already	not	clear	1-C	month
		Oh, you've already been unclear for one month						

L 101	wu	tian	a.
	5	day	EXC
	five days.		

L 102	S:	Bu	shi.	Wo	*ϕ*	$_{III}$jiali	$_{I}$[yige][13]	*$_{III}$wu-*ϕ*	yue.
		Not	be	I	(at)	home-in	altogether	five(-C)	month
		No. I home May altogether.							

L 103 E: Ou zhei yangzi, a.
EXC this way EXC
Oh is that right.

L 104 S: Dui.
right
Right.

L 105 E: Ou. Hao.
EXC good
Oh. Ok.

L 106 Exp2: Che huo shenmo shihou fasheng?
car accident what time happen
When was the car accident?

L 107 Fam: Shiyue ershiba.
10-month 28
October 28th.

L 108 E: Qunian, shi bu shi?
go-year be not be
Last year, right?

L 109 Fam: Qunian.
go-year
Last year.

L 110 E: You chezi zhuangdao ni, shi bu shi?
have car hit-arrive you be not be
A car hit you, right?

L 111 S: Dui. Wo tou... ϕ hao duo le$_1$.
right I head (now) good much ASP
Right. My head... much better.

L 112 Wo tou $_{II}$limian xiao le$_1$.
I head inside reduce ASP
The inside of my head has gone down.

L 113 $_{II}$Huangshuiye ϕ hao duo le$_1$.
yellow-water-liquid (now) good much ASP
The pus much better.

[13] For *yigong*.

L 114	E:	Ou,	zhende.			
		EXC	really			
		Oh really.				

L 115	S:	Dui.				
		right				
		Right.				

L 116	E:	Ou	zhei	yangzi,	a.	
		EXC	this	way	EXC	
		Oh is that right.				

L 117	S:	Wo	$_{II}$YANJING	$_{II}$ZUOBIAN	ϕ[14]	$_{II,IV}$tuchule$_v$.
		I	eye	left-side	MOD	protrude-out-ASP
		My eye left stuck out.				

L 118	E:	Hm,	hm.			
		AFF	AFF			
		Hm, hm.				

L 119	S:	Hao	duo.	$_{II}$Yanjing	$_{II,IV}$tuchule$_v$.	
		very	much	eye	stick-out-ASP	
		A lot. My eye stuck out.				

L 120	E:	Ou	zhei	yangzi.		
		EXC	this	way		
		Oh is that right.				

L 121	S:	Dui.				
		right				
		Right.				

L 122	E:	Buguo	ni	xianzai	kanqilai	bucuo
		but	you	now	look-rise-come	not-bad
		But now you look pretty good,				

L 123	ma,	dui bu dui?	
	EXC	right not right	
	right?		

[14] The sentence should read: *Wo zuobian de yanjing tuchule.*

L 124 S: Dui.
right
Right.

L 125 E: Ni kan ni yanjing ye shi hao de.
you see you eye also be good EMP
See, your eye is also better.

L 126 S: Wo $_{II}$zuobian, $_{II}$youbian...
I left-side right-side
My left side and right side...

L 127 E: Kande qingchu ma?
see-ADV clear Q
Can see clearly?

L 128 S: ...dou ???.
all ???
...are all ???.

L 129 E: Hao, zhei bian shi shenmo dongxi? Ou zhei
good this side be what thing EXC this
Ok, what's over here? Oh, is that

L 130 yangzi. Hao, women xunlian ni jiang hua. 'Bí'.
way good I-PL train you speak speech nose
right. Ok, let's do some speech practice. 'Nose'.

L 131 S: 'Bí'.
nose
'Nose'.

L 132 E: Mm, hao.
AFF good
Mm, good.

L 133 S: $_{II}$Zuiba, $_{II}$yanjing.
mouth eye
Mouth, eye.

L 134 E: Mm... mei...
AFF eye-
Mm...eyebr-...

L 135	S:	Zhe	$_{II}$laoshi...					
		this	teacher					
		This teacher... (referring to E2)						

L 136	E:	Mm.	
		AFF	
		Mm.	

L 137	S:	⋈*$_{IV}$Gai⋈le$_v$[15]	⋈dian⋈.
		cover-ASP	electricity
		He covered electricity.	

L 138	E:	Mm.	'Meimao'.
		AFF	eyebrow
		Mm. 'Eyebrow'.	

L 139	S:	Bu	shi.	Ni	jiang...	*$_{III}$<dian>...	◇*$_{III}$<dian>liao◇.	
		not	be	you	say	electric-	electric-cure	
		No. You say... elec-...electrotherapy.						

L 140	Zhe	$_{II}$laoshi	zuo	$_{II}$pangbian	ϕ	◇*$_{III}$<dian>liao◇[16].	
	This	teacher	sit	side	(do)	electric-cure	
	This teacher sits on the side electrotherapy.						

L 141	E:	Hao,	dianliao.
		good	electric-cure
		Ok, electrotherapy.	

L 142	S:	Mm.	
		AFF	
		Mm.	

L 143	E:	Hao,	ni	shuo	'dianliao'.
		good	you	say	electric-cure
		Ok, say 'electrotherapy'.			

L 144	S:	$_{II}$Dianliao.
		electric-cure
		Electrotherapy.

---

[15] The subject uses inflection with a jargon word. The jargon word is an anticipation of *dianliao* in 140.

[16] The target is the word *zhiliao* 'treat, cure'.

L 145	E:	Hao.	'Ji'.
		good	chicken
		Good. 'Chicken'.	

L 146	S:	Ni....
		you
		You...

L 147	E:	Hao,	meiyou	guanxi.
		good	not-have	relation
		Ok, don't worry about it.		

L 148	S:	Ta	ϕ	mei	zuo.
		he	(still)	not	sit
		He didn't sit. (referring to E2)			

L 149	E (to E2):	Ni	zui	hao	zuoxialai.
		you	most	good	sit-down-come
		You'd better sit down.			

L 150	S:	$_I$Meiyou.	Ta	zhi$_I$	ϕ	$*_{IV}$zhan-ϕ.
		not-have	he	only	(be)	stand(-ASP)
		No. He just stand.				

L 151	$*_{IV}$Zhan-ϕ	hao	◇duo◇[17].
	stand(-ASP)	very	much
	Stand a lot.		

L 152	E:	Li Xinzheng,	lai,	ni	ting	wo	shuo...
		Li Xinzheng	come	you	listen	I	speak
		Li Xinzheng, come, listen to me...					

L 153	S:	Ta	ϕ	mei	zuo.
		he	(still)	not	sit
		He didn't sit.			

L 154	E:	Lai,	ni	ting	wo	shuo,	a.	Pei	xiansheng
		come	you	listen	I	speak	EXC	Pei	Mr.
		Come, listen to me. Mr. Packard's							

[17] The target was *jiu* 'a long time', which is semantically related to *duo* 'a lot'.

L 155 zuo zai neige zhuozi shangmian. Ni kan ta
sit at that-C table top you see he
sitting on that table. Look at him

L 156 xianzai zuo zai zhuozi shangmian.
now sit at table top
sitting on that table now.

L 157 S: ∇zùo xiè nǐ... ge∇... Ni ◇zhan◇. Ni zuo.
??? you stand you sit
??? You stand. You sit.

L 158 E: Pei xiansheng ta shenti bucuo.
Pei Mr. he health not-bad
Mr. Packard's a healthy person.

L 159 Ta zhanyixia meiyou guanxi.
he stand:awhile not-have relevance
It's ok if he stands awhile.

L 160 S: Ta zhan hao jiu le,.
he stand very long:time ASP
He's been standing for a long time.

L 161 E: Ta zhan hao jiu.
he stand very long:time
He's been standing for a long time.

L 162 S: Ta ϕ mei zuo.
he (still) not sit
He didn't sit.

L 163 E: Mm, hao. Meiyou guanxi. Hao. Lai, women
AFF good not-have relevance good come I-PL
Mm, ok. That's ok. Good. Come, let's

L 164 xianzai yao zuo lianxi.
now want do practice
practice now.

.... end ....

A.2 Interlinear Translation of Guo Jiande

G 1 S: Mm.. mm.. yong.. yong $_{III}$yizhi shou.
HES HES use use 1-C hand
Mm.. mm use.. use 1 hand.

G 2 E: Nayizhi?
which-1-C
Which one?

G 3 S: *$_{III}$Liang-ϕ $_{I}$bijiao $_{III}$pangde.
two(-C) compare fat-MOD
Couple relatively fat ones.

G 4 E: Zheizhi haishi zheizhi?
This-C or this-C
This one or this one?

G 5 S: $_{I}$Bi.. $_{I}$BIJIAO $_{III}$NEIGE.. $_{III}$NEIGE.. *$_{III}$NEIϕ $_{III}$PANGD
com- compare that-C that-C that(-C) fat-MOD
More.. that.. that.. fat.. fatter that one.

G 6 E: Bijiao pang de neizhi a?
compare fat MOD that-C EMP
That fatter one?

G 7 S: Ei. Mm.
AFF AFF
Mm-hm.

G 8 E: Nayizhi bijiao pang?
which-1-C relative fat
Which one's fatter?

G 9 S: Ei.
AFF
Uh-huh.

G 10 E: Zheizhi, shi bu shi?
this-C be not be
This one, right?

G 11 S: Ei. $_{III}$Zheizhi $_{I}$bijiao pang.
AFF this-C compare fat
Uh-huh. This one's fatter.

G 12	E:	Zheizhi,	a?				
		this-C	Q				
		This one?					

G 13	S:	Mm.
		AFF
		Mm.

G 14	E:	Haishi	zheizhi?
		or	this-C
		Or this one?	

G 15	S:	Zhe..	YE	$_{III}$ZHEIZHI[18]	$_{I}$bijiao	pang.
		this	also	this-C	compare	fat
		This.. this one is relatively also fat.				

G 16	E:	Nayizhi?
		which-1-C
		Which one?

G 17	S:	∇diǎng..diáng∇	$_{III}$zheizhi	a.
		???	this-C	EXC
		??? this one.		

G 18	E:	Ni	yong	neizhi?
		you	use	which-C
		Which one do you use?		

G 19	S:	Yong	$_{III}$zheizhi.
		use	this-C
		I use this one.	

G 20	E:	Yong	zheizhi	na... na	chanzi.
		use	this-C	hold	spoon
		You use this one to hold.. hold a spoon.			

G 21	S:	Ei.
		AFF
		Uh-huh.

[18] The order of *zheizhi* and *ye* should be reversed.

G 22	E:	Na	ni	kuaizi	ne?	Yong	nayizhi	shou?	
		then	you	chopstick	Q	use	which-1-C	hand	
		And what about chopsticks? Which hand do you use?							

G 23	S:	$_{II}$Kuaizi	shi	$_{I}$bijiao	ϕ
		chopsticks	be	compare	(use)
		Chopsticks, I more			

G 24	*$_{III}$<yi>[19]zhi	shou	ma.
	one-C	hand	AFF
	one hand.		

G 25	E:	Nayizhi?
		which-1-C
		Which hand?

G 26	S:	⋈Diăn..diăn⋈	$_{III}$yizhi	shou.
		count..count	one-C	hand
		Count..count one hand.		

G 27	Wo..	wo..	wo..	de..	de..	[zh.. zh..]	$_{II}$kuaizi.
	I	I	I	MOD	MOD	???	chopstick
	I.. I.. I.. my.. my.. ??? chopsticks.						

G 28	E:	Zheizhi	a?
		this-C	Q
		This one?	

G 29	S:	*$_{III}$ZHE-ϕ	$_{II}$KUAIZI	WO..	WO	DOU	ϕ	$_{IV}$NAZHE[20]
		this(-C)	chopsticks	I	I	all	(use)	hold-ASP
		This, chopsticks, I.. I always hold.						

G 30	E:	Ou,	zhei	yangzi.
		AFF	this	way
		Oh, is that right.		

G 31	S:	Mm..	mm.
		AFF	AFF
		Mm, mm.	

[19] This should be a demonstrative such as 'this' rather than a number.
[20] It should be: ***Wo dou yong zheizhi nazhe kuaizi.***

G 32 E: Suoyi ni shi yong you shou a.
so you be use right hand Q
So you use your right hand.

G 33 S: Eh.. eh.. eh.
AFF AFF AFF
Eh, eh, eh.

G 34 E: Ni meiyou yong zuo shou a?
you not-have use left hand Q
You don't use your left?

G 35 S: $_I$Meiyou.
not-have
No.

G 36 E: Ni jia you meiyou ren yong zuo shou?
you home have not-have person use left hand
Does anyone in your family use their left hand?

G 37 S: Mm.. $_I$meiyou.
HES not-have
Mm.. no.

G 38 E: Meiyou a.
not-have Q
No.

G 39 S: Wo dou yong.. yong you shou.
I all use use right hand
I only use.. use my right hand.

G 40 E: You shou a. Hao. Na ni
right hand EMP good then you
Right hand. Ok. Now, how

G 41 you jige xiaohai a?
have many:Q-C child Q
many children do you have?

G 42 S: Wo $_I$XIANZAI $_I$BUGUO[21] jiu you
I now however only have
I now but have only

G 43 *$_{III}$<yi.. $_{III}$yizhi shou>[22]. Ho. $_{III}$Neige...
AFF that-C one- one-C hand
one.. one hand. See. That...

G 44 *$_{I}\phi$-guo ta $_{II}$sishi... $_{II}$sishiji nian
(how-)ever she 40 40-few year
-ever, she forty... for forty-something years

G 45 ta.. ta.. ta.. ta.. ta you kan
she she she she she have see
she.. she.. she.. she.. she has seen a son,

G 46 $_{II}$erzi, ta.. ta $_{I}$ziji zhi zhei $_{II}$yangzi.
son she she self only this way
she.. she herself is just like that.

G 47 E: Ou, zhei yangzi a.
AFF this way EXC
Oh, is that right.

G 48 S: Ei.
AFF
Uh-huh.

G 49 E: Dengyideng a.
wait-one-wait EMP
Wait a minute.

G 50 S: Mm.
AFF
Mm.

G 51 E: Wo wen ni, ni you jige xiaohai?
I ask you you have many:Q-C child
I asked, how many kids do you have?

G 52 S: Ta dou you $_{III}$liangge.
she all have two-C
She has 2 in all.

---

[21] The order should be: *Buguo wo xianzai...*

[22] Instead of 'child', the word for 'hand' is used perseveratively, including the appropriate classifier.

G 53	E:	Liangge.
		2-C
		Two.

G 54	S:	Mm.
		AFF
		Mm.

G 55	E:	Ni	you	liangge	xiaohai.
		you	have	2-C	child
		You have 2 kids.			

G 56	S:	Mm.
		AFF
		Mm.

G 57	E:	Nande	hai	nude?	Nande?
		male-MOD	or	female-MOD	male-MOD
		Boys or girls? Boys?			

G 58	S:	Wo...	wo	dou	you	$_{III}$liuge.	Shi bu ϕ	$_{III}$liuge...
		I	I	all	have	6-C	be not (be)	6-C
		I.. I have 6 in all. Isn it 6...						

G 59	$_{III}$liangge...	$_{III}$liangge..	$_{III}$liuge.	$_{III}$Keneng
	2-C	2-C	6-C	maybe
	2... 2.. 6. Maybe			

G 60	$_{III}$liuge..	$_{III}$liuge.
	6-C	6-C
	6.. 6.	

G 61	E:	Ni	you	liuge?
		you	have	6-C
		You have 6?		

G 62	S:	Mm.	You	$_{III}$liuge	ta..	ta	jiu	ϕ	$_{III}$yige.
		AFF	have	6-C	she	she	only	(have)	1-C
		Mm. I have 6 she.. she only 1.							

G 63	Ta..	ta..	ta..	ta	you	$_{III}$liangge.	Ta	ϕ
	she	she	she	she	have	2-C	she	(have)
	She.. she.. she.. she has 2. She							

G 64 $_{III}$liangge $_{III}$sange.
2-C 3-C
two three.

G 65 E: Mm hm.
AFF AFF
Mm hm.

G 66 S: Ta [s-...] ta mm.. Wo $_{I}$meiyou *$_{III}$ne⊗ge⊗mo[23]
she s-... she HES I not-have that-C-so
She s-.. she mm.. I don't have thatso

G 67 duo a.
many EMP
many.

G 68 E: Mm hm.
AFF AFF
Mm hm.

G 69 S: Ta.. ta dou you *$_{III}$liangϕ.. $_{III}$liangge.
she she all have 2(-C) 2-C
She.. she has two.. two in all.

G 70 E: Shei? Shei you liangge?
who who have 2-C
Who? Who has 2?

G 71 S: Eh.. Wo $_{I}$xianzai ϕ a.
HES I now (have) EMP
Eh.. I now.

G 72 E: Hm.
AFF
Hm.

G 73 S: Ta jiu you $_{III}$liangge.
she only have 2-C
She only has 2.

[23] This is a word formation error in which the word *nemmo* 'so' is split apart by an intrusive classifier *-ge*. The probable source of the error is the fact that the demonstrative *na* often cooccurs with *-ge* as *neige* 'that'. Note that since both *nemmo* and *neige* are formed at lexical level III, a word formation error in which parts of these words are interchanged might be expected.

G 74	E:	Uh-huh.
		AFF
		Uh-huh.

G 75	S:	Ta..	ta..	ta..	ta..	ta	yao..	yao..	yao..
		she	she	she	she	she	want	want	want
		She.. she.. she.. she.. she wants.. wants.. wants..							

G 76	yao..	yao	wen..	wen..	wen	ta,	ho.
	want	want	ask	ask	ask	he	EMP
	wants.. wants to ask.. ask.. ask him, see.						

G 77	E:	Uh-huh.
		AFF
		Uh-huh.

G 78	S:	Ta	shuo	jiao	wo	$_{III}$liangge...	$_{II,III}$shisange...
		she	say	tell	I	2-C	13-C
		She said told me two... 13...					

G 79	[sh*$_{I}$yigong]...	Ta	<SHI>	$_{I}$YIGONG	$_{I}$XIANZAI[24]
	is-altogether	she	be	altogether	now
	tsaltogether... She now is altogether				

G 80	$_{III}$sange	ou.
	three-C	EXC
	three.	

G 81	E:	Ou.	Ni	you	sange	xiaohai.
		AFF	you	have	3-C	child
		Oh. You have 3 kids.				

G 82	S:	Mm..	mm..	mm.
		AFF	AFF	AFF
		Mm mm mm.		

G 83	E:	Zhei	yangzi.
		this	way
		Is that right.	

[24] The order should be *xianzai yigong you.*

G 84	S:	Mm.						
		AFF						
		Mm.						

G 85	E:	Ni	taitai	ti	ni	sheng	jige	xiaohai?
		you	wife	for	you	bear	many:Q-C	child
		Your wife had how many kids for you?						

G 86	S:	Wo	$_{II}$taitai...
		I	wife
		My wife...	

G 87	E:	Sheng	jige	xiaohai?
		bear	many:Q-C	child
		Had how many kids?		

G 88	S:	Wo	$_{II}$taitai	dou...	$_{I}$xianzai	dou	you	$_{III}$sange.
		I	wife	all	now	all	have	3-C
		My wife in all... now has 3 in all.						

G 89	E:	Ou,	sange	a.
		AFF	3-C	EXC
		Oh, 3.		

G 90	S:	You	$_{III}$sige	*$_{III}$nei⊗ge⊗yang[25]	ren.
		have	4-C	that-C-C:type	person
		There are four of that-one type of person.			

G 91	E:	Sige,	a?!	Sange	haishi	sige?
		4-C	EXC	3-C	or	4-C
		Four!? Three or four?				

G 92	S:	$_{III}$Sige.
		4-C
		4.

[25] The erroneous form **neigeyang* 'that-C-C:type' is a combination of *neiyang* 'that kind' and *neige* 'that-C'. Its occurrence may be attributed to the fact that the demonstrative *nei-* so often occurs with the classifier *-ge* that the subject inserted that classifier even though the slot was already filled by another classifier. Note that both classifiers are posited to be affixed at the same lexical level (viz., level III). This provides an explanation for their propensity to be misused in conjunction with one another.

G 93	E:	Na,	jige	nande?				
		then	many:Q-C	male-MOD				
		Then, how many boys?						

G 94	S:	$_{III}$Sige...	uh..	$_{III}$jige	$_{III}$neiyangrde	uh.		
		4-C	HES	many:Q-C	that-way-MOD	HES		
		Four... uh.. like, how many, uh.						

G 95		$_{III}$Sige...	$_{III}$sige..	aw.				
		4-C	4-C	EXC				
		4... 4.. aw.						

G 96	E:	Uh.	Na,	nansheng	ne?			
		AFF	then	male-child	Q			
		Uh. Then, what about boys?						

G 97	S:	*$_{II}$Nanϕ..	*$_{II}$nanϕ..	$_{II}$nansheng	jiu	ϕ	$_{III}$sige.	
		male(-child)	male(-child)	male-child	only	(have)	4-C	
		Boy.. boy.. boys just 4.						

G 98	E:	Na,	nude	ne?				
		then	female-MOD	Q				
		And, what about girls?						

G 99	S:	Jiu..	jiu..	jiu	you	$_{III}$yige..	$_{III}$yige	
		only	only	only	have	1-C	1-C	
		There's just.. just.. just one..						

G 100		$_{III}$nude	a.					
		female-MOD	EXC					
		girl.						

G 101	E:	A,	na	ni	you	wuge,	shi bu shi?	
		EXC	then	you	have	5-C	be not be	
		So you have 5, right?						

G 102	S:	$_{III}$Yige..	$_{III}$yige..	$_{III}$yige..	$_{III}$yige	$_{III}$nude.		
		1-C	1-C	1-C	1-C	female-MOD		
		One.. one.. one.. one girl.						

G 103	E:	Yige	nude.					
		1-C	female-MOD					
		One girl.						

G 104	S:	Ei.						
		AFF						
		Uh-huh.						
G 105	E:	Na	ni	yigong	you			
		then	you	altogether	have			
		So how many kids						
G 106		jige	xiaohai	a?				
		many:Q-C	child	Q				
		do you have altogether?						
G 107	S:	Ta	$_{I}$xianzai	zhi	you	$_{III}$sange.		
		she	now	only	have	3-C		
		She only has 3 now.						
G 108	E:	Xianzai	sange.					
		now	3-C					
		3 now.						
G 109	S:	Ei.	Ta..	ta	hai	you	$_{III}$yige...	
		AFF	she	she	still	have	1-C	
		Yeah. She.. she also had one... that's						
G 110		$_{I}$yijing	$_{I}$meiyou	le,.				
		already	not-have	ASP				
		already gone.						
G 111	E:	Ou.						
		AFF						
		Oh.						
G 112	S:	Hai	you	$_{III}$yige	yòu	yao	*$_{IV}$⋈huā⋈zhe[26]	
		also	have	one-C	again	want	spend-ASP	
		There's also one that we again wanted to spend						
G 113		ta,	$_{I}$buguo	$_{I}$xianzai	$_{I}$meiyou	le,.		
		it	but	now	not-have	ASP		
		it, but now it's gone.						

[26] This is an example of jargon that is properly inflected.

G 114 E: Xianzai dou meiyou le?
now all not-have ASP
It's all gone now?

G 115 S: Ei. $_{I}$Xianzai...
AFF now
Uh-huh. Now...

G 116 E: Nadiao[27], shi bu shi?
take-away be not be
Taken away, right?

G 117 S: $_{I}$Meiyou. *$_{II}$Na-ϕ $_{III}$yige.
not-have take(-away) one-C
No. Take one.

G 118 E: Na yige a. Nadiao yige.
take one-C EMP take-away one-C
Take one. Took away one.

G 119 S: Ei. *$_{II}$Na-ϕ $_{III}$yige. *$_{II}$Na-ϕ $_{III}$yige jiu...
AFF take(-away) one-C take(-away) one-C then
Take one. Take one then...

G 120 JIU TA.. TA[28] ϕ $_{III}$yige.. $_{III}$yige.
then he he (leave) one-C one-C
then she.. she one.. one.

G 121 E: Ou.
AFF
Oh.

G 122 S: Ta.. ta $_{I}$xianzai a, you la.
she she now EXC have EXC
She.. she now has one.

G 123 E: A?
Q
What?

---

[27] Slang for an aborted pregnancy.
[28] The word order should be *ta jiu*.

G 124	S:	$_{I}$Xianzai..	ta	⊗$_{I}$xianzai⊗...	dou			
		now	she	now	all			
		Now.. she now... doesn't						
G 125		$_{I}$meiyou	le$_{s}$,	⊗$_{I}$xianzai⊗.				
		not-have	ASP	now				
		have any, now.						
G 126		⊗Wo⊗	$_{I}$buguo	ta	$_{III}$neige	jiu...		
		I	however	she	that-C	then		
		I however she that just...						
G 127	E:	Uh-huh.						
		AFF						
		Uh-huh.						
G 128	S:	...hai	$_{III}$yige..	$_{III}$yige	*$_{III}$nu-ϕ.	$_{III}$Nude		
		also	one-C	one-C	female(-MOD)	female-MOD		
		There's also a.. a g-. Girl.						
G 129		la.	Hai	$_{III}$yige...	$_{III}$liangge	$_{III}$nude	la.	
		EMP	still	1-C	2-C	female-MOD	EXC	
		There's also one... two girls.						
G 130	E:	Uh-huh.						
		AFF						
		Uh-huh.						
G 131	S:	Ta	$_{I}$xianzai...	hai	da..da	ϕ[29].		
		she	now	also	hit	(DO)		
		Now she also hit..hit.						
G 132		$_{I}$Buguo	$_{III}$liangge	qiao	*$_{II}$bian-ϕ..			
		but	two-C	stick:up	braid(-NOM)			
		But two kick the buck[30]..						
G 133		qiao	*$_{II}$bian-ϕ.	Na	gai	you	$_{III}$yige	la.
		stick:up	braid(-NOM)	then	should	have	1-C	EXC
		kick the buck. So there should be one.						

[29] A direct object is obligatory here, and was omitted.

[30] Cf. 'kicked the bucket'. *Qiào biànzi* 'stick up the braids' is a euphemism for death in Mandarin.

G 134 E: Ou, zhende.
EXC really
Oh, really.

G 135 S: Mm.
AFF
Mm.

G 136 E: Benlai liangge nude,
originally 2-C female-MOD
There were originally 2 girls,

G 137 houlai shengxia yige.
after left-down 1-C
then there was 1 left.

G 138 S: Ei.
AFF
Uh-huh.

G 139 E: Ou, zhei yangzi.
EXC this way
Oh, is that right.

G 140 S: Ei.
AFF
Uh-huh.

G 141 E: Na, nansheng sheng jige?
then male-child bear many:Q-C
Then how many boys did she have?

G 142 S: $_{II}$Nansheng dou si $_{III}$yige la ⊗de⊗. Hai you
male-child all die one-C EXC MOD also have
Of the boys, one that died. There's also...

G 143 $_{III}$yige le$_{s}$. Hai you... $_{III}$yige le$_{s}$. Hai you
one-C ASP still have one-C ASP still have
...another. There's also... another. There's also...

G 144 $_{III}$zheige... ⊗$_{I}$xianzai⊗... $_{I}$buguo $_{III}$tade...
this-C now but him-MOD
this... now... but his...

G 145 dou $_{I}$meiyou le$_{I}$.
all not-have ASP
is all gone.

G 146 E: Nande ye dou meiyou le.
male-MOD also all not-have ASP
There aren't any boys either.

G 147 S: Mm.
AFF
Mm.

G 148 E: Ni pian wo. Ni bu shi you yige
you trick me you not be have 1-C
You're kidding me. Don't you have a

G 149 erzi yao jiehun ma?
son want marry Q
son who's getting married?

G 150 S: Ta $_{II}$erzi yao $_{III}$jiehun la. Ta
he son want marry EXC he
Her son's getting married. Her

G 151 $_{II}$ERZI $_{III}$YIGE.. $_{III}$yige $_{II}$erzi yao $_{III}$jiehun la.
son 1-C 1-C son want marry EXC
son one.. one son is getting married.

G 152 E: Uh-huh.
AFF
Uh-huh.

G 153 S: ⊗Jiu⊗.. ⊗jiu⊗.. ⊗jiu⊗.. ⊗JIU⊗ $_{I}$BUGUO TA
only only only only but he
Only.. only.. only.. only but she

G 154 jiu hai $_{III}$yige la.
only still 1-C EXC
still only has one.

G 155 E: Hai you yige.
still have 1-C
She still has one.

G 156	S:	$_{III}$Yige	ta..	ta..	ta..	ta	fu	<$_{III}$yige>[31].
		one-C	he	he	he	he	serve	one-C
		One he.. he.. he.. he.. served one.						

G 157	FU	$_{III}$YIGE	TA[32].
	serve	one-C	he
	Served one he.		

G 158	E:	Yige	jiehun	sheng	yige.
		1-C	marry	leave	1-C
		One's getting married, and one is left.			

G 159	S:	Ei.
		AFF
		Uh-huh.

G 160	E:	Ou	zhei	yangzi	a.
		EXC	this	way	Q
		Oh is that right.			

G 161 E2 (English): Of course we can't necessarily believe what he says.

G 162	E:	Wo	zhidao	ni	you	hao	duo	xiaohai	a.
		I	know	you	have	very	many	child	EXC
		I know you've got a lot of kids.							

G 163	Xianzai	dou	gaobuqingchu	a,	nayige
	now	all	make-not-clear	EXC	which-1-C
	Right now you can't remember which				

G 164	shi	nayige.
	be	which-1-C
	is which.	

G 165	S:	Ni	$_{I}$xianzai...	ni	$_{I}$xianzai	yao bu yao?
		you	now	you	now	want not want
		You now... do you want one now?				

G 166	E:	Wo	yao bu yao	shenmo?
		I	want not want	what
		Do I want what?		

---

[31] *Yige* was improperly used in the place of the noun *bingyi* 'military'.

[32] This sentence seems to be a 'scrambled' version of the previous incorrect utterance.

G 167	S:	$_{I}$Xianzai,	$_{III}$zheige	$_{II}$xiaohair,	ni					
		now	this-C	child	you					
		Now, this child, do you								

G 168	yao bu yao	<yong>[33]?	
	want not want	use	
	want to use it?		

G 169	E:	Bu	yao,	wo	bu	yao	yong.	Wo	zhi	shi
		not	want	I	not	want	use	I	only	be
		No, I don't want to use it. I only								

G 170	xiang	zhidao	ni	you	jige	xiaohai.
	think	know	you	have	many:Q-C	child
	want to know how many kids you have.					

G 171	S:	Wo	$_{I}$xianzai	hai y-..y-..y-...	jiu	hai	you..
		I	now	still	only	still	have
		I now still h-.. h-.. h-... still only have..					

G 172	hai	you	$^{*}{}_{III}$yiϕ..	$^{*}{}_{III}$yiϕ	$_{III}$liangge.
	still	have	one(-C)	one(-C)	2-C
	still have one.. one two.				

G 173	E:	Liangge	hai	mei	jiehun,	shi bu shi?
		2-C	still	not	marry	be not be
		Two still haven't gotten married, right?				

G 174	S:	Mm..	mm..	mm..	mm.
		AFF	AFF	AFF	AFF
		Mm mm mm mm.			

G 175	E:	Zhei	yangzi	a.
		this	way	Q
		Is that right.		

G 176	S:	Ei.	$_{I}$Buguo	ta..	ta..	ta	shi	$_{III}$zheige
		AFF	but	he	he	he	be	this-C
		Uh-huh. But he.. he.. he's this						

[33] The verb *yong* 'use' improperly used in place of the verb *sheng* 'to give birth'.

G 177 *$_{II}$yang-ϕ a. Jiu shi $_{III}$liangge, fu $_{II}$bingyi
way(-NOM) EXC only be 2-C serve military
way. It's just that two, served in the military.

G 178 Ta.. ta.. ta ⊗de⊗ fu ⊗de⊗ $_{II}$bingyi a.
he he he MOD serve MOD military EXC
He.. he.. his military that he served.

.... next session..............................

Description of 'Cookie Theft' picture.

G 179 E: Wo bang ni lu yin, hao bu hao?
I help you record sound good not good
I'll record for you, ok?

G 180 S: Hao.
good
Ok.

G 181 E: Ni zhi-bu-zhidao jintian women yao
you know-not-know today I-PL want
Did you know that today we're going to

G 182 lianxi shuo hua?
practice speak speech
practice speaking?

G 183 S: Ei, hen hao, hen hao.
AFF very good very good
Ah, very good, very good.

G 184 E: Hen hao, a.
very good EXC
Good.

G 185 S: Ei, ei, ei.
AFF AFF AFF
Mm-hm, mm-hm, mm-hm.

G 186 E: Na women xian rang ni kan yizhang
then I-PL first let you see 1-C
Now first let us show you a

G 187 tupian, hao bu hao?
picture good not good
picture, ok?

G 188 S: Hao, hao, hao.
good good good
Ok, ok, ok.

G 189 E: Na gaosu women tupian limian shuo shenmo.
then tell I-PL picture inside say what
Now tell us what the picture says.

G 190 S: Ei, ei.
AFF AFF
Uh-huh, uh-huh.

G 191 E: Hao, ni kan. Ni xian kankan zheige tupian.
good you look you first look-look this-C picture
Ok, look. First take a look at this picture.

G 192 S: Mm. Wo $_{III}$shenshang you $_{I}$meiyou $_{II}$tupian?
HES I body-on have not-have picture
Mm. Do I have a picture on my body?

G 193 E: Ou, tupian.
AFF picture
Oh, a picture.

G 194 S: $_{II}$Tupian.
picture
Picture.

G 195 E: Zhe limian shuo shenmo gushi?
this inside say what story
What story is being told in here?

G 196 S: Ou, ou. XI WAN *$_{III}$ZHEIϕ.. $_{III}$ZHEIGE[34] ϕ
EXC wash dish this(-C) this-C (be)
Oh, oh. Washing dishes th-.. this.

G 197 [*$_{I}$Duanshi] [de]... $_{III}$Zheige.. hai $_{IV}$xide
however he this-C still wash-ADV
Chowever dee... This is also washed

G 198 dou shi a.
all be EXC
all over the place.

G 199 E: Mm. Ranhou lei?
AFF after Q
Mm. What else?

G 200 S: *$_{I}$Ranhou shi shuo...* *$_{IV}$shuole$_{v}$...* *$_{I}$zenmo sh- zh-*
then be say say-ASP how
Then to say... said... how

G 201 *$_{III}$zheige...* *...$_{I}$putong dou.. dou gàn $_{I}$yihuir, ho.*
this-C usually all all do awhile AFF
this... usually is always done for awhile, huh?

G 202 E: Mm.
AFF
Mm.

G 203 S: Mm.
AFF
Mm.

G 204 E: Hao. Ranhou lei?
good after Q
Ok. Then what?

G 205 S: $_{I}$Ranhou hai you $_{I}$shenmo?
after still have what
What else is there?

G 206 E: Dui, hai you shenmo a? Zheige tupian
right still have what Q this-C picture
Right, what else is there? In this picture

G 207 hai you shuo shenmo?
still have say what
what else is going on?

[34] The order should be *Zheige shi ('is') xi wan.*

G 208 S: Mmm. Yao... wen... *${}_{III}$zheiϕ.. ${}_{III}$zheige...
AFF want ask this(-C) this-C
Mm. You want to... ask... this...

G 209 shi ${}_{I}$shenmo, a.
be what Q
what th-.. this... is.

G 210 E: Mm.
AFF
Mm.

G 211 S: Na zhei.. zhei jiu ${}_{III}$zheige, ${}_{I}$yuanlai
then this this only this-C originally
So this.. this just this, originally

G 212 shi fu ${}_{I}$shenmo?
be append what
was attached to what?

G 213 E: Mm. Na, hai you ne?
AFF then still have Q
Mm. Now, what else?

G 214 S: HAI YOU ${}_{I}$YUANLAI[35] *${}_{III}$nei<ge>[36] shu a,
also have original that-C book EXC
There was also originally that book,

G 215 ${}_{II}$zidian a.
dictionary EXC
and dictionary.

G 216 E: Ou, shu gen zidian.
EXC book and dictionary
Oh, a book and dictionary.

G 217 S: Mm, mm, mm.
AFF AFF AFF
Mm, mm mm.

[35] The order should be *Yuanlai hai you...* .
[36] The proper classifier for book is *-ben*.

G 218 E: Shu gen zidian zenmoyang?
book and dictionary what:about
What about the book and dictionary?

G 219 S: *Mm... Ni shuo yao gen shu*
HES you say want with book
How did you say you want to want the dictionary

G 220 $_{I}$*zenmoyang yao* $_{II}$*zidian?*
how:way want dictionary
with the book?

G 221 E: Ou yao zidian a.
EXC want dictionary Q
Oh, want the dictionary.

G 222 S: Mm, mm.
AFF AFF
Mm, mm.

G 223 E: Hao. Na ta zai gan ma? Zheige
good then he now do what this-C
Ok. So what's he doing? This

G 224 dongxi zai gan ma?
thing now do what
thing, what's it doing?

G 225 S: Ou, $_{I}$yuanlai yao.. yao
EXC originally want want
Oh, originally it was

G 226 $_{IV}$chaile$_{v}$ $_{II}$zidian a.
take:apart-ASP dictionary EXC
taken out of a dictionary.

G 227 E: Ou, zhei yangzi. Ranhou lei? Yuanlai
EXC this way after Q originally
Oh, is that right. What else? Originally

G 228 yao zhei yangzi. Ranhou lei? Houlai zenmoyang?
want this way after Q after how:way
it was that way. And afterward? What happened afterward?

G 229 S: Ou $_{I}$yuanlai $_{IV}$nimen shi $_{I}$zenmoyang wen
EXC originally you-PL be how:way ask
Oh originally how is it you're asking

G 230 zhe $_{II}$zidian a?
this dictionary EXC
about this dictionary?

G 231 E: Mm. Ou zhei yangzi, a.
AFF EXC this way EXC
Mm. Oh is that right.

G 232 S: Mm, mm.
AFF AFF
Mm, mm.

G 233 E: Na hai you meiyou qita de ne?
then still have not-have other MOD Q
Now is there anything else?

G 234 Ni zai zixi kankan. Hai you ou!
you again careful look-look still have EXC
Look again carefully. There's more!

G 235 S: Ni shuo $_{I}$yuanlai shi yao $_{I}$zenmoyang?
you say originally be want how:way
What did you say you wanted originally?

G 236 $_{III}$*Nemmo yao.. yao* *<you>* $_{II}$*zidian* $_{I}$*zenmoyang...*
then want want have dictionary how:way
Then what do you want to have about the dictionary...

G 237 $_{III}$*Zheige... zhe... wen shei wen...*
this-C this ask who ask
This... th-... ask who ask...

G 238 E: Ou zhei yangzi a.
AFF this way Q
Oh is that right.

G 239 S: Mm.
AFF
Mm.

G 240 E: Yuanlai zhei yangzi. Na ni xiang zenmoyang?
originally this way then you think how:way
It was this way at first. Now what do you think of it?

G 241 S: *Wo* $_{IV}$*chenzhe* $_{I}$*xianzai* *shi* *xiang* *a,* *shi* *deng*
I avail-ASP now be think EXC be wait
I'm taking the opportunity now to think, to wait for

G 242 $_{III}$*cuxin...* $_{I}$*yuanlai* $_{III}$*cuxin...* $_{I}$*yuanlai* $_{I}$*shenmo*
careless originally careless originally what
careless... originally careless... originally kind of

G 243 $_{III}$*xixin* *de.*
careful EMP
careful.

G 244 E: A.
AFF
Oh.

G 245 S: $_{I}$*Zenmoyang* *rang..* *rang..* *rang* $_{III}$*tade,* *ou.*
how:way let let let him-MOD EXC
How do I let.. let.. let his.

G 246 E: Ou zhei yangzi.
EXC this way
Oh, is that right.

G 247 S: Ei.
AFF
Uh-huh.

G 248 E: Hao, hao.
good good
Good, good.

G 249 S: $_{III}$Zheige $_{I}$yuanlai $_{I}$meiyou le,.
this-C originally not-have ASP
This was nothing all along.

G 250 E: A.
AFF
Oh.

.... end................................

A.3 Interlinear Translation of Yang Xifeng

Y 1	E:	Ou,	zhei	yangzi.				
		AFF	this	way				
		Oh, is that right.						

Y 2	S:	*Wo*	*cong*	$_{II}$*xiaohaizi*	*de*	$_{II}$*shihou*	
		I	from	small-child	MOD	time	
		From the time I was a child					

Y 3	*la,*	*dou*	$_{IV}$*cuole*$_v$*,*	$_{I}$*shenmo*
	EXC	all	wrong-ASP	something
	I was always wrong, something			

Y 4	∇*diān*∇	$_{III}$*nèige*	∇*xiǎn fēn*∇	*a.*	$_{III}$*Nèige*	⋈*$_{IV}$*líu*⋈*le*$_v$[37]
	insane	that-C	danger part	EXC	that-C	left-ASP
	insane that danger part. That left...					

Y 5	*...*$_{III}$*neige*	$_{I}$*shenmo*	⋈*fēng xiá*⋈	⋈*yǒu*	*sè*⋈	*a?*
	that	what	wind canyon	have	color	Q
	... that whatever wind canyon has color?					

Y 6	⋈*Diǎn*⋈	*de*	$_{II}$*shihou,*	*aw!...*	*[de]*
	count	MOD	time	EXC	all
	When one counted, oh. It was oll				

Y 7	$_{I}$*bijiao*	*cha*	$_{III}$*yidian.*
	compare	lacking	one-bit
	a bit lacking.		

Y 8	E:	Zhende!
		real-MOD
		Really!

Y 9	S:	$_{I}$*Wèishénmò*	*wǒ*	$_{I}$*qítā*	*dė*	$_{II}$*shíhòu*	∇*fŭ dīn*∇	*ȧ?*
		why	I	other	MOD	time	???	Q
		Why did I ??? at other times?						

Y 10	*Na*	∇*bù qióng*∇	*wo*	*dou*	$_{I}$*meiyou*	*ma.*
	that	not poor	I	all	not-have	EXC
	That unpoor, I didn't have any.					

[37] Inflection of a jargon word.

Y 11	*Dou*	*shi*	*◇èr◇*	*φ*	*de*	$_{II}$*shihou*	$_{I}$*nianqing*		
	all	be	two	(year)	MOD	time	young		
	I was always a young one when I was couple.								

Y 12	*de*	*ma.*	$_{I}$*Nianqing*	*de*	$_{II}$*shihou*	*dou*	$_{III}$*xiaode.*	
	EMP	EXC	young	MOD	time	all	know	
	When I was young, I knew it all.							

Y 13	*Ei?*	*Ni*	*kan!*	*Ei,*	*wo*	$_{II}$*taitai!*
	EXC	you	look	EXC	I	wife
	Huh? Look! Hey, my wife!					

Y 14	*Jiu*	$_{III}$*xiaode*	*ren*	*zhi*	*xiang.*
	only	know	person	MOD	appearance
	She only knows people's appearance.				

Y 15	E:	Ou.
		AFF
		Oh.

Y 16	S:	*Ta*	$_{I}$*zuihou*	*dou*	*cha*	$_{III}$*yidian.*
		she	most-after	all	lacking	one-bit
		In the end, she comes up a bit short.				

Y 17	E:	Zhei	yangzi.	Hao.	Wo	wen	ni	lingwai
		this	way	good	I	ask	you	other
		Is that right. OK. Let me ask you another						

Y 18	yige	wenti.	Nin	gui	xing?	Ni	xing	shenmo?
	1-C	question	you	dear	name	you	name	what
	question. What's your name? What's your last name?							

Y 19	S:	Wo	shi	Yang Xi... Yang Xifeng.
		I	be	(name)
		I am Yang Xi... Yang Xifeng.		

Y 20	E:	Ou,	Yang Xifeng,	shi bu shi?
		AFF	(name)	be not be
		Oh, Yang Xifeng, right?		

Y 21	S:	A.	Yang Xi...Yang Xifeng	a...	ai...
		AFF	(name)	EXC	EXC
		Mm-m. Yang Xi...Yang Xifeng.			

Y 22 E: Ou, Yang Xifeng.
AFF (name)
Oh, Yang Xifeng.

Y 23 S: ⋈Dǎ⋈ gė ▽xiǎn xián jīn fù▽.
hit M danger salty gold father
Hit a danger salty gold father.

Y 24 E: Ou, zhei yangzi. Ranhou ni jinnian
AFF this way after you this-year
Oh, is that right. Now, this year

Y 25 ji sui?
many:Q year
how old are you?

Y 26 S: Wo ⊗shi⊗ $_{II}$sishi... $_{III}$yinggai shi... $_{II}$ershier sui.
I be forty should be twenty-two year
I'm forty... make that twenty-two years old.

Y 27 E: Ershier sui, a...
22 year Q
Twenty-two years (old)...

Y 28 S: Ei.
AFF
Mm-hm.

Y 29 E: ...haishi...
or
...or...

Y 30 S: Wo $_{I}$yijing $_{II}$sishi...s-..s-... $_{II}$ershi.. *$_{I}$◇cóngnián◇[38]
I already forty twenty from-year
I'm already forty...f-..f-... twenty.. past year

Y 31 shi $_{II}$sishi sui ma. Si sui, $_{IV}$women
be forty year EMP four year I-PL
I was forty years old. Four years old, at that time

[38] The proper way to say 'last year' in Mandarin is *qunian* 'gone-year'. The subject improperly substitutes the semantically related *cóng* 'from' for *qu* 'go'.

Y 32

$_{III}$neige	$_{II}$shihou	$_{IV}$duole$_v$	liang	nian	ma.
that-C	time	more-ASP	two	year	EMP

we had two more years.

Y 33 E:

Uh-huh.
AFF
Uh-huh.

Y 34 S:

LIǍNG	NIÁN	∇*$_{IV}$SÌ∇LE$_v$[39].	∇Dāng qiān sì∇.
two	year	four-ASP	become thousand four

Two years foured. Became thousand four.

Y 35 E:

Ou.
AFF
Oh.

Y 36 S:

Wo	zhi	shi	◇*$_{II}$liǎng◇shí[40]sì...
I	only	be	couple-ten-four

I'm only couplty-four...

Y 37

◇*$_{II}$liǎng◇shíèr	◇nián◇[41]	a.
couple-ten two	year	EMP

...couplty-two years.

Y 38 E:

Ou.
AFF
Oh.

Y 39 S:

Wo	*lai*	*de*	$_{II}$*shihou*	*wo*	*shi*	$_{III}$*tongji*	*de*
I	come	MOD	time	I	be	register	MOD

When I came when I was registered...

Y 40

$_{II}$*shihou*	*wo*	*shi*	*a...*	*Ei?*
time	I	be	EXC	EXC

I was uh... huh?

[39] This is an example of an inflected neologism (*sìle*) used in a sentence with bad word order. The order should be *VERB-le liang nian.*

[40] There are two words for 'two' in Mandarin. *Er* is used in the formation of larger numbers, while *liang* is used only with classifiers. Here the subject used the wrong (but semantically related) form in saying the larger number 'twenty'.

[41] The subject improperly uses the semantically related *nian* 'years' for *sùi* 'years of age'.

Y 41 $_{I}$*Mashang* *yao* *jin* *la!* *Ei?* *Wo* *shuo*
immediately want enter EXC EMP:Q I say
We're going in right now! Huh? I said

Y 42 $_{III}$*zheige.* *Ou,* *wo* *shuo* ∇*wéi pó*∇.
this-C EXC I say surround woman
this. Oh, I said surround the woman.

Y 43 *A,* $_{I}$*suoyi* *de,* $_{III}$*neige* $_{IV}$*women...* $_{III}$*neige*
EXC so MOD that-C I-PL that-C
Uh-huh, so, that our... that

Y 44 $_{II}$*lianzhang* *zai* *ma.* $_{II}$*Lianzhang*
company-commander present EMP company-commander
company commander of ours was there. The company commander,

Y 45 *a,* *ta* *shuo...* *ken* $_{III}$*neige* ∇*jiā jīn*∇ *ma.*
EMP he say willing that-C house money EMP
he said... he was willing that house money, y'know.

Y 46 ∇*Jiā jīn*∇ *yǔ* $_{III}$*neige...* ∇*dìng ge*∇ *ma.*
house money and that-C set M EMP
The house money and that set one y'know.

Y 47 *Wo* *you* $_{II}$*jiàndao* $_{III}$*yige* $_{III}$*jiade.*
I again see-attain one-C fake-MOD
I saw a fake one again.

Y 48 $_{I}$*Meiyou* *jiǎn* $_{III}$*yidian.* *You* $_{IV}$*duole*$_{v}$ *$_{III}$*yi[zhèn].*
not-have reduce one-bit again more-ASP one-C:needle.
It didn't go down a bit. Again one beedle too many.

Y 49 *Dāng* *gė* $_{III}$*bàngė* *duō* ⋈$_{II}$*cèsuǒ*⋈ ∇*sēn* hǒ∇.
become M half-C more toilet forest ???
Became a more than half a toilet forest ??? .

Y 50 E: Uh-huh.
AFF
Uh-huh.

Y 51 S: Zuo $_{III}$haoxie le$_{s}$.
do lot-PL:M ASP
Did a lot.

Y 52 E: Uh-huh.
AFF
Uh-huh.

Y 53 S: *$_{II,IV}$[Chèn][42]xiàláile$_v$ ma.
left-down-come-ASP EMP
It was reft over, see?

Y 54 E: Ou, chènxià[43], na ni...
AFF left-down then you
Oh, reft over, then you...

Y 55 S: $_{II}$[CHÈN]XIALAI DE $_{II}$SHIHOU $_{III}$LIANGGE..
left-down-come MOD time 2-C
When it was reft over two..

Y 56 $_{III}$LIANGGE ⋈DIÀN⋈[44] a...
2-C store EXC
two stores...

Y 57 E: Uh-huh.
AFF
Uh-huh.

Y 58 S: Shi $_{III}$lianggen.
be two-C:shot
It was two shots.

Y 59 E: Qian liang dian.
before 2 dot
Two times before.

Y 60 S: *$_{III}$Sì.. $_{III}$sìguǎn. Zhi $_{III}$neige $_{III}$sìguǎn [dà]
four-C:bottle only that-C four-C:bottle inject
Four..four bottles. Only those four bottles infected

---

[42] For *Shèng*
[43] The experimenter repeats the error.
[44] The order should be *Chenxialai liangge dian de shihou...*

Y 61 [nián] [zì] [nǐa] $_{III}$liǎng[jiān].
two four two two-C:needle
in boo pore boo two deedles.

Y 62 E: Ou, zhei yangzi.
AFF this way
Oh, is that right.

Y 63 S: Wo da de $_{II}$shihou $_{I}$bijiao cha $_{III}$yidian.
I inject MOD time compare bad one-bit
When I got the shot, I was a little worse.

Y 64 Aiya, wo shou bu xing a.
EXC I hand not good EMP
Oh gosh, my hand is no good.

Y 65 E: Xianzai hao duo le, a.
now good much ASP EMP
It's a lot better now, though.

Y 66 S: DOU $_{I}$XIANZAI DE $_{II}$SHIHOU[45]
all now MOD time
Always at the time of now,

Y 67 $_{I}$xianzai wo $_{II}$yanjing hen cha lei.
now I eye very bad EXC
now my eyes are very bad.

Y 68 E: Ou.
AFF
Oh.

Y 69 S: Wo dou shi $_{I}$nianqing de $_{II}$shihou, a,
I all be young MOD time EXC
Always when I was young

Y 70 ⊗dou⊗ bu $_{III}$renshi ϕ[46] lie.
all not recognize (DO) EXC
I always didn't recognize.

---

[45] The structure *X de shihou* acts as a time adverbial, and means 'at the time of X'. The structure takes either clock time or an event in the *X* slot. The subject erred here in placing a time adverbial in the *X* slot. In addition, the time adverbial slot in this sentence is already occupied by the following *xianzai*. Also, the word order of the sentence is bad because the adverbial *dou* cannot precede the time adverbial.

Y 71 E: Na, dengyideng a. Ni jinnian ji sui?
then wait-1-wait EXC you this-year many:Q year
Now wait a minute. How old are you this year?

Y 72 S: $_{I}$Jinnian. $_{I}$*Jinnian* *[sī]* *jiǎn.* *Sì* *diǎn*
this-year this-year four minus four dot
This year. This year I'm minus pour. 33 or

Y 73 $_{II}$*sanshisan* *f-...* $_{II}$*sanshi* *san* *si* *fen.*
thirty-three f-.. thirty three four minute
four minutes after four.

Y 74 E: Dengyideng a. Wo shuo, ni jinnian
wait-1-wait EMP I say you this:year
Wait a minute. I said, this year

Y 75 ji sui? Ji sui?
many:Q year many:Q year
how old are you? How old?

Y 76 S: Aiyo, $_{I}$xianzai wo $_{III}$neige $_{II}$yanjing... ni kan...
EXC now I that-C eye you look
Oh my, now those eyes of mine...look...

Y 77 $_{I}$xianzai shi hen re le[46], ni kan.
now be very hot ASP you look
now it's real hot, take a look.

Y 78 Ni $_{IV}$momo kan. Dui bu dui, ni $_{IV}$momo kan.
you feel-feel look right not right you feel-feel look
Feel it and see. Right? Feel it and see.

Y 79 E: Ou dui. Hen re.
EXC right very hot
Oh, right. Very hot.

Y 80 S: $_{IV}$Rere you $_{III}$neige *$_{II}$xueϕ.. $_{II}$xuehong.
hot-hot have that-C blood(-red) blood-red
It's hot, and has that blood..bloody red.

Y 81 E: Ou zhei yangzi. Ni shi bu shi sishijiu sùi?
EXC this way you be not be 49 year
Oh, is that right. Aren't you forty-nine years old?

---

[46] Obligatory direct object omitted.

Y 82 S: $_{II}$Sìshísān [dùi]! $_{II}$Sìshísān [hùi] la!
forty-three year forty-three year EXC
Forty-three beers old! Forty-three cheers old!

Y 83 Yang Xifeng la, Yang Xifeng.
(name) EXC (name)
Yang Xifeng, Yang Xifeng.

Y 84 E: Ni shi bu shi wushier sui?
you be not be fifty-two year
Aren't you 52?

Y 85 S: A. $_{I}$Dengyu shi $_{II}$sishier a, $_{II}$sishi... Bu!
EXC equal be forty-two EXC forty NEG
Ah. It's equal to 42... 40... No!

Y 86 *Wo shi da* ⋈$_{II}$*gongsi*⋈.
I be big company
I'm a big company.

Y 87 E: Wushi ji sui?
fifty many:Q year
Fifty what?

Y 88 S: *Lian* $_{III}$*neige* $_{II}$*shihou* ⋈$_{II}$*shenjing*⋈ $_{III}$*neige*
even that-C time nerve that-C
Even at that time, that nerve

Y 89 $_{I}$*dongxi a, shi* $_{II}$*ershier [hùi].*
thing EXC be twenty-two years
thing was 22 cheers old.

Y 90 E: Ou zhei yangzi ha.
EXC this type EXC
Oh, is that so.

Y 91 S: $_{II}$Ershisi ∇dēng∇[47].
twenty-four light
Twenty-four light.

[47] This is categorized as a neologism rather than jargon because although it is a possible word, it does not occur in a syntactically correct context since there is no classifier preceding it.

Y 92	E:	Hm,	hm.						
		AFF	AFF						
		Um-hm, um-hm.							

Y 93	S:	$_{I}$Xianzai	wo	$_{III}$neige	$_{II}$yanjing	dou	$_{I}$chajin[48]	a,	
		now	I	that-C	eye	all	bad-very	EXC	
		Now those eyes of mine are very bad, there's							

Y 94	mei	$_{II}$banfa	la.	
	no	method	EXC	
	nothing I can do.			

Y 95	E:	Bu	hui	bu	hui,	hen	hao.	Ni	jiangde	
		not	able	not	able	very	good	you	talk-ADV	
		No, no, it's ok. You speak								

Y 96	hen	qingchu.	Na,	ni	yiqian	zuo	shenmo	shi?	
	very	clear	then	you	before	do	what	matter	
	really clearly. Now, what work did you do before?								

Y 97	S:	Dou	shi	$_{II}$xiaohair	ma.	Dou	gen	$_{II}$renjia	ma.
		all	be	child	EXC	all	with	people	EXC
		I was always a child. Always with people.							

Y 98	$_{III}$Neige	$_{II}$shihou	$_{II}$xiaohair	ma.	Dou
	that-C	time	child	EXC	all
	At that time a child. We all..				

Y 99	s-..dou	$_{III}$renshi	ta.
	all	know	him
	all knew him.		

Y 100	E:	Eh,	uh-huh.	Hao,	dengyideng.
		AFF	AFF	good	wait-1-wait
		Eh, uh-huh. Ok, wait a minute.			

Y 101	S:	Dou	bu	$_{III}$xiaode	wo	$_{I}$zìjǐ	◇hǎo	dūo◇[49]	sùi.
		all	not	know	I	self	very	many	year
		I don't even know a lot of years that I myself am.							

---

[48] Categorized as a level I word, because it is a non-productive resultative.

[49] The subject incorrectly uses *hao duo* 'very many' in place of the semantically related question word *ji* 'how many'. The target is 'I don't even know how old I myself am.'

Y 102 $_{I}$Shenmo shi wo dou *$_{IV}$wang-ϕ.
what matter I all forget(-ASP$_v$)
I've forget everything.

Y 103 E: Na ni yiqian shi
then you before be
Then what work

Y 104 zuo shenmo gongzuo?
do what work
did you do before?

Y 105 S: [Zǔ] $_{II}$[yījīn] a. ∇Sì xīn∇ a. Aiyo,
do doctor EXC four heart EXC EXC
I wiz a docpor. Four hearts. Oh my,

Y 106 $_{II}$jintian dou bu xing. A... $_{II}$jintian...
today all not good EXC today
today nothing's right. Y'know...today...

Y 107 E: Bu hui, bu hui, bu hui.
not able not able not able
No, no, no.

Y 108 S: $_{II}$Jintian ni kan, ni $_{IV}$momo kan. Wo
today you look you feel-feel look I
Today, take a look, feel it and see. Aren't

Y 109 shi bu shi zong shi $_{III}$rede?
be not be always be hot-MOD
I always hot?

Y 110 E: Wo ye shi rede.
I also be hot-MOD
I'm hot too.

Y 111 S: $_{I}$Haoxiang $_{III}$rede, ni kan. $_{III}$Rede. $_{I}$*Yiqian*
seem hot-MOD you look hot-MOD before
It seems hot, take a look. Hot. Before

Y 112 *dou* $_{III}$*baide.* $_{III}$*Zheici* $_{I}$*bijiao* *cha* $_{III}$*yidian.*
all white-MOD this-C:time compare poor one-bit
it was all white. This time it's a little worse.

.... different session..........................

Y 113 E: Ni xianzai jiang hua
you now talk speech
Now when you talk do you have

Y 114 you meiyou kunnan?
have not-have difficulty
difficulty?

Y 115 S: Aiyayo. $_{I}$Tamade. ∇Zī mǎ∇
EXC-EXC-EXC him-mother-MOD capital horse
Oh-me-my. Goddam it. Capital horse's

Y 116 de... $_{II}$wandan. Haha ni xie $_{I}$shenmo zi
MOD finish-egg (laughs) you write what word
done for. Haha... the words you write,

Y 117 a, dou dong.
EXC all understand
I understand them all.

Y 118 E: Ou, meiyou, zhe shi yinggai de.
EXC not-have this be should MOD
Oh, no, this should be done.

Y 119 S: Na $_{I}$shenmo?
that what
What's that?

Y 120 E: Zhe shi ni de mingzi.
this be you MOD name
This is your name.

Y 121 S: Zhe shi wo de ◇Yang Xifeng◇[50].
this be I MOD Yang Xifeng
This is my Yang Xifeng.

Y 122 E: Zhe shi ni de nianling, ha. Wushier sui,
this be you MOD age EXC 52 year
This is your age, see. Fifty-two,

[50] Instead of the word for 'name', the subject incorrectly inserts his actual name.

Y 123 dui bu dui? Zheli shuo ni jiang hua
right not right here say you talk speech
right? Here it says that you speak

Y 124 hen qingchu.
very clear
clearly.

Y 125 S: Hai $_{III}$qingchu!? $_{I}$Xianzai
still clear now
Oh clearly, yet!? Now

Y 126 $_{IV}$chale$_{v}$ hao duo le$_{s}$!
poor-ASP very much ASP
I'm much worse!

Y 127 Fam: Zhuyi ting xiaojie.
notice listen girl
Listen to the young lady.

Y 128 E: Xianzai lianxi.
now practice
Now we'll practice.

Y 129 S: $_{III}$Xiexie. Aiya $_{IV}$zaode yi da $_{III}$hutu a,
thank-thank EXC mess-ADV one big muddle EXC
Thanks. Oh gosh, I'm really messed up,

Y 130 $_{IV}$zaole$_{v}$ $_{III}$bantian.
mess-ASP half-day
I'm always messed up.

Y 131 E: Ni hui bu hui lei?
you able not able tired
Are you tired?

Y 132 S: $_{I}$Youde $_{II}$shihou you $_{III}$yidian a[51]. You shi
some time have one-bit EXC have time
Sometimes a little. Sometimes

[51] The subject misunderstands the temporal reference. The experimenter's question clearly refers to the present time, while the subject misunderstands it as meaning 'in general'.

Y 133	$_{I}$zaoshang	$_{I}$wanshang	$_{II}$qilai,	a.	
	morning	evening	rise	EXC	
	in the morning and the evening I get up.				

Y 134	E:	Mm.
		AFF
		Mm.

Y 135	S:	◇$_{I}$Shenmo◇[52]	jiang	a.	You	$_{III}$yige
		what	speak	EXC	have	one-C
		What do you say. There's a				

Y 136	$_{I}$shenmo	$_{III}$neige	$_{I,IV}$mălícēcēle$_{v}$	$_{II}$xiaobian.
	what	that-C	stimulating-ASP	urinate
	like that kind of good feeling urinating.			

Y 137	YE	NI[53]	$_{IV}$zuoguo	de	a.
	also	you	do-ASP	EMP	EMP
	You've done also it before.				

Y 138	Wo	$_{III}$nage	shi	$_{I}$yiqian	$_{IV}$zuoguo	de.
	I	that-C	be	before	do-ASP	MOD
	That was something I've done before.					

Y 139	Na	$_{I}$mali	hai	zhen...	∇zī diàn∇	dou
	that	feeling	still	real	capital shop	all
	That feeling was really... capital shops I've all					

Y 140	$_{IV}$chiguole$_{v}$.	Wo	dou	hui	chi	de.
	eat-ASP-ASP	I	all	can	eat	MOD
	eaten before. I can eat everything.					

Y 141	E:	Na	ni	yiqian	mei	zai	Rong-...
		then	you	before	not	at	(name)
		Now you've never before at Veteran's...					

Y 142	S:	Dou	$_{IV}$chiguo,	ei!
		all	eat-ASP	EXC
		I've eaten them all before!		

---

[52] The subject uses 'what' for the semantically related 'how'.

[53] The word order should be *Ni ye...* .

Y 143 E: Ou, chiguo shenmo?
AFF eat-ASP what
Oh, eaten what before?

Y 144 S: Wo dou $_{IV}$chiguole$_{v}$. $_{I}$Xianzai dou
I all eat-ASP-ASP now all
I've eaten them all. Now

Y 145 shi... $_{I}$Xianzai dou $_{IV}$nongde ⊗dou⊗ you
be now all do-ADV all have
it's all... it's all gotten all

Y 146 $_{III}$yidian $_{III}$chade. Dou you $_{III}$chade.
one-bit bad-MOD all have bad-MOD
a bit bad. It's all bad.

Y 147 Dou shi $_{IV}$ruanruande $_{III}$yidian.
all be soft-soft-MOD one-bit
It's always a little soft.

Y 148 E: Ou, ruanruande, zhei yangzi. Ou, ni shuo
EXC soft-soft-MOD this way EXC you say
Oh, soft, is that right. Now, you say that

Y 149 ni yiqian dou daguo zhen, shi bu shi?
you before all inject-ASP needle be not be
you got a shot before, right?

Y 150 S: Ei! Ye cai $_{III}$liangci de. You
EXC also only two-C:time MOD have
Yeah! But only twice.

Y 151 $_{III}$yici ni kan, $_{III}$zheli hai you
one-C:time you look here still have
One time, take a look, here there's still

Y 152 $_{III}$yigen a, hai zai $_{III}$zheli.
one-C:mark EXC still at here
a mark, it's still here.

Y 153 E: Zhende!
real-MOD
Really!

Y 154 S: *You* $_{III}$*yici,* *chuan* $_{III}$*neige* $_{II}$*Fuzhou..* $_{III}$*neige*
have one-C:time wear that-C Fuzhou that-C
Once I was wearing that Fuchow.. that

Y 155 *dai* $_{III}$*neige* $_{I}$*dongxi* a.
wear that-C thing EXC
wearing that thing.

Y 156 E: Uh-huh.
AFF
Uh-huh.

Y 157 S: *Dai..* *dài* $_{III}$*liangci* *de.* *Dài* $_{III}$*yige* *dà..*
wear wear two-C:time MOD wear one-C big
Wore..wore it twice. Wore a big..

Y 158 *dà..* $_{III}$*neige..* $_{III}$*neige* ⋈$_{II}$*zhijia*⋈ *dà* *$_{III}$*[niǎng][ci]*[54].
big that-C that-C fingernail big two-C:time
big..that..that fingernail big boo dimes.

Y 159 $_{IV}$*Dàle*$_{v}$ *dou..* *dou* $_{I}$*dàbiàn* *a!* $_{I}$*Dàbiàn*
big-ASP all all big-convenience EXC big-convenience
It got so big it even..even took a shit! The shit

Y 160 *yi...* $_{III}$*neige...* $_{II}$*jiěbuchulai.* $_{II}$ *Wōbuchulai.*
one that-C release-not-exit-come push-not-exit-come
as soon as... that... I couldn't go. I couldn't push it out.

Y 161 *Dou* *sheng* $_{III}$*nenmo* $_{III}$*yidian.* $_{I}$*Dongxi* *mei* *dǎo*
all left this one-bit thing not invert
This little bit was left over. I didn't complete

Y 162 $_{I}$*dàodǐ.* *Bǎi* *zai* $_{II}$*limian.* *Dou* *shi* *zhei*
completely place at inside all be this
the thing. It was inside. It was all this

Y 163 $_{II}$*yangzi.* *Ba* *ta* *diu* *zai* $_{II}$*limian.*
way OBJ it lose at inside
way. I lost it inside.

[54] For *liǎngci.*

Y 164 *Dou shi* ∇*shuāng fāng*∇ *<ge>*[55] *a.*
all be double side M EXC
It was all a bilateral.

Y 165 *Na dai* $_{III}$*neige* $_{I}$*dongxi* $_{II}$*náqilai.*
then carry that-C thing carry-up-come
Then I carried that thing and brought it up.

Y 166 E: Ou, zhei yangzi.
EXC this way
Oh, is that right.

Y 167 S: *Shì* $_{I}$*xianzai* $_{IV}$*nongde dou* $_{III}$*zheyang* $_{IV}$*chide,*
matter now do-ADV all this-way eat-MOD
The matter is now done and eaten in this way,

Y 168 $_{I}$xianzai a, $_{IV}$haode duo a. $_{I}$Xianzai.
now EXC good-ADV much EXC now
now it's much better. Now.

Y 169 E: Mm-hm.
AFF
Mm-hm.

Y 170 S: Chi $_{III}$zhexie $_{I}$dongxi $_{IV}$chide dou shi
eat this-C:pl thing eat-ADV all be
Eating these things is all done

Y 171 $_{I}$bijiao [sǎng][56] $_{III}$yidian.
relative smooth one-bit
a little more smeethly.

Y 172 E: Mm-hm.
AFF
Mm-hm.

Y 173 S: Dou dai $_{III}$nage.. $_{III}$nage yang de.
all carry that-C that-C kind MOD
They all have that..that kind.

[55] A verbal paraphasia for the modifier *de*.
[56] For *shuǎng*.

Y 174 $_{III}$Zheige ∇biǎn∇. $_{III}$Zheige...
this-C flat this-C
This flat. This...

Y 175 E: Nèige bijiao you liliang.
that-C relative have strength
That one (hand) is stronger.

Y 176 S: $_{III}$Zheige hao. Dou shi $_{III}$zheige hao. $_{III}$Zheige
this-C good all be this-C good this-C
This one's good. This one's always better.

Y 177 ruan $_{III}$yidian $_{I}$xianzai, ni kan. $_{III}$Zheige.. $_{III}$zheige
this-C soft one-bit now you look this-C
This one's a little weak now, look. This.. this

Y 178 ruan $_{III}$yidian. Ni kan $_{III}$zheige
soft one-bit you look this-C
one's a little weak. Look, this one's

Y 179 $_{IV}$haode hen.
good-ADV very
very good.

Y 180 E: Mm. Na zheige...
AFF then this-C
Mm. And this one...

Y 181 S: Dou shi $_{III}$zheige na $_{I}$bijiao shuǎi[57].
all be this-C hold relative weak
This one always holds a little weakly.

Y 182 E: You meiyou zuo yundong?
have not-have do exercise
Do you do exercises?

Y 183 S: Jiu shi $_{III}$zheige a!
just be this-C EXC
It's just this!

[57] The proper form for 'weak' is *shuāi*. The subject's production reflects either his dialectal pronunciation or a tonal paraphasia.

Y 184 E: Ou, you meiyou zuo yundong?
EMP have not-have do exercises
Oh, do you do exercises?

Y 185 S: $_{III}$Zheige $_{I}$bijiao ruan. Dou [sǎ] $_{III}$yidian, a.
this-C relative soft all weak one-bit EXC
This one's a little soft. All a little wake.

Y 186 Bu shi! $_{III}$*Neige jiu* $_{I}$*meiyou wā zhēn a!*
not be that-C just not-have dig needle EXC
No! That one wasn't dug by a needle!

Y 187 *Ta shuo [sŭa]* $_{IV}$*shŭale*$_{v}$ $_{III}$*jǐcì a.*
he say play play-ASP few-C:time EXC
He said ploy play it a few times.

Y 188 *Xia* $_{III}$*yici,* $_{III}$*zhenmo yi chi.* $_{IV}$*Chide...*
next one-time this one eat eat-ADV
The next time I ate this way. I ate so that...

Y 189 E: Ni you meiyou zuo zheige yundong?
you have not-have do this-C exercise
Do you do those exercises?

Y 190 S: *...lian* $_{III}$*neige* $_{II}$*dabian dou zhi dao*
even that-C big-convenience all straight invert
...even that shit I simply pushed it right up

Y 191 $_{III}$*neige qi. Ei, ye mei* $_{II}$*banfa! Dou shi* $_{III}$*nayi*
that up EXC also no way all be that-one
there. There was no way! It was all on that

Y 192 *tian a. Ta dou dai de* $_{I}$*dongxi... gei*
day EXC he all bring MOD thing give
day. Everything he brought for

Y 193 *wo chi. Wo shuo wo mei* $_{II}$*banfa chi.*
me eat I say I no way eat
me to eat. I said... there's no way I could eat.

Y 194 *Wo shuo* $_{II,III}$*yixiazi... ta dou you* $_{III}$*neige*
I say awhile he all have that-C
I talked awhile...and he even had that

Y 195	$_{I}$*shenmo*	*Yú*	$_{III}$*neige*	$^{*}{}_{II}$*[sìfēng]*[58]	$_{I}$*yiyang*
	what	(name)	that-C	stone-powder	same
	whatever 'Yu' that medicine powder like that				

Y 196	$_{III}$*neige...*	$_{I}$*dongxi*	⊗$_{I}$*yiyang*⊗	*de,*	*dou*	*shi*
	that-C	thing	same	MOD	all	be
	kind of thing, and it was all					

Y 197	∇*diǎo*∇	*dou*	*zhenmo*	∇*diǎo*∇.	*Zhe*	$_{IV}$*daole*$_{v}$
	???	all	this	???	this	arrive-ASP
	???, all ??? like this. This in the					

Y 198	$_{I}$*wanshang*	$_{III}$*gaosu*	$_{III}$*neige*	$_{II}$*daifu,*	$_{II}$*yisheng*	*a.*
	evening	tell	that-C	doctor	doctor	EXC
	evening I told to that doctor, the doctor.					

Y 199	E:	Mm-hm.
		AFF
		Mm-hm.

Y 200	S:	Ta	dou	wen.	Ta	shuo	'ni	$_{III}$yige	da
		he	all	ask	he	say	you	one-C	shot
		He asked. He said, 'you got a shot							

Y 201	$_{II}$qianbian	a'?	Wo	shuo	'you	a!	Wo	shi
	front-side	EXC	I	say	have	EXC	I	be
	in the front'? I said 'I did! I got							

Y 202	da	$_{II}$qianbian	de,	you	la'.	$_{II}$Shijian
	shot	frontside	MOD	have	EXC	time
	a shot in the front, I sure did.' At the same time.					

Y 203	$_{I}$yiyang	de.	Zhei	shi	$_{II}$yisheng	de	hua.
	same	MOD	this	be	doctor	MOD	speech
	These were the doctor's words.						

Y 204	*Dia!*	*F-..aiyou!*	*Ba*	*ta*	$_{I}$*dongxi*	*dou*	$_{II,IV}$*nadiaole*$_{v}$*!*
	INT	INT	OBJ	he	thing	all	pull-away-ASP
	Pow! Ouch! He pulled his thing out!						

---

[58] According to my informant, this is a phonological paraphasia for *shí fēn* 'stone powder', a kind of medicine.

Y 205 E: Zhei yangzi. Hao, wo xie yige
this way good I write 1-C
Is that right. Ok, I'll write

Y 206 dongxi gei ni kan, a. ....
thing give you look EXC
something for you to look at.

Y 207 S: Wo ⊗dou⊗ kan dou $_{II}$kanbujian.
I all look all look-not-see
I anything can't see anything

....(end of session) ....

Y 208 S: *Na* *$_{II}$*[xiǎojiān]* *nǐ* *dė* *∇tǎo∇* *dė*
that girl you MOD get MOD
That kirl your noodles you

Y 209 *∇miàn∇* $_{III}$*nèmmo* *hǎo.*
noodle that good
got were so good.

Y 210 E: Dui. Wo bu hao. Hao.
right I not good good
Right. I'm no good. Ok.

Y 211 S: $_{II}$Zaogao lei. Wo $_{I}$zenmo ai?
EXC EXC I how EXC
Oh, drat. What's happened to me?

Y 212 E: Wo zhi yao wen ni jige wenti.
I only want ask you few-C question
I only want to ask you a few questions.

Y 213 S: Wo $_{I}$zenmo $_{III}$zhidao...
I how know
How do I know...

Y 214 E: Hei. Wo zhi yao wen ni jige wenti.
AFF I only want ask you few-C question
Ok. I only want to ask you a few questions.

Y 215 Hao, wo xianzai wen, ni jintian hao bu hao?
good I now ask you today good-not-good
Ok, let me ask, how are you today?

Y 216 S: Wǒ ∇hóu∇ nǐ ∇sān dēn∇ hěn hǎo.
I monkey you three ??? very good
I monkey you three ??? very well.

Y 217 E: Hao, hen hao. Ni you meiyou kanguo wo?
good very good you have not-have see-ASP I
Ok, very good. Have you ever seen me before?

Y 218 S: Wo dou shi *$_{II}$tǐngbu[dōng]... -dǒng a.
I all be hear-not-understand understand EXC
I don't underpand... understand anything I hear.

Y 219 E: A. Ni kanguo wo meiyou?
AFF you see-ASP I have-not
Ok. Have you ever seen me before?

Y 220 S: Dui.
right
Right.

Y 221 E: Ni...
you
You...

Y 222 S: Wo bu hui.
I not able
I can't.

Y 223 E: Ni you meiyou kanguo wo?
you have not-have see-ASP I
Have you ever seen me before?

Y 224 S: Bu hui bu hui. ∇Hee ha∇.
not able not able ???
I can't, I can't. ??? .

Y 225 E: Hei. Zhei yang. Hao. Na, ni you meiyou
AFF this way good then you have not-have
Ok. Is that right. Ok. Then, do you

Y 226 juede women yiyuan de ren, women zheli
feel I-PL hospital MOD person I-PL here
feel the people in our hospital, the people here

Y 227 yiyuan de ren neng bangzhu ni?
hospital MOD person able help you
in our hospital, can help you?

Y 228 S: Wo dou shi wo Yang Xifeng de ∇guai wei∇.[59]
I all be I Yang Xifeng MOD ???
I'm all my Yang Xifeng's ??? .

Y 229 E: A.
AFF
Oh.

Y 230 S: Bu hui gei *//*renjia jiang.
not able give people talk
I can't talk to people.

Y 231 E: Women zheli...
I-PL here
We here...

Y 232 S: Hei.
AFF
Yes.

Y 233 E: ...neng bu neng bangzhu ni?
can not can help you
...can we help you?

Y 234 S: Dui. Wo.. wo de.. wo de.. Yang Xifeng
right I I MOD I MOD Yang Xifeng
Right. I..my..my..m-.. Yang Xifeng's

Y 235 de ∇wài∇ *///*yidian.
MOD outside one-bit
a little outside.

[59] Both spoken with a mid-level tone, which does not properly occur in Mandarin.

Y 236 E: Uh-huh.
AFF
Uh-huh.

Y 237 S: $_{I}$Keshi wo $_{III}$yinggai $_{III}$keyi $_{II}$jiangchuqu de.
but I should able speak-exit-go MOD
But I should be able to speak it out.

Y 238 E: Hao, ni de zhiliao shenmo shihou zuowan?
good you MOD cure what time do-finish
Ok, when will your therapy be finished?

Y 239 S: Ou, zhe bu dong la. Wo shi $_{II}$xuehui
EXC this not understand EXC I be study-able
Oh, this I don't understand. I learned it.

Y 240 la. $_{II}$Xiaohaizi dou bu hui dong a.
EXC child all not able understand EXC
None of the children can understand.

Y 241 E: Ou zhei yangzi.
EXC this way
Oh, is that right.

Y 242 S: Dui!
right
Right!

Y 243 E: Wo xiwang bu hui tai jiu. Qing ni
I hope not able too long please you
I hope it won't be too long. Please would you

Y 244 gaosu wo ni jiao shenmo mingzi.
tell me you call what name
tell me what your name is.

Y 245 S: Wǒ ⋈tǔ⋈. Wǒ Yang Xifeng.
I spit I Yang Xifeng
I spit. I'm Yang Xifeng.

Y 246 E: Hao, dui.
good right
Good, right.

Y 247 S: ⋈Zhuàn⋈, dùi bù dùi?
spin right not right
Spin, right?

Y 248 E: Dui, hao. Ni zhu nali?
right good you live where
Right, fine. Where do you live?

Y 249 S: Wo de... $_{II}$Sanchongshi.
I MOD Sanchong-city
My...Sanchong city.

Y 250 E: A. Sanchongshi.
AFF Sanchong-city
Ah. Sanchong City.

Y 251 S: Dui.
right
Right.

Y 252 E: Hao.
good
Ok.

Y 253 S: Yang Xifeng.
(name)
Yang Xifeng.

Y 254 E: Sanchongshi ji lu?
Sanchong-city many:Q road
What number road in Sanchong city?

Y 255 S: Ei, dui, dui, dui.
EXC right right right
Uh, right, right, right.

Y 256 E: Nayitiao lu?
which-one-C road
Which road?

Y 257 S: Shi san... $_{III}$*sizhong* $_{III}$*sandui* *ma.*
be three four-C:kind three-C:pair EXC
It's three... four kinds and three pairs.

Y 258 E: Ji hao? Ji hao?
many:Q number many:Q number
What number? What number?

Y 259 S: N-... *$_{III}$liangϕ... $_{III}$lianggen... $_{III}$liangzhen,
two(-C) two-C two-C:needle
T-..two...two of them...two needles,

Y 260 shi bu shi a? Wo *$_{IV}$wangϕ.. $_{IV}$wanggeli[60].
be not be EXC I forget(-ASP) forget-ASP
right? I forget.. forgot.

Y 261 E: Ou, wangle, huh.
EXC forget-ASP Q
Oh, you forgot.

Y 262 S: Ei.
AFF
Uh-huh.

Y 263 E: Na ni weishenmo lai yiyuan?
then you why come hospital
Now, why did you come to the hospital?

Y 264 S: *Wo dong, lao* $_{I}$*xiansheng lai qian*
I understand old man come before
I understand, before the old man came,

Y 265 *gen wo* ∇*wei jiao feng ei*∇ *[*$_{I}$*yīzhēn]*[61]...
with I ??? opinion
with me ??? obinion,

Y 266 $_{III}$*neige* $_{II}$*yisheng de [*$_{I}$*yìzhèn]...*
that-C doctor MOD opinion
that doctor's obinion...

Y 267 E: Ou, yisheng, huh.
EXC doctor AFF
Oh, the doctor, eh?

---

[60] Double particle indicating finality in Sichuan Mandarin.
[61] For *yìjiàn*.

Y 268 S: ...diǎn [tián]... $_{III}$neige diǎn zhēn...
drop medicine that-C drop medicine
...medicine plops...those medicine drops...

Y 269 dian.. gei $_{IV}$women chi.
drop give I-PL eat
drops given us to take.

Y 270 E: Ou.
AFF
Oh.

Y 271 S: Ou, ∇yū∇ $_{III}$nemmo.. ∇sǒu zhēng∇ a,
EXC ??? then ??? EXC
Oh, ??? then.. ???,

Y 272 da zhen a, bá ya... dou
inject needle EXC pull EXC all
giving shots, pulling it out, they did

Y 273 $_{IV}$gǎole$_{v}$ $_{III}$naxie $_{I}$dongxi.
do-ASP this-PL thing
all those things.

Y 274 E: Ou, zhei yangzi.
AFF this way
Oh, is that right.

Y 275 S: ∇Lǎo shēng, lǎo shēng∇. Ta you ∇yān shēng∇.
old sound old sound he have smoke sound
Old noises, old noises. He has smoke noises.

Y 276 E: A.
AFF
Oh.

Y 277 S: Ei.
AFF
Uh-huh.

Y 278 E: Na, ni yiqian zuo shenmo shi?
then you before do what matter
Now, what work did you do before?

Y 279	S:	Wo	dou	∇zī zī∇	na	∇shǎo gēn∇	a.	
		I	all	???	that	few root	EXC	
		I always ??? those few roots.						

Y 280	Bang..	∇shǎo zhōu∇.	∇Diào lǒng bāt∇[62]	$_{III}$liangzhi..	
	help	few state	fall hold ???	two-C	
	Helping.. few states. Fall hold ??? two..				

Y 281	$_{III}$liangzhi	$_{IV}$dăle$_v$.	Ou,	dǎ	$_{III}$yici
	two-C	inject-ASP	AFF	inject	1-C:time
	two shots. Oh, gave me one shot,				

Y 282	ou,	∇$_{IV}$kāikāi∇.	Au!	Ooh!
	EXC	open-open	EXC	EXC
	oh, open it up. Ow! Ooh!			

Y 283	E:	Hen	tong,	shi bu shi?
		very	hurt	be not be
		It hurt a lot, didn't it?		

Y 284	S:	Ou,	zai	$_{III}$diyici.	Zai	⋈kān⋈.
		EXC	again	ORD-1-C:time	again	watch
		Oh, did it once first time. Watch again.				

Y 285	⋈*$_{IV}$Kăn⋈[63]le$_v$	$_{III}$yici.	You.	Ta	$_{III}$zheli..	$_{III}$zheli
	chop-ASP	1-C:time	have	he	here	here
	Chopped once. Yes. He here.. here					

Y 286	⋈gài⋈	$_{III}$yici	∇diān∇	diǎn	diǎn	zhēn.
	build	1-C:time	crazy	drop	drop	medicine
	built crazy dropping medicine drops.					

Y 287	E:	Uh-huh.
		AFF
		Uh-huh.

Y 288	S:	Dou	shi	zhei	$_{II}$yangzi.	Dou	hao.
		all	be	this	way	all	good
		It was all this way. All good.					

[62] The syllable *bāt* in this neologistic sequence violates the phonotactic rules of Mandarin syllable structure, since non-nasal stops are not allowed in syllable-final position.

[63] This instance of jargon is phonologically perseverative, following the pronunciation of the previous word.

Y 289 E: Hao. Wo xianzai gei ni kan yige tupian.
good I now give you see 1-C picture
Good. Now I'll give you a picture to look at.

Y 290 S: Wo dou shi bu $_{III}$duizhun lei.
I all be not focus EXC
I can't focus at all.

Y 291 E: Na ni jiu kanyikan jiu keyi, a.
then you then look-1-look then can EXC
Then just take a look and that's OK.

Y 292 S: Ye shi $_{III}$yige.. $_{III}$yige *$_{II}$[zhǔ]ϕ..
also be 1-C 1-C bamboo(-stool)
It's also a.. a bim..

Y 293 *$_{II}$[zhǔ]ϕ.. *$_{II}$[zhǔdēng][64]. $_{III}$Zheli $_{II}$fangshangqu
bamboo(-stool) bamboo-stool here put-on-go
bim.. bimboo stole. Here putting something up,

Y 294 $_{III}$zheli $_{III}$tūokǔa, $_{I}$meiyou ∇*$_{IV}$cāng∇hao[65].
here fall not-have ???-well
here falling, he hasn't ??? well.

Y 295 E: A.
AFF
Oh.

Y 296 S: Dui bu dui?
right not right
Right?

Y 297 E: Ei.
AFF
Uh-huh.

Y 298 S: Zhe kan. $_{III}$Yinggai dou $_{IV}$huǎi[66]le$_{v}$ ma.
this look should all bad-ASP EXC
Look here. Everything's going wrong.

[63] For *zhúdèng*.
[65] This is another example of an inflected neologism.

Y 299	E:	A.					
		AFF					
		Ah.					
Y 300	S:	Ba	$_{III}$zheige	ren	dou	$_{II,IV}$huáqule$_{v}$.	
		OBJ	this-C	person	all	slip-go-ASP	
		She made this person slip down.					
Y 301	E:	Ou.					
		AFF					
		Oh.					
Y 302	S:	Zhe	dou	$_{II,IV}$huáxialaile$_{v}$,	dui bu dui?		
		this	all	slip-down-come-ASP	right not right		
		Here he's slipping down, right?					
Y 303	E:	Ei.					
		AFF					
		Uh-huh.					
Y 304	S:	Na,	$_{III}$neige	[dēng]			
		then	that-C	stool			
		Then, that stole					
Y 305	E:	Uh-huh...					
		AFF					
		Uh-huh.					
Y 306	S:	Shi bu shi	a?				
		be not be	Q				
		Right?					
Y 307	E:	Dui.					
		right					
		Right.					
Y 308	S:	$_{III}$Neige	$_{I}$dongxi	hui...			
		that-C	thing	can			
		That thing will...					
Y 309	E:	Hai	you	ne?			
		still	have	Q			
		What else?					

[66] Dialectal pronunciation of *huài* 'bad'.

Y 310 S: Ei.
AFF
Uh-huh.

Y 311 E: Hai you ne?
still have Q
What else?

Y 312 S: $_{III}$Neige hai you $_{III}$yige $_{II}$xiaojie.
that-C also have one-C girl.
There's also a girl.

Y 313 E: A.
AFF
Ah.

Y 314 S: $_{II}$Xiaojie zai $_{III}$zheli *$_{IV}$[fū][67]zhōng[68] ta.
girl at here support-ASP him
The girl is here sapporting him.

Y 315 E: Mm.
AFF
Mm-hm.

Y 316 S: Jiào tā bú yào <bǎng>[69].
make him not want tie:up
To keep him from getting tied up.

Y 317 E: A.
AFF
Uh-huh.

Y 318 S: Ta $_{III}$neige ren.
he that-C person
That person.

Y 319 E: Ni jiangde hen hao.
you talk-adv very good
You speak very well.

---

[67] For *fú*.

[68] According to my informant, *zhōng* is a dialectal variant of the progressive aspect marker *zhe*.

[69] The target word here is probably something like *shuāi* 'fall'.

Y 320 S: Ha ha ha ha.
(laughs)
Ha ha ha ha.

Y 321 E: Zheli ne? Zheige ne?
here Q this-C Q
And here? What about this?

Y 322 S: $_{III}$Neige shi ∇sān dēng∇ ma.
that-C be three light EXC
That's three light.

Y 323 E: A, gan ma?
AFF do what
Oh, what's it for?

Y 324 S: ∇Sān dēng∇ de..de..de...de $_{III}$zheige ma.
three light MOD this-C EXC
The three-lighted... this.

Y 325 E: Ei.
AFF
Oh.

Y 326 S: ∇Yīn nǐ tē dǐ∇
sound you ??? low
Sound you ??? low.

Y 327 E: Uh-huh. Hao. Na zai zhei bian ne? Zhei
AFF good then at this side Q this
Uh-huh. Good. What about over here? Over here

Y 328 bian you shenmo shiqing?
side have what matter
what's going on?

Y 329 S: $_{III}$Zheige. $_{III}$Neige $_{III}$zheige $_{II}$xiaojie.
this-C that-C this-C girl
This. That's this girl.

Y 330 E: Uh-huh.
AFF
Uh-huh.

Y 331 S: E, hen hao la.
HES very good EXC
Ah, very good.

Y 332 E: Ta zai gan ma?
she at do what
What's she doing?

Y 333 S: Ta zai $_{IV}$duānzhe.. ta zai
she at serve-ASP she at
She's serving.. she's

Y 334 $_{IV}$duānzhede hen hao.
serve-ASP-ADV very good
serving very well.

Y 335 E: Uh-huh. Ta zai zuo shenmo?
AFF she at do what
Uh-huh. What's she doing?

Y 336 S: Ei. Zùo... ∇zhì... chuáng sì∇...
AFF do cure bed four
Eh. Doing... cure... bed four.

Y 337 E: Mm-hm.
AFF
Mm-hm.

Y 338 S: ∇Dì∇ hao.. h-..hao. ∇Dì∇ hao.
floor good good floor good
Floor good..good. Floor good.

Y 339 E: Ta zuo shenmo?
she do what
What's she doing?

Y 340 S: Ei. $_{I}$Bijiao hao.
AFF compare good
Uh-huh. Quite good.

Y 341 E: Ta zuo shenmo?
she do what
What's she doing?

Y 342	S:	Ei.	$_{IV}$Zuode	hen	hao	a.		
		AFF	do-ADV	very	good	EXC		
		Uh-huh. She's doing it very well.						
Y 343	E:	Zuode	hen	hao.				
		do-ADV	very	good				
		She's doing it very well.						
Y 344	S:	Ei.						
		AFF						
		Uh-huh.						
Y 345	E:	Zheige	ne?	Zheli.				
		this-C	Q	here				
		What about this? Over here.						
Y 346	S:	$_{III}$Zhexie	$_{I}$dongxi,	ou.	$_{III}$Zheige			
		this-C:PL	thing	EXC	this-C			
		These things, uh. This						
Y 347	[du]	[be]	*$_{III}$dùi[jǐ]	le,.				
	all	not	focus	ASP				
	I capt focooz at oll.							
Y 348	E:	Uh.						
		AFF						
		Oh.						
Y 349	S:	Wo	$_{III}$zhende	$_{II}$kanbudao	lei.			
		I	real-MOD	see-not-arrive	EXC			
		I really can't see it.						
Y 350	E:	Ou	kanbudao.	Yanjing	bu	hao,	shi bu shi?	
		AFF	see-not-arrive	eye	not	good	be not be	
		Oh you can't see it. Your eyes are bad, right?						
Y 351	S:	Mm.	$_{IV}$Laole$_v$	ma.	$_{II}$Naozi	ye...	Ei,	
		AFF	old-ASP	EXC	brain-NOM	also	EXC	
		Mm. I'm old. Also my mind... Hey,						
Y 352	ni	kan,	dou	bai	∇yè∇	le,.		
	you	look	all	white	page	ASP		
	look, it's all white page.							

Y 353 E: Ou, hui se de.
EXC gray color MOD
Oh, grey-colored.

Y 354 S: Dou bai le$_s$, dou $_{II}$kanbudao le$_s$.
all white ASP all see-not-arrive ASP
It's all white and I can't see.

Y 355 E: Ou. Na ta gen tamen liangge
EXC then she with he-PL 2-C
Oh. Now what relation is there between

Y 356 you shenmo guanxi?
have what relation
her and these two?

Y 357 S: $_{III}$Zheige...
this-C
This...

Y 358 E: Uh-huh.
AFF
Uh-huh.

Y 359 S: $_{III}$Zheige [dā]-[70]...
this-C big
This one's pig...

Y 360 E: Ta gen tamen you shenmo guanxi?
he with he-PL have what relation
What does she have to do with them?

Y 361 S: $_{III}$Zheige shi [duǎi].. $_{III}$neige xiao de.
this-C be big that-C small MOD
This one's pik.. that one's small.

Y 362 E: Uh-huh. Dui.
AFF right
Uh-huh. Right.

[70] For *dà*.

Y 363 S: $_{III}$Liangge $_{I}$yiqi.
two-C together
They're both together.

Y 364 E: Dui.
right
Right.

Y 365 S: Dui ba?
right Q
Right?

Y 366 E: Dui.
right
Right.

Y 367 S: $_{III}$Neige lao de la. $_{III}$Neige [duài]...
that-C old MOD EXC that-C big
That one's old. That one's bik...

Y 368 $_{III}$neige.. $_{III}$neige dà de, $_{III}$neige xiao de.
that-C that-C big MOD that-C small MOD
that.. that's a big one, that's a small one.

Y 369 E: Uh-huh.
AFF
Uh-huh.

Y 370 S: $_{III}$Neige $_{I}$bijiao hao le.
that-C compare good ASP
That one's better.

Y 371 E: Dui. Hao. Hai you meiyou?
right good still have not-have
Right. Good. Is there anything else?

Y 372 S: Ei. Bu $_{I}$youde $_{II}$shihou.. bu $_{I}$youde..
AFF not some time not some
Eh. But sometimes.. but some..

Y 373 hen.. hen shao bu $_{III}$rongyi zuo la.
very very few not easy do EXC
are very.. very few are not easy to do.

Y 374	E:	Ou	dui.
		EXC	right
		Oh, right.	

Y 375	S:	Mei	$_{II}$banfa	le,.
		no	way	ASP
		There's no way.		

Y 376	E:	Dui.
		right
		Right.

Y 377	S:	Ei	wo	de	$_{II}$yanjing	ye	$_{II}$kanbuqing.
		EXC	I	MOD	eye	also	see-not-clear
		Eh, my eyes also can't see clearly.					

Y 378	E:	Ou	zhei	yangzi.
		EXC	this	way
		Oh is that right.		

Y 379	S:	Ei!
		AFF
		Uh-huh!

Y 380	E:	Hao.
		good
		Ok.

Y 381	S:	$_{III}$Xiexie.
		thank
		Thanks.

Y 382	E:	Meiyou,	meiyou.	Wo	xianzai	you	shi,	ho.
		not-have	not-have	I	now	have	matter	EXC
		Not at all, not at all. I have something to do now.						

Y 383	S:	∇Yē nuǒ∇.	Wo	$_{II}$shetou	$_{IV}$mazhe...	$_{II}$yanjing
		coconut ???	I	tongue	numb-ASP	eye
		Coconut ??? . My tongue is numb... and my eyes				

Y 384	ye	$_{II}$kanbudao.	Na	$_{I}$dongxi	a,	ye	bu
	also	see-not-arrive	that	thing	EXC	also	not
	can't see. That thing, I also don't						

Y 385	dong.	$_{II}$Xiaohaizi	zhù	bu	jìn	ne.
	understand	child	live	not	close	ASP

understand. The kids don't live close by.

Y 386	E:	Ou.
		AFF

Oh.

Y 387	S:	Dou	bu	hui	⋈xiè⋈	ma.	Dou	bu
		all	not	able	diarrhea	EXC	all	not

I can't have the runs. I can't

Y 388	neng	∇yè∇,	∇*$_{II}$yě∇bùqǐlái[71]	a.
	able	page	wild-not-rise-come	EMP

have pages. I can't get wild.

Y 389	E:	Ou.
		AFF

Oh.

Y 390	S:	$_{III}$Yige	$_{I}$dongxi	$_{II}$chulai	⊗$_{I}$dongxi⊗	dou	bu
		one-C	thing	out-come	thing	all	not

Something comes out something and you don't even

Y 391	$_{III}$xiaode.	$_{IV}$Women	$_{II}$xiaohaizi	de	$_{II}$shihou	cong...
	know	I-PL	child	MOD	time	from

know. When we were kids from...

Y 392	$_{II}$waiguo	a...	$_{I}$shenmo...	ren	lai..
	abroad	EXC	what	person	come

abroad... the things that some... person came..

Y 393	lai	zuo	de	$_{II}$shiqing	a.
	come	do	MOD	thing	EXC

came to do.

Y 394	$_{IV}$Women	⊗dou⊗	jiang	dou	bu	hui	jiang.
	I-PL	all	speak	all	not	able	speak

As for all talking, we couldn't even talk at all.

---

[71] This is another example of an affix occurring on a neologistic form.

Y 395 E: Ou, na xianzai ne?
AFF then now Q
Oh, what about now?

Y 396 S: Dou bu gan jiang. Bu hui ma.
all not dare talk not able EXC
I don't dare talk at all. I can't.

Y 397 Bu hui jiang ma. Cong $_{II}$xiaohaizi de
not able talk EXC from child MOD
I can't talk. From the time I was

Y 398 $_{II}$shihou ▽lū▽.. $_{IV}$laole, dou bu $_{III}$jide ma.
time ??? old-ASP all not remember EXC
a child ???.. I'm now old, I don't remember.

Y 399 E: Ou zhe shi xiaohaizi de shihou.
EXC this be child MOD time
Oh, this is when you were a child.

Y 400 S: Dou bu hui zùo ma. [*$_{II}$Zǔo]buqilai. *Z-..zùo*
all not able do EXC do-not-rise-come do
I can't do anything. I can't poo it. D..do

Y 401 ⋈$_{II}$*lǎojiàn*⋈[72]. *Na* $_{I}$*xianzai...* *dà* *èr* $_{III}$*neige*
callous that now big two that-C
callouses. Now, big two that

Y 402 ⋈*pái jiàn*⋈.. $_{II}$*baba..* $_{II}$*mama* $_{III}$*naxie..* *zhe*
align sword dad mom that-C:PL this
line up a sword.. daddy.. mommy those.. this

Y 403 *shi* $_{III}$*keyi* $_{III}$*jide,* $_{IV}$*laole,* $_{III}$*keyi* *ji.* *Tai*
be can remember old-ASP can recall too
I can remember, when old, you can remember. Too

Y 404 *duo* $_{III}$*keneng* *ye* $_{IV}$*nongde* *dou* *bu* ▽*qù*▽.
much maybe also do-ADV all not go
much maybe it's also can't go it.

[72] Sichuan Mandarin pronunciation of the word 'callous'.

Y 405 E: Ou.
AFF
Oh.

Y 406 S: Dou hui $_{II}$wangdiao le$_{s}$.
all can forget-away ASP
I forget it all.

Y 407 E: Jiu shi xiaohaizi de shihou naxie
just be child MOD time that-C:PL
You mean you forgot all those

Y 408 shiqing dou wangdiaole.
matter all forget-away-ASP
things about when you were a child.

Y 409 S: Dou $_{II,IV}$wangdiaole$_{v}$. Ei dou $_{II,IV}$wangdiaole$_{v}$.
all forget-away-ASP AFF all forget-away-ASP
I forgot them all. Uh-huh, I forgot them all.

Y 410 E: A.
AFF
Ah.

Y 411 S: Wo bu $_{III}$zhidao lao le$_{s}$. Dou lao le$_{s}$. Ni
I not know old ASP all old ASP you
I don't know old. I'm all old.

Y 412 kan. $_{II}$Yanjing dou *$_{II}$kan-ϕ..
look eye all see(-not-arrive)
Look. My eyes can't see..

Y 413 $_{II}$kanbudao le. Dou ∇yī dǐng∇ ei.
see-not-arrive ASP all clothes top EXC
see anything. The top of clothes, uh.

Y 414 *$_{II}$Kan-ϕ ei $_{II}$kanbudao le$_{s}$.
see(-not-arrive) HES see-not-arrive ASP
I can..can't s-.. see.

Y 415 E: Ou. Ni xianzai ji sui?
AFF you now how:many year
Oh. How old are you now?

Y 416	S:	Wo..wo	$_{I}$yijing..	$_{II}$liushi-...	$_{II}$liushier..	$_{II}$ershi
		I	already	sixty-	62	20
		I..I'm already.. sixty-... sixty-two.. twent-..				

Y 417	duo	le$_{,}$.	Wo	$_{I}$yijing...	ni	kan...	na	dou..
	more	ASP	I	already	you	look	that	all
	more than twenty. I'm already... look... that's all..							

Y 418	na..na	dou	hei	le$_{,}$,	ni	kan.
	that	all	dark	ASP	you	look
	that.. that's all dark, look.					

Y 419	Na	$_{II}$yanjing	a,	lai	dian	yan	de	$_{II}$shihou
	that	eye	EXC	come	light	smoke	MOD	time
	And my eyes, when I go to light a cigarette,							

Y 420	a,	ni	kan..	ni	kan...	$_{II}$Nongbuqilai.
	EXC	you	look	you	look	do-not-rise-come
	look.. look... I can't do it.					

Y 421	E:	A.	Xiaohaizi	bu	yiyang.
		AFF	child	not	same
		Oh, not the same as a child.			

Y 422	S:	Aiya,	⊗bu⊗	$_{II}$kanbuqilai	le$_{,}$.
		EXC	not	see-not-up-come	ASP
		Darn, I can't not see.			

Y 423	Dou	$_{II}$kanbudao	le$_{,}$.	Dou	$_{II}$jibude	le$_{,}$.
	all	see-not-arrive	ASP	all	recall-not-attain	ASP
	I can't see anything. I can't remember anything.					

Y 424	YE	DOU	$_{II}$XIAOHAIZI[73]...	Ou4	$_{II}$xiaohaizi,	ni
	also	all	child	EXC	child	you
	The also children all... Oh, the children,					

Y 425	kan	mm	$_{IV}$diǎndiān	dà.	$_{III}$Nemmo..	$_{III}$nemmo
	look	HES	little-little	big	so	so
	look um, little too big. That.. that					

[73] The order should be *xiaohaizi ye dou.*

Y 426 $_{IV}$diǎndiān dà. $_{I}$Haishi [*$_{III}$chǎngde][74] le,.
little-little big or long-MOD ASP
a little too big. It's still rong.

Y 427 Ni jiang $_{II}$baba! Ni xing $_{I}$shenmo?
you talk father you name what
You say, 'Daddy! What's your name?'

Y 428 Ta jiu dǒng. $_{III}$Neige zǒng bu hui
he then understand that-C always not able
Then he understands. That, I can never

Y 429 jiang a. Wo shi $_{III}$zheige $_{II}$xiaohaizi gen ni
talk EMP I be this-C child with you
say. I'm always this kid

Y 430 jiang, ei. Wo dao $_{I}$zuihou dou bu $_{III}$zhidao.
talk EXC I arrive most-end all not know
talking with you. In the end, I know nothing.

Y 431 E: Ou. Ni you meiyou xiaohaizi?
EXC you have not-have child
Oh. Do you have any children?

Y 432 S: $_{II}$Xiaohai. $_{II}$Xiaohai $_{I}$xianzai wu..wu sui a.
child child now 5 year EXC
Children. My child is five.. five years old now.

Y 433 E: Wu sui.
5 year
Five years old.

Y 434 S: Ei. $_{II}$Nuhaizi.
AFF female-child
Uh-huh. A girl.

Y 435 E: Ou, ta wu sui.
EXC she 5 year
Oh, she's five years old.

---

[74] For *chángde*.

Y 436 S: A wu a wu..wu [hùi]. Wo $_{III}$neige $_{II}$shihou
AFF 5 EXC 5 year I that time
Uh, five uh, five..five.. cheers old. At that time I

Y 437 lè shi a. Où! ∇Zā∇. Où! $_{II}$Xiaohai!
happy affair EXC EXC bind EXC child
was happy. Oh! Tied. Oh! Children!

Y 438 Ta ye $_{III}$xiaode $_{II}$baba lai le,. Dou
he also know father come ASP all
They also know Daddy's coming. They all

Y 439 [zhī] yong wo ⋈zhǐ⋈ de.. $_{III}$zhī-bu-zhīdao $_{I}$shenmo
only use I point MOD know-not-know what
unly use me to point.. whether they know anything or not

Y 440 $_{I}$dongxi wo ye bu $_{III}$zhidao.
thing I also not know
I don't know at all.

Y 441 E: Ou!
EXC
Oh!

Y 442 S: Na $_{II}$xiaohair, dou $_{III}$xiaode a. Dang
that child all know EXC be
The kids all know. Those who

Y 443 $_{II}$baba de.. $_{II}$baba de $_{II}$haizi lai le,.
father MOD father MOD child come ASP
are fathers... father's children come.

Y 444 $_{II}$Xiaohaizi lai le,, $_{II}$xiaohaizi lai le,,
child come ASP child come ASP
Children are coming, children are coming, they

Y 445 dou..dou $_{III}$xiaode.
all know
all know.

Y 446 E: Ou.
AFF
Oh.

Y 447 S: $_{I}$Xianzai $_{I}$MASHANG YAO... $_{I}$MASHANG YAO... YAO
now immediate want immediate want want
Now we're about to... about to... to

Y 448 $_{IV}$WOMEN[75] $_{II}$huiqu le$_{s}$. Dou shi... $_{III}$neige
I-PL return-go ASP all be that-C
we're going back. It's all... that

Y 449 *$_{I}$shen- ∇tǎngbúlīn∇ a, $_{II}$huilai.
what ??? EXC return-come
whatev- ??? come back from.

Y 450 Ei, $_{II}$xiaohaizi $_{II}$huilai le$_{s}$.
AFF child return-come ASP
Ah, the kids have returned.

Y 451 E: Mm.
AFF
Mm.

Y 452 S: Ou, ∇già∇[76], $_{II}$baba $_{II}$huilai le$_{s}$. A,
EXC ??? father return-come ASP EXC
Oh, ???, Daddy's come back. Ah,

Y 453 $_{III}$nǎyí ∇qìu∇. Wo $_{II}$xiaohaizi $_{II}$huilai le$_{s}$.
which-one ??? I child return-come ASP
which one ???. My child has returned.

Y 454 E: Ta hui gaoxing.
she can happy
She'll be happy.

Y 455 S: Dui, a! Jiu zhei $_{II}$yangzi. ∇Ha hi ha∇.
right EXC just this way ???
Right! That's the way it is. ??? .

Y 456 E: Ta ye hui gaoxing ma.
she also can happy EXC
She'll be happy, too.

---

[75] The order should be *...women mashang yao....*

[76] This syllable is phonotactically impermissible in Mandarin, since the high front vowel [i] cannot be preceded by a velar consonant.

Y 457 S: ∇Ha ha∇. Wo dou bu hui a. Aiya,
??? . I all not able EXC. EXC
??? . I can't do anything. Darn,

Y 458 WO DUI $_{II}$XIAOHAIZI DOU BU NENG[77] jiang a.
I to child all not able speak EMP
I can't even to children talk.

Y 459 E: Yinggai zai yiqi.
should at together
You should be together.

Y 460 S: $_{I}$Xianzai $_{II}$xiaohair, a. ∇Tóng∇ na $_{I}$shenmo...
now child EXC with that what
Now the child. With that whatever...

Y 461 ∇$_{II}$gūozhēn∇ a, na $_{I}$shenmo. $_{III}$Neiju
pot-needle EXC that what that-C:sentence
pot needle, that whatever. That sentence

Y 462 hua jiao tai duo le$_{,}$, wo
speech said too much ASP I
was said too much, I

Y 463 dou mei $_{II}$banfa le$_{,}$.
all no way ASP
had no way.

Y 464 E: Ou.
AFF
Oh.

Y 465 S: Tai duo le$_{,}$.
too much ASP
Too much.

Y 466 E: Mm. Ta wu sui, shi bu shi?
AFF he 5 year be not be
Mm. She's five, right?

[77] The order should be *Wo dou bu neng dui xiaohaizi jiang.*

Y 467 S: Mm. Wo de *$_{II}$tai-ϕ...(coughs).
AFF I MOD wife(-wife)
Mm. My wi-...(coughs).

Y 468 Ai. Wan le$_s$. Ou!
EXC finish ASP EXC
Uh. We're finished. Oh!

Y 469 E: Dagai meiyou biede shiqing.
probably not-have other matter
There's probably nothing else.

Y 470 S: Mm, [*$_{II}$zuǒ]buqǐlái, tai duo le$_s$, mei $_{II}$banfa.
AFF do-not-rise-come too much ASP no way
Mm, I can't stew it, it's too much, no way.

Y 471 E: Wo tai mafan ni, bizhe ni zuo shiqing.
I too trouble you force-ASP you do thing
I've troubled you too much, making you do things.

Y 472 S: $_{I}$Youde $_{II}$shihou wo tai bu hui jiang
some time I too not able talk
Sometimes I really can't talk at all,

Y 473 a, $_{I}$meiyou $_{II}$banfa.
EXC not-have way
there's no way.

Y 474 E: Ni hui jiang, zhi shi tai lei
you can talk only be too tired
You can talk, it's just you're too tired,

Y 475 eryi. You shihou hui wangdiao.
only have time can forget-away
that's all. Sometimes you forget.

Y 476 S: *$_{II}$Laoϕ.. $_{II}$laoshi yao lai, wo
teach(-er) teacher want come I
When the therapist comes, I

Y 477 dou mei $_{II}$banfa. $_{I}$Youde dou bu hui
all no way some all not able
can't do it at all. Some things I can't

Y 478 jiang, ⋈$_{II}$nòngbùqǐlái nòng⋈[78].
speak do-not-up-come do
say at all, I can't do it up to do it.

Y 479 E: Qishi, ni hui jiang, you shihou...
actually you can talk have time
Actually, you can talk, but sometimes...

Y 480 S: A, dou shi $_{II}$nòngbùqǐlái ma, bu xing.
EXC all be do-not-rise-come EXC not good
Ah, I just can't do it, it's no good.

.... end ....

[78] The Mandarin grammatical structure *VERB$_1$ buqilai VERB$_2$* means 'to be unable to VERB$_1$ in order to VERB$_2$'. The subject not only improperly uses the same verb in both the VERB$_1$ and VERB$_2$ slots, the verb he uses is one of the most semantically empty verb in Mandarin, *nong* 'make or do'.

A.4 Interlinear Translation of Zheng Youjuan

Z 1	E:	Qingwen	ni	gui	xing?	Ni	xing	shenmo?
		please-ask	you	dear	surname	you	surname	what
		May I ask, what is your name? What's your name?						

Z 2	S:	Xing	Zheng.
		surname	Zheng
		My name's Zheng	

Z 3	E:	Zheng...	wo	yinggai	zenmo	chenghu?
		(name)	I	should	how	call
		Zheng...how should I address you?				

Z 4	E2:	Zheng...Zheng	da	niang.
		(name)	big	lady
		Zheng... Mrs.Zheng.		

Z 5	S:	Jiao	wo	$_{II}$mingzi.
		call	I	name
		Call me by my first name.		

Z 6	E:	Jiao	shenmo	mingzi?
		call	what	name
		What's your name?		

Z 7	S:	Zheng	Youjuan.
		Zheng	Youjuan
		Zheng Youjuan.	

Z 8	E:	Zheng	Youjuan.	Ni	renshi bu renshi	wo?
		name	name	you	know not know	me
		Zheng Youjuan. Do you know me?				

Z 9	S:	*$_{III}$Shangϕ..	$_{III}$shangci	bu	jian..
		top(-C:time)	top-C:time	not	see
		Last..last time didn't we meet..			

Z 10	jian	$_{III}$yihui	a?
	see	one-C:time	EXC
	meet once?		

Z 11 E: Ni jianguo wo, shi bu shi?
you see-ASP me be not be
You've met me before, right?

Z 12 S: A.
AFF
Mm-hm.

Z 13 E: Na, jitian yiqian?
then many:Q-C:day before
Then, how many days ago?

Z 14 S: Na wo jiu bu [*$_{III}$yì]-ϕ[79] le$_s$.
that I just not remember(-attain) ASP
That I just don't lememb- .

Z 15 E: A, na shi liang tian yiqian de shiqing.
EXC that be 2 day before MOD matter
That was two days ago.

Z 16 S: Liang tian $_{I}$yiqian.
two day before
Two days ago.

Z 17 E: Liang tian yiqian. Ni xianzai you
2 day before you now have
Two days ago. Do you now

Z 18 meiyou juede bi neige shihou hao?
not-have feel compare that-C time good
feel better now than you did then?

Z 19 S: Zhe shi bu $_{IV}$haoshuo. Wo...
this matter not good-speak I
It's hard to say about that. I...

Z 20 E: Ou.
EXC
Oh

[79] For *jìdé*.

Z 21	S:	Yi	shuo	hua	a...	
		one	speak	talk	EXC	
		As soon as I talk...				

Z 22	E:	Hm.
		AFF
		Oh.

Z 23	S:	...jiu	$_{III}$nenggou...
		then	able
		...then it might be...	

Z 24	E:	Hm.
		AFF
		Oh.

Z 25	S:	...bu	dui.
		not	right
		...wrong.	

Z 26	E:	Ou.	Nayi	fangmian	bu	dui?
		AFF	which-1	aspect	not	right
		Oh. Which part's wrong?				

Z 27	S:	$_{I}$Yihuer	$_{I}$huoyǒuxǔ[80].. $_{I}$yǒuxǔ		dui	le$_{,}$.
		awhile	perhaps		right	ASP
		For awhile, maybe.. maybe it's right.				

Z 28	E:	Uh-huh.
		AFF
		Uh-huh.

Z 29	S:	∇Chéng $_{II}$aìreń∇.
		become spouse
		Become a spouse.

Z 30	E:	Zhe	you	yidiar...
		this	have	one-C:bit
		This is a little...		

---

[80] Both *hùoyǒuxǔ* and the following *yǒuxǔ* are Peking Mandarin dialectal equivalents for *yěxǔ* 'perhaps'.

Z 31 S: Zhe h-..hua, $_{II}$shuochulai ⊗zhe hua⊗[81] dui.
this talk speak-out-come this talk right
These words, they're coming out these words right.

Z 32 E: Uh.
AFF
Uh.

Z 33 S: Quan dui.
complete right
Completely right.

Z 34 E: Quan dui.
complete right
Completely right.

Z 35 S: A. Her[82] zai shuo $_{I}$huoyouxu bu dui la.
AFF but then speak perhaps not right EXC
Uh-huh. But when I say something else, maybe it's wrong.

Z 36 E: Youxie bu dui. Na shenmo
have-C:PL not right then what
Some is wrong. Now, what

Z 37 difang bu dui ne?
place not right Q
part's wrong?

Z 38 S: Jiu bu $_{III}$zhidao ne. Wo jiu bu $_{III}$zhidao.
just not know ASP I just not know
I just don't know. I just don't know.

Z 39 Wo jiu *$_{II}$shuobu-ϕ-lai... $_{II}$shuobuchulai.
I just speak-not(-out-)come speak-not-out-come
I just can't say out... say it out.

Z 40 E: Zhe yangzi. Na wo tingde
this way then I hear-ADV
Is that right. Well, it sounds

[81] The topic of the sentence, *zhe hua*, cannot occur in both places.
[82] This is a Peking Mandarin dialectal form of *keshi* 'but'.

Z 41 hen dui. Hen zhengque.
very right very correct
right to me. Very correct.

Z 42 S: Ni $_{IV}$tīngde t-..tǐng dui.
you hear-ADV very right
You hear really well.

Z 43 E: Ou.
AFF
Oh.

Z 44 S: Na ker[83] YÒU WO[84] ya, yao shuo
then but again I EXC want speak
But if again I, want to talk,

Z 45 ya, jiu bu $_{III}$zhidao le,.
EXC just not know ASP
then I just don't know.

Z 46 E: Ou zhe yangzi. Xinli zuoyong.
EXC this way heart-in effect
Oh is that right. It's in your mind.

Z 47 S: Wo jiu bu [*$_{III}$zhào][85] le,.
I just not know ASP
I just don't noo-oh.

Z 48 E: Na wo kanbuchulai keneng
then I see-not-out-come maybe
Well, if I can't see it maybe

Z 49 shi ni xinli de.
be you heart-in MOD
it's in your mind.

---

[83] This is another Peking Mandarin dialectal form of *keshi* 'but'.

[84] The order should be *...wo you...* .

[85] The word for 'know' in Mandarin is *zhīdào*. In producing the form *zhào*, the subject merged the two syllables of the target word, combining the initial of the first syllable with the final and tone of the second syllable.

Z 50 S: Ei... ei, ei ei dui le. Ni shuo de hua..
AFF right ASP you speak MOD talk
Uh-huh, uh-huh, uh-huh, uh-huh, right. What you say..

Z 51 wo shuo de hua.. wo shuo de hua
I speak MOD talk I speak MOD talk
what I say.. when I say

Z 52 $_{IV}$duozhe ne, $_{III}$haoxie.. $_{III}$haoxiege bu dui.
much-ASP ASP much much-C not right
a lot, a good deal.. a good deal of it's wrong.

Z 53 E: Ou. Ni xiang shuo shenmo,
AFF you think say what
Oh. You want to say something,

Z 54 shuobuchulai, shi bu shi?
speak-not-out-come be not be
and you can't say it, right?

Z 55 S: A dui le,.
EXC right ASP
Mm right.

Z 56 E: Na jiaru fasheng nenmo yige shiqing, jiu
then suppose happen that 1-C matter then
When that happens, that is,

Z 57 shuo hua, shuobuchulai, haishi jinliang shuo.
speak talk speak-not-out-come still utmost speak
wanting to talk but not getting it out, try hard to say it anyway.

Z 58 S: Dui, dui, dui
right right right
Right, right, right.

Z 59 E: Wo zhi shi baituo ni jinliang
I only be implore you utmost
I'm just asking you to do your best

Z 60 shuo, hao bu hao? Kan shuochulai shenmo hua...
talk good not good see speak-out-come what speech
to talk, ok? By seeing what you can say...

Z 61 S: $_{IV}$Shuobuliao a!
speak-not-able EXC
I can't talk!

Z 62 E2: Ta shuo dai huer a, ta
he say wait moment EXC he
He's saying that in a moment, he's going to

Z 63 gei ni jieshi jinliang rang ni...
give you explain utmost make you
explain something to you to get you to...

Z 64 S: Wo $_{III}$zhidao. Ta $_{IV}$shuole$_v$ ne dui.
I know he speak-ASP ASP right
I know. He said it right.

Z 65 Ta shuo de hua.. ta..t-..ta shuo
he speak MOD talk he speak
What he said.. he.. what h-.. he said

Z 66 de hua wo quan $_{IV}$dongle$_v$.
MOD talk I complete understand-ASP
I understood completely.

Z 67 E2: Ni dong a.
you understand AFF
You understand.

Z 68 S: Quan dong.
complete understand
I understand completely.

Z 69 E: Suoyi wo jiangde bu qingchu...
so I speak-ADV not clear
So if I speak unclearly...

Z 70 S: Quan dong. Bu, ni $_{IV}$shuode
complete understand no you speak-ADV
I understand completely. No, you speak

Z 71 hen $_{III}$qingchu de. Ting hao de.
very clear MOD very good MOD
very clearly. Very good.

Z 72 E: He yidian shui ma?
drink 1-C:bit water Q
Have a little water?

Z 73 S: Wo bu.. wo bu he shui.
I not I not drink water
I don't..I don't drink water.

Z 74 He shui bu xing. Zhe zui ya,
drink water not good this mouth EXC
Drinking water's not good. This mouth,

Z 75 shuo hua ya, lao shi a...
speak talk EXC always be EXC
when I talk, is always...

Z 76 *$_{I}$You-ϕ[86] shuo bu dui.
some(ϕ) speak not right
Some is incorrect.

Z 77 E: Ou. Ni shuo weishen-...
AFF you say why
Oh. Tell us why...

Z 78 S: Shuo bu.. wo shuo bu dui ne,
speak not I speak not right ASP
I speak in-..speak incorrectly,

Z 79 $_{I}$keshi wo mei $_{II}$shuochulai.
but I not speak-out-come
but I didn't get it out.

Z 80 E: Ou. Hai mei shuochulai, hai zai limian ne.
AFF still not speak-out-come still at inside ASP
Oh. You didn't say it out, it's still inside.

Z 81 S: Gēn[87] $_{II}$litou ne. Mei $_{II}$shuochulai.
at inside ASP not speak-out-come
Inside. I didn't say it out.

[86] This should be *youde* 'some'.
[87] *Gēn* is a colloquial Peking Mandarin dialectal form for *zai* 'at'.

Z 82 E: Ni xianzai duo da suishu?
you now many:Q big year-count
How old are you now?

Z 83 S: $_{II}$Liushisan.
63
Sixty-three.

Z 84 E: Liushisan sui.
63 years
Sixty-three years old.

Z 85 S: Ei, dui le$_s$.
AFF right ASP
Mm-hm, right.

Z 86 E: You jige xiaohar?
have many:Q-C child
How many kids do you have?

Z 87 E2: Shuo ba.
speak SUG
Say it.

Z 88 E: Zenmo shuo ne? Zhenmo duo[88], shi bu shi?
how say Q this much be not be
How do you say it? This many, right?

Z 89 S: *$_{III}$Jiuϕ.. $_{III}$jiuge.
nine(-C) nine-C
Ni-..nine.

Z 90 E: Jiuge xiaohar.
9-C child
Nine kids.

Z 91 S: Dui le$_s$! $_{II,IV}$Shuochulaile$_v$.
right ASP speak-out-come-ASP
Right! I got it out.

[88] Refers to the number of fingers being held up by the experimenter.

Z 92 E: Laotour ji sui?
husband many:Q year
How old's your husband?

Z 93 S: $_{II}$Laotour $_{II}$jinnian $_{II}$liushiqi.. bu shi!
husband this-year 67 not be
This year my husband's sixty-seven.. no!

Z 94 Aiya, $_{II}$liushi... $_{II}$liushisan.
EXC sixty- sixty-three
Oh my, sixty... sixty-three.

Z 95 E: Liushisan.
63
Sixty-three.

Z 96 S: Hm.
AFF
Uh-huh.

Z 97 E: Hao. Na ni jiali ne, qingkuang zenmoyang?
good then you home Q condition how-way
Ok. Now as for your home, what's the situation like?

Z 98 S: [Tū wū][89] ting hao la.
all very good EXC
Overy ting's very good.

Z 99 E: A, ting hao.
EXC very good
Ah, very good.

Z 100 S: [Tū] $_{IV}$haozhe ne.
all good-ASP ASP
Everyting's going well.

Z 101 E: Hen gaoxing, shi a?
very happy be Q
Very happy, right?

[89] The word for 'all' (*dōu*) is produced with a [t] instead of a [d]. The word is also split into two syllables, both of which carry the level tone over the syllable coda [ū]. The nuclear vowel [o] is omitted.

Z 102	S:	Mm.	Dou	hao.					
		AFF	all	good					
		Mm, everything's fine.							
Z 103	E:	Xianzai	you	jige	xiaohar	gen	ni	zhu?	
		now	have	many:Q-C	child	with	you	live	
		How many children do you have living with you now?							
Z 104	S:	Jiu	$_{III}$yige.						
		only	one-C						
		Only one.							
Z 105	E:	Yige.							
		1-C							
		One.							
Z 106	S:	Uh.							
		AFF							
		Mm.							
Z 107	E:	You	yige.	Ta	duo	da?			
		have	1-C	he	many:Q	big			
		You have one. How old is he?							
Z 108	S:	San..	$_{II}$jinnian	a...	$_{II}$sanshisan..				
		3-	this-year	EXC	33				
		Thir-..this year... thirty-three.							
Z 109	E:	Sanshi..	gen	wo	yiyang.				
		30	with	me	same				
		Thirty-.. the same as me.							
Z 110	S:	Dui,	dui,	dui,	dui,	dui,	dui.		
		right	right	right	right	right	right		
		Right, right, right, right, right, right.							
Z 111	E:	Ta	shi	nande	haishi	nude?			
		he	be	male-MOD	or	female-MOD			
		Is it a boy or a girl?							
Z 112	S:	$_{II}$Nanhair.							
		male-child							
		A boy.							

Z 113 E: Nanhair, a. Hao.
male-child EXC good
A boy. Good.

Z 114 S: You $_{III}$yige $_{II}$xiaohaizi a, you $_{III}$yige
have one-C child EXC have one-C
There's a child, and a

Z 115 $_{II}$erxifer, zai wo ϕ.
son-wife at I (home)
daughter-in-law at my.

Z 116 E: Sunzi, ne?
grandson Q
What about grandsons?

Z 117 S: $_{I}$Yilāzi[90] zai $_{II}$waibiar ne.
altogether at outside ASP
All on the outside.

Z 118 E: A, zai waibiar. Neng bu neng bang wo
AFF at outside can not can help me
Ah, outside. Can you

Z 119 shuoming yixia ni nage bingli? Jiu shi
explain 1-time you that-C sick-history just be
explain for me a little about your case? That is

Z 120 shuo ni neitian shengbing de shihou
say you that-day produce-sick MOD time
to say, what happened the day

Z 121 fasheng shenmo shiqing?
happen what matter
you got sick?

Z 122 S: Mei... ei?
not Q
Not... huh?

---

[90] Colloquial Pekingese for 'altogether'.

Z 123 E: Fa bing yiqian fasheng shenmo shi?
start sick before happen what matter
What happened before you got sick?

Z 124 S: Aiya!
EXC
Oh my!

Z 125 E: Ni jibuqingchu ye wusuowei.
you recall-not-clear also not:matter
If you don't remember clearly, that's ok.

Z 126 E2: Ni dei jiangjiang ni de
you must talk-talk you MOD
You should talk a little about your

Z 127 bing de jingguo.
sick MOD experience
illness history.

Z 128 S: Wo $_{IV}$shuole$_{v}$. $_{III}$Natian $_{II}$zaochen ne,
I speak-ASP that-day morning ASP
I've said it. That morning,

Z 129 QIÁO DE $_{II}$SHIHOU, $_{III}$ZHEIGE[91]... $_{I}$wanbanshar[92]
watch MOD time this-C evening
I when was watching this... evening...

Z 130 a... QIAO DE $_{II}$SHIHOU $_{III}$NAGE[93]... ai..aiyou,
EXC watch MOD time that-C EXC
I when was watching that... oh.. oh my,

Z 131 yòu $_{II}$shuobushanglai le$_{s}$.
again speak-not-up-come ASP
once again, I can't say it.

Z 132 E: Manman lai, manman lai.
slow-slow come slow-slow come
Take it easy, take it easy.

---

[91] The order should be *...qiao zheige de shihou...*
[92] Colloquial Pekingese for 'evening'.
[93] The order should be *...qiao nage de shihou...*

Z 133 Obs: Ni shuo cong yi kan dianshi natian
you say from 1 look television that-day
You said that as soon as you started watching TV

Z 134 wanshang jiu...
evening then
that night then...

Z 135 S: Jiu shi a.
precise be EXC
Exactly.

Z 136 E2: Dou you yixie bu shufu
all have 1-C:PL not comfortable
There was a little discomfort,

Z 137 a, zenmo jiang...
EXC how say
how would you say...

Z 138 S: Nage *$_{II}$dianϕ.. $_{II}$dianshi $_{III}$natian $_{I}$wanbanshanr
that-C electric(-view) television that-day dusk
That tele-..television that evening

Z 139 *$_{III}$yanϕ.. $_{III}$yande shi $_{III}$nage... $_{I}$shenmolaide...
play(-MOD) play-MOD be that-C what-come-MOD
was play-.. playing that... whaddiyacallit...

Z 140 $_{II}$shuobushanglai. Zhe shi $_{I}$mafan le,.
speak-not-up-come this be trouble ASP
I can't get it out. This is a pain.

Z 141 E2: Dianshi yan de neirong shi shenmo ma?
television play MOD content be what EXC
What was playing on the TV?

Z 142 S: Jiu shuo shi na... wo ye.. shuo de
just say be that I also speak MOD
I was just saying it's that... I also..say

Z 143 $_{III}$nage.. *$_{III}$naϕ r-..$_{III}$nage *$_{II}$shuobu-ϕ-ϕ
that-C that(-C) that-C speak-not(-out-come)
That.. th- that can't speak it

Z 144	E2:	Shuobuchulai.					
		speak-not-out-come					
		You can't speak it out.					

Z 145	E:	Meiyou	guanxi.				
		not-have	relationship				
		That's ok.					

Z 146	E2:	Jiezhe	jiang	ba!	Qi	bing	de
		connect-ASP	talk	SUG	start	sick	MOD
		Go on! When you					

Z 147		shihou	hai	you	shenmo...		
		time	still	have	what		
		got sick, what else...					

Z 148	S:	$_{II}$Shuobushanglai	le,.	$_{II}$Shuobushanglai	le,,	lou!	
		speak-not-up-come	ASP	speak-not-up-come	ASP	EXC	
		I can't get it out. I can't get it out!					

Z 149		Dai	huer	zai	shuo	ba.	
		wait	awhile	again	speak	SUG	
		In awhile I'll try again.					

Z 150	E:	Hao.	Dai	yihuir	zai	shuo	xing.
		good	wait	awhile	again	speak	good
		Ok. Trying again in awhile is ok.					

Z 151	S:	Hao	ma?				
		good	Q				
		Ok?					

Z 152	E:	Mei	guanxi.	Xiangqi	jiu	shuo-shuo.	Hao.
		no	relation	think-up	then	say-say	good
		That's ok. When it comes to you, then say it. Ok.					

Z 153	S:	Rang	ta	gei	wo	$_{III}$nage	$_{II}$penr,
		make	her	give	I	that-C	pan
		Have her get me that pan,					

Z 154		wo	sa	pao	niao.		
		I	spray	M	urine		
		so I can take a leak.					

——————————— next session ———————————

Z 155	E2:	Dui.	Jiu	shi	ni	zai	jiangjiang
		right	just	be	you	again	talk-talk
		Right. Just say a little					

Z 156	fa	bing	de	jingguo.
	start	sick	MOD	experience
	about the history of your illness again.			

Z 157	S:	$_{I}$Wanbanshangr	a,	$_{IV}$qiaole$_{v}$	$_{III}$yige
		evening	EXC	watch-ASP	1-C
		In the evening, watching a			

Z 158	$_{I}$shenmode..	$_{I}$shenmolaide...
	something	what-come-MOD
	something.. whaddiyacallit...	

Z 159	E:	Mm.
		AFF
		Mm.

Z 160	S:	Zhe	$_{I}$shenmode..	$_{I}$shenmo..	$_{I}$shenmo	∇dì shí∇
		this	something	what	what	earth rock
		This whatever..what..what earth rock				

Z 161	wo	jiu	zai	hui	$_{II}$shuobushanglai	le,.
	I	then	again	can	speak-not-up-come	ASP
	now I can't talk again.					

Z 162	E:	Ou,	ou,	dui.
		AFF	AFF	right
		Oh, oh, right.		

Z 163	S:	Shuo	ya.	Hai..	hai	mei...	∇jié.. jié zhào∇
		speak	EXC	still	still	not	???
		Talk. I still..still haven't... ??? .					

Z 164	E:	Hai	mei	jīedào?
		still	not	receive-arrive
		Still haven't received?		

Z 165 S: Bu shi, bu shi. Dui.
not be not be right
No, no. Right.

Z 166 E2: Na shi ni fa bing
that time you start sick
At that time when you got sick,

Z 167 dangshi shi zai zuo shenmo?
that-time be at do what
what were you doing?

Z 168 Zenmo fa bing de? Naxie bu shufu?
how start sick EMP which-C:PL not feel:good
How did you get sick? Where did you feel bad?

Z 169 S: Fā ∇fū shí∇ wo.. fa.. $_{IV}$fale$_{v}$.. $_{IV}$fale$_{v}$..
start ??? I start start-ASP start-ASP
Get ??? I get..got..got..

Z 170 fa.. sh- fa.. fa ϕ de $_{II}$shihou,
start ??? start start (sick) MOD time
get.. get..when I got,

Z 171 ai, bu dui!
EXC not right
darn, it's wrong!

Z 172 E: Mm. Mei guanxi. Ni xinli
AFF no relation you heart-in
Hm. That's ok. In your mind

Z 173 zhidao bu dui, shi ba?
know not right be Q
you know it's wrong, right?

Z 174 S: Dui.
right
Right.

Z 175 E: Keshi ni hai yao jiang hua.
but you still want talk speech
But you still have to speak.

Z 176		Bu	guan	dui	haishi	bu	dui.		
		but	not	care	right	or	not	right	
		No matter if it's right or wrong.							
Z 177	S:	Bu	dui	$_{I}$zenmo	shuo	ya?			
		not	right	how	speak	EXC			
		If it's not right, how do I say it?							
Z 178	E:	Mm?							
		Q							
		Huh?							
Z 179	S:	Bu	dui	zenmo	shuo	ya?			
		not	right	how	speak	EXC			
		If it's not right, how do I say it?							
Z 180	E2:	'Bu	dui	zenmo	shuo'.	Ta	jiu	shuo	
		not	right	how	speak	EXC	she	just	say
		'If it's not right, how do I say it'. She's just saying							
Z 181		'bu	dui	wo	jiu	$_{,}$shuobuxiaqu	le'.		
		not	right	I	just	speak-not-down-go	ASP		
		'if it's wrong then I can't say it'.							
Z 182	S:	$_{II}$Shuobuxiaqu	a.						
		say-not-down-go	EXC						
		I can't say it.							
Z 183	E:	A	shuobuxiaqu.						
		AFF	say-not-down-go						
		Oh, you can't say it.							
Z 184	S:	A.							
		AFF							
		Um-hm.							
Z 185	E:	Na	shenmo	hua	shuochulai	jiu	keyi.		
		then	what	speech	speak-out-come	then	can		
		Then whatever you can say is ok.							
Z 186	S:	Shuo	na	shi	qiao..qiao				
		say	that	time	watch				
		I said at that time I was watch...							

Z 187 $_{III}$nahuir qiao..qiao $_{II}$dianshi a.
that-C:time watch television EXC
at that time watch.. watching the TV.

Z 188 E: Mm.
AFF
Mm.

Z 189 S: $_{III}$Qiaode shi $_{I}$shenmolaide...
watch-MOD be what-come-MOD
I was watching that whaddiyacallit...

Z 190 E2: Jiu fanzheng neitian wanshang
just anyway that-day evening
Anyway, that evening

Z 191 zai qiao dianshi ma.
at watch television EMP
you were watching TV.

Z 192 S: Zhe $_{II}$dianshi shi $_{I}$shenmo ya? ∇Gé gē bìng∇..
this television be what EXC revolution song sick..
What was on the TV? Revolution song sick..

Z 193 ∇Gé gē bìng∇.. ∇gé gē bìng jiā∇.. ..∇jiāshàng∇.
revolution song sick revolution song sick home home-on
Revolution song sick.. revolution song sick home.. at home.

Z 194 E: Hm.
AFF
Hm.

Z 195 S: Bu dui.
not right
Wrong.

Z 196 E2: Shi 'Gémìng Jīatíng' ma?
be revolution family Q
Was it 'Revolutionary Family'?

Z 197 S: Bú shì. ∇Fù lù hù∇ ∇$_{II}$gémìng $_{II}$jiàshǐ∇..
not be ??? revolution pilot
No. ??? revolutionary pilot..

Z 198 ∇bié jiā zhài zhǎ dė hòu∇. Ss!
don't home debt fry MOD thick EXC
Don't house debt fried thick. Ss!

Z 199 E2: Mei guanxi. Jiangbuchulai
no matter speak-not-out-come
It's ok. If you can't say it,

Z 200 jiu jiangbuchulai haole.
then speak-not-out-come good-ASP
then you can't say it, it's ok.

Z 201 S: Boooonnn... bu shi, bu shi, bu..
??? not be not be not
???... no, no, no..

Z 202 aiya! $_{I}$Zenmo shuo ne?
EXC how speak Q
darn! How do I say it?

Z 203 E: Hai you, houlai shei song ni
still have after who escort you
Also, afterward who took you

Z 204 dao yiyuan lai? Ni ziji laide?
arrive hospital come you self come
to the hospital? Did you come yourself?

Z 205 S: Bu shi. Wo $_{II}$guinu [dùi][94] wo lai de.
not be I daughter take I come EMP
No. My daughter teak me.

Z 206 E: Shei?
who
Who?

Z 207 E2: Guinu.
daughter
Daughter.

[94] For *dài* 'take'.

Z 208 S: Da..da $_{II}$guinu... lai...
big daughter come
My old-..oldest daughter came...

Z 209 E: Ta yige ren?
she 1-C person
By herself?

Z 210 S: $_{II}$Toutian shi.. $_{II}$toutian $_{I}$wanshang
head-day be head-day evening
The first day it was..the first evening the

Z 211 da $_{II}$xiaozi lai de.
big son come EMP
oldest son came.

Z 212 E: Mm-hm.
AFF
Mm-hm.

Z 213 S: $_{III}$Dier tian $_{I}$zaoshang shi... $_{III}$dier $_{I}$zaoshang
ORD-two day morning be ORD-two morning
The second morning it was...the second morning it

Z 214 shi $_{II}$guniang $_{IV}$laile$_{v}$...
be daughter come-ASP
was my daughter that came...

Z 215 E: Hm.
AFF
Mm.

Z 216 S: Er $_{II}$guinu.. er $_{II}$guinu $_{IV}$laile$_{v}$.
two daughter two daughter come-ASP
My second daughter..second daughter came.

Z 217 E2: Ni kan dianshi de shihou juede
you watch TV MOD time feel
When you were watching TV, how did you feel,

Z 218 zenmode, na shi?
how that time
at that time?

Z 219 S: A?
Q
Huh?

Z 220 E2: Ni zenmode le, juede?
you how ASP feel
How did you feel?

Z 221 S: Jiu shi [shuā][95] bu..bu..bu $_{III}$mingbai la.
just be talk:speech not clear EXC
It's just I could not..not..not spalk clearly.

Z 222 E: Ou.
AFF
Oh.

Z 223 S: Bu dui a.
not right EXC
Wrong.

Z 224 E: Shuo hua shuobuchulai.
say talk say-not-out-come
In talking, you can't get it out.

Z 225 S: A, bu, dui a.
EXC not right EXC
Uh, no, right.

Z 226 E: Ou.
AFF
Oh.

Z 227 S: Yi shuo hua jiu *$_I$hú... *$_I$hú.. *$_I$hú..
one say talk just confuse- confuse- confuse-
As soon as I talk it's con-.. con-.. con-..

Z 228 *$_I$HÚDÀO SH-.. *$_I$HÚ ϕ DÀO SHŪO[96] le,.
confuse-speak confuse(-eight-)speak-talk ASP
con-totally-fused speech.

[95] The target is the two-word expression *shuō huà* 'speak words'. The subject merges the initial consonant ([ʂ]) and the high level tone ([¯]) of the first word with the nuclear vowel of the second ([a]). This dissociation of tone from nuclear vowel is discussed in section 3.4.2 of the text.

Z 229		Jiu	na	yangr	le,.		
		just	that	way	ASP		
		It's just that way.					
Z 230	E2:	Ni	xianzai	yòu	zhidao	gai	
		you	now	again	know	should	
		Mm. Do you know					
Z 231		gai	shuo	shenmo	ma?		
		should	say	what	Q		
		what to say again now?					
Z 232	S:	$_{III}$Zhidao	ϕ	jiang	a.		
		know	(how)	speak	EXC		
		I know say.					
Z 233	E2:	Zhidao	gai	shuo	shenmo	ma?	
		know	should	say	what	Q	
		You know what you should say?					
Z 234	S:	Gai	jiang	*$_{III}$zheiϕ..	$_{III}$zheiju	hua	
		should	speak	this(-C:phrase)		this-C:phrase	talk
		This.. this sentence I should say					
Z 235		neng..neng	$_{II}$shuochulai.				
		can	speak-out-come				
		I can..can say it out.					
Z 236	E:	Mm.					
		AFF					
		Mm.					
Z 237	S:	Jiu	ϕ	$_{IV}$zanmen	$_{III}$neihuir		
		just	(like)	we-PL	that-C:time		
		Just we were talking					
Z 238		shuo	hua	$_{I}$yiyang...			
		speak	talk	same			
		that time...					

[96] In this very interesting speech error, the target is the common four-syllable phrase, *hú-shuō-bā-dào* (lit. confused-speak-eight-talk) 'to talk nonsense'. The subject uses the wrong morpheme order and omits a syllable.

Z 239 E: Mm.
AFF
Mm.

Z 240 S: Jiu bu hui shuo ma! Bu hui la.
just not can speak EXC not can EXC
I just can't talk! I can't.

Z 241 $_{IV}$Huibuliao le$_{,}$.
can-not-able ASP
I'm not able.

Z 242 E: Mei guanxi.
no relation
That's ok.

Z 243 S: Yao[97] $_{I}$zenmo you bing le$_{,}$ ne?
want how have sick ASP Q
Otherwise, why would I be considered sick?

Z 244 E: Hm?
AFF
Huh?

Z 245 S: Ta[98] jiu gūi[99] you bing la. Jiu gui
she just return have sick EXC just return
That's just why I'm sick. That's just

Z 246 you bing le$_{,}$, zui $_{II}$litou you bing le$_{,}$.
have sick ASP mouth inside have sick ASP
why I'm sick, why there's a sickness in my mouth.

Z 247 E2: Ta jiu shuo 'yinwei shuobuliao
she only say because speak-not-able
She's just saying 'because I can't talk,

Z 248 suoyi wo zhidao you bing le'.
so I know have sick ASP
therefore I know I'm sick.'

---

[97] Short for *yaoburan* 'otherwise'.
[98] The 3rd person pronoun can refer to self in colloquial Pekingese.
[99] Colloquial Pekingese for 'for this reason'.

Z 249 S:

Ei,	jiu	you	bing	le$_s$.
AFF	then	have	sick	ASP

Uh-huh, so I'm sick.

Z 250 E:

Mm-mm.
AFF

Mm-hm.

Z 251 S:

Ni	shuo...	bu	suan	shi	bing.
you	say	not	consider	be	sick

You say... you don't consider it an illness.

Z 252 E:

Mm-mm.
AFF

Mmm.

Z 253 S:

Wo	ye	bu	xiang	[zhi]..	ye..ye..ye	quan
I	also	not	think	be	also	complete

I also don't think itsh.. also..also.. also totally

Z 254

dou	bu	[dǎng]	ϕ..	bu	[dǎng]	ϕ..
all	not	think	(COMP)	not	think	(COMP)

don't dink.. don't dink..

Z 255

bu	dǎng	ϕ[100]	le$_s$.
not	think	(COMP)	ASP

don't dink.

Z 256 E:

Mm-hm.
AFF

Mm-hm.

Z 257 S:

Jiu	bu	hui	shuo	$_{III}$zheiju	hua.
just	not	able	speak	this-C:phrase	speech

I just can't say this sentence.

Z 258 E:

Mm-hm.
AFF

Mm-hm.

---

[100] In this and the previous utterance, the verb *xiǎng* 'think' (which the subject produces as **dǎng*) should take a sentential complement (such as 'think I'm sick), but it is omitted by the subject.

Z 259 S: Dai huir jiu shuo bu hui
wait moment then say not able
After a minute if you say you can't do it,

Z 260 le$_s$, ni $_{I}$zenmo ban ne?
ASP you how do Q
what can you do?

Z 261 E: Mm-mm.
AFF
Mm-hm.

Z 262 S: $_{III}$Zhāojí ye $^{*}_{IV}$[pái]ϕ.. $^{*}_{IV}$[pái]ϕ.. $^{*}_{IV}$[pái]ϕ..
worry also vain(-ASP) vain(-ASP) vain(-ASP)
Worrying is just for moth-.. moth-.. moth-..

Z 263 $^{*}_{IV}$[pái]ϕ.. $^{*}_{IV}$[pái]ϕ.. $^{*}_{IV}$[pái]ϕ.. $^{*}_{IV}$[pái]zháo[101].
vain(-ASP) vain(-ASP) vain(-ASP) vain-ASP
moth-.. moth-.. moth-.. mothing.

Z 264 E: Mm.
AFF
Mm.

Z 265 S: Ni $_{I}$shenmo nong a? Jiu zhei yangr.
you what do EXC just this way
What do you do? That's the way it is.

Z 266 Zan you bu shuo le$_s$.
we again not talk ASP
We won't say any more.

Z 267 E: Mm.
AFF
Mm-hm.

Z 268 S: Haishi bu shuo le$_s$.
still not speak ASP
I'm still not talking.

[101] The **pái* should be *bái* ('in vain, for nothing'), and *zháo* is an alternate pronunciation of *zhé* 'progressive aspect'.

Z 269	E:	Bu	shuo	le.
		not	speak	ASP
		You're not talking.		

Z 270	S:	Bu	shuo	le,.
		not	speak	ASP
		I'm not talking.		

Z 271	E2:	Bu	shuo	le.
		not	speak	ASP
		She's not talking.		

Z 272	S:	Bu	shuo	le,.
		not	speak	ASP
		I'm not talking.		

Z 273	E:	Jiangbuchulai.
		speak-not-out-come
		You can't get it out.

Z 274	S:	$_{II}$Jiangbuchulai.
		speak-not-out-come
		I can't get it out.

Z 275	E:	Mm.	Ni	neige	guinu	duo	da	suishu?
		AFF	you	that-C	daughter	much:Q	big	age-count
		Hm. How old is that daughter of yours?						

Z 276	S:	$_{II}$Guinu	$_{III}$yige	$_{II}$sishiyi	de.
		daughter	1-C	41	EMP
		The daughters, one is 41.			

Z 277	E:	Sishiyi	a.
		41	EXC
		41.	

Z 278	S:	Xiao	de	$_{III}$yige	$_{II}$sishi..s-..	er	san	de.
		small	MOD	1-C	40	2	3	EMP
		The young one is forty-two or three.						

Z 279	E:	Mm.	Sanshi.
		AFF	30
		Hm. 30	

Z 280 S: Zhe shi [*$_{I}$liă][102]dà no.
this be old-big EXC
This is the ildest

Z 281 E: Mm.
AFF
Uh-huh

Z 282 S: $_{III}$Neige...
that-C
That...

Z 283 E: Ni gen tamen de guanxi ting hao ma?
you and them-PL MOD relation very good Q
You get along with them well?

Z 284 S: Bu hao a.
not good EXC
No.

Z 285 E: Bu hao.
not good
No.

Z 286 S: Dui wo $_{III}$qinre.. $_{III}$qinre... shi leng ??? .
right I intimate be cold ???
Right, our intimate..intimate... it's cold ???.

Z 287 E: Shide, shide.
be-EMP be-EMP
Yes, yes.

Z 288 S: $_{II}$Ershi ϕ ϕ tou da $_{II}$erzi.
twenty (years) (bear) first big son
Twenty my first child.

Z 289 E: Mm-hm.
AFF
Mm-hm.

[102]For *lăo*.

Z 290	S:	Zui	xiao	de	shi	*$_{II}$sanshi-s-..s-..	$_{II}$sānshí[sèr][103]
		most	small	MOD	be	thirty(-four)	thirty-four

The youngest is thirty-f.. f-.. thirty-fer.

Z 291	E:	Mm.
		AFF

Uh-huh.

Z 292	S:	A	*$_{II}$san-ϕ..	$_{II}$sanshisan.
		EXC	3(-ten)	33

Thir.. 33.

Z 293	E2:	Sanshisan.	Zui	xiao	de
		33	most	small	MOD

33. The youngest child,

Z 294	erzi	le,	jiu..	laojiu.
	son	ASP	9	old-9

nine.. the ninth child.

Z 295	S:	Mm,	dui.
		AFF	right

Mm, right

Z 296	E2:	Shi	laojiu	ma?
		be	old-9	Q

Is he the ninth?

Z 297	S:	A.
		AFF

Uh-huh.

Z 298	E2:	Zui	da	de	ne?
		most	old	MOD	Q

What about the oldest?

Z 299	S:	*$_{II}$Erϕ..	$_{II}$ershi	a.
		2(-ten)	20	EXC

Twent-..twenty.

---

[103] For *sì*.

Z 300	E2:	Laoda	ya?!						
		old-big	Q						
		The oldest?!							

Z 301	S:	*II*Laoda	shi	a,	wo	*II*ershi	ϕ	deng..	wo...
		old-big	be	EXC	I	20	year	wait	I
		Yeah, the oldest, I was when 20 I...							

Z 302	E2:	Ni	ershi	de	shihou	sheng	ta?
		you	20	MOD	time	bear	him
		You had him when you were 20?					

Z 303	S:	A.	Dui.
		AFF	right
		Uh-huh. Right.	

Z 304	E2:	Na	ta	duo	da	ne	ya?
		then	he	much:Q	big	Q	EXC
		So how old is he?					

Z 305	S:	*II*Sishijiu	a.
		49	EXC
		49.	

Z 306	E2:	Sishijiu,	dui	la.	Ni	ganggang
		49	right	EXC	you	just
		49, right. You just				

Z 307	shuo	zui	da	de	ershi.	Ni	shi
	say	most	big	MOD	20	you	be
	said the oldest was 20. You						

Z 308	shuo	ni	ershi	sui	de	shihou	sheng	ta.
	say	you	20	year	MOD	time	bear	him
	mean you had him when you were 20.							

Z 309	S:	A.
		AFF
		Uh-huh.

Z 310	E2:	Dui	ba,	ta	xianzai	sishijiu	sui	ba.
		right	EMP	he	now	49	year	EMP
		Right, now he's 49.						

Z 311 S: $_{II}$Sanshis-.. $_{II}$sanshis-.. si s-...
34 34 4
Thirty-f..thirty-f.. for-...

Z 312 E2: Ni bu jiuge ma?
you not 9-C Q
Don't you have 9?

Z 313 S: Shi $_{III}$jiuge $_{III}$zheige...
be 9-C this-C
There's 9 these...

Z 314 E2: Laoda...
old-big
The oldest...

Z 315 S: Jiu <*$_{II}$dă>[104]dà.. <*$_{II}$dă>dà ...uh...
only hit-big hit-big HES
He's just the doldest..doldest..uh..

Z 316 Obs: Lǎodà jinnian sishisan.
old-big this-year 43
The oldest is 43 this year.

Z 317 S: Ei, $_{II}$sishisan la. $_{II}$Sishisan la. $_{I}$Xianzai
AFF 43 EXC 43 EXC now
Uh-huh, 43. 43. Now

Z 318 [zúi][105] xiao.. [zúi] xiao de jiu shi... er.. $_{II}$ershi.
most small most small MOD only be 2 20
the youngarst.. youngarst is only twen-.. twenty.

Z 319 E2: Ershi sui.
20 year
Twenty years old.

Z 320 S: Ei, zùi[106] xiao de $_{III}$zheige $_{II}$ershi... $_{II}$ershi..
AFF most small MOD this-C 20 20
Uh-huh, the youngest is twenty-.. twenty-..

---

[104] The target here is the word *lǎo* 'old' as in *lǎo dà* 'the oldest'. The subject gets the target tone (˘) correct, but gets the consonant-vowel sequence incorrect, in anticipation of the word *dà* 'big'.

[105] For *zùi* .

Z 321 $_{II}$ershi, $_{III}$yige, $_{III}$yige s-..$_{II}$sishisan.
20 1-C 1-C 43
one is twenty, one is f-.. forty-three.

Z 322 E: Mm.
AFF
Mm-hm.

Z 323 E2: Ni xinli haishi mingbai de ma?
you heart-in still understand EMP Q
Are you clear in your mind?

Z 324 S: A.
AFF
Mm-hm.

Z 325 E2: Na ni neng jiangjiang tamen shu
then you can talk-talk he-PL belong
Then can you say what sign of the zodiac

Z 326 shenmo ne ma? Laoda shu shenmo?
what Q Q old-big belong what
they're under? What sign is the oldest under?

Z 327 Lao er shu shenmo?
old 2 belong what
What sign is the second oldest under?

Z 328 S: Shu ji de.
belong chicken EMP
Under the chicken.

Z 329 E2: Laoda shu ji.
old-big belong chicken
The oldest is under the chicken.

Z 330 S: Sh-..f-..fa-.. shu.. $_{III}$touyige
??? belong ORD-1-C
??? under.. the first one,

Z 331 na shi xiao..xiao long.
that be small dragon
that's a little..little dragon.

[106] She corrects the tone of this word improperly produced in her previous utterance.

Z 332	E2:	Diyi	shu	shenmo?				
		ORD-1	belong	what				
		What's the first under?						

Z 333	S:	Ei..	shu...	yang.				
		HES	belong	sheep				
		Um.. he's under... the sheep.						

Z 334	E2:	Diyige	shu	yang.	Dierge	ne?		
		ORD-1-C	belong	sheep	ORD-2-C	Q		
		The first is under the sheep. And the second?						

Z 335	S:	∇zuo di..do..di..do∇	///yige..///yige..///yige...					
		???	1-C					
		??? one.. one.. one..						

Z 336	E2:	Mm.						
		AFF						
		Uh-huh.						

Z 337	S:	///Yige	bu	shi..	///yige	shu	lao..	
		1-C	not	be	1-C	belong	old	
		One, no.. one is under the old..						

Z 338		shu...	bu	dui	ba.			
		belong	not	right	EMP			
		under... wrong.						

Z 339	E2:	Ni	shi	shu	shenmo	de?		
		you	be	belong	what	EMP		
		What sign are you under?						

Z 340	S:	Shu	ji	de.				
		belong	chicken	EMP				
		I'm under the chicken.						

Z 341	E2:	Shu	ji	de.				
		belong	chicken	EMP				
		Under the chicken.						

Z 342	S:	Ei.						
		AFF						
		Uh-huh.						

Z 343 E2: Ou, shu ji de. Na ni
EXC belong chicken EMP then you
Oh, you're under the chicken. So you're

Z 344 xianzai shi liushier.
now be 62
62 now.

Z 345 S: A.
AFF
Uh-huh.

Z 346 E2: Dui ba.
right EMP
Right.

Z 347 S: Dui, dui, dui, dui, dui. Wo zhei er $_{II}$guniang
right I this 2 daughter
Right, right, right, right, right. My second daughter

Z 348 gen wo $_{I}$yìbiār[107] da.
with I one-side big
is the same age as me.

Z 349 E2: A?
Q
Huh?

Z 350 S: Wo zhei er $_{II}$guniang gen wo.. gen wo..
I this 2 daughter with I with I
My second daughter is the same.. same..

Z 351 er..er.. $_{I}$yibiar da.
2 1-side big
uh.. uh.. age as me.

Z 352 E2: Ni er guniang gen ni yibar da?
you 2 daughter with you 1-kind big
Your second daughter is the same age as you?

---

[107] Colloquial Pekingese for *yìbān* 'the same'.

Z 353 S: A.
AFF
Uh-huh.

Z 354 E2: Ta shi shenmo yisi? Qishi
she be what meaning actually
What does she mean? Actually,

Z 355 shi shuxiang shi yiyang.
be zodiac be same
it's their zodiac signs that are the same.

Z 356 S: Ei, *I*yiyang.
AFF same
Uh-huh, the same.

Z 357 E2: A ta shuxiang shi yiyang.
EXC she zodiac be same
Ah, their signs are the same.

Z 358 S: Shi *I*yiyang.
be same
They're the same.

Z 359 E2: Dou shi shu ji de.
all be belong chicken EMP
They're both under the chicken.

Z 360 S: A.
AFF
Uh-huh.

——————— next session ———————

'Cookie Theft' Picture Description

Z 361 E: Gei ni kan zheige tupian. Ni
give you see this-C picture you
I'll show you this picture. Can you

Z 362 kande qingchu ma?
see-ADV clear Q
see it ok?

Z 363 E2: Ni ziji shou nazhe, keyi.
you self hand hold-ASP can
You can hold it with your own hand.

Z 364 Neige shou na keyi.
that-C hand hold can
You can hold it with that hand.

Z 365 S: Bu yong, bu yong. Zhe shi $_{II}$xiaohair...
not use not use this be child
No need, no need. This is a child...

Z 366 E: Ei.
AFF
Uh-huh.

Z 367 S: Dui.
right
Right.

Z 368 E: Ni kan shenmo jiu shuo shenmo.
you see what only say what
Say whatever you see.

Z 369 S: Zhe shi... zhei ye shi $_{II}$xiaohair.
this be this also be child
This is... this is also a child.

Z 370 E: Shide.
be-EMP
Right.

Z 371 S: Shi ba?
be Q
Isn't that so?

Z 372 E: Shi. Mei cuo.
be no wrong
Right. Exactly.

Z 373 S: Zhe shi $_{II}$daren.
this be big-person
This is an adult.

Z 374 E: Ei.
AFF
Uh-huh.

Z 375 S: Na $_{III}$yige ba... zhe shi.. zhe shi
hold 1-C SUG this be this be
Holding a.. it seems.. this is.. this is

Z 376 $_{I}$shenmo $_{II}$quanr..$_{II}$quanr.
what circle
some kind of circle..circle[108].

Z 377 E: Ei.
AFF
Uh-huh.

Z 378 S: Shi ba?
be SUG
Right?

Z 379 E: Mm.
AFF
Uh-huh.

Z 380 S: $_{I}$Meiyou $_{I}$shenmo.. $_{I}$meiyou $_{I}$shenmo le,.
not-have what not-have what ASP
There's nothing.. there's nothing.

Z 381 $_{I}$Meiyou $_{I}$shenmo $_{I}$biede la.
not-have what other EXC
There's nothing else.

Z 382 E: You de. Limian you shiqing fasheng.
have EMP inside have matter happen
Yes there is. There's something going on in there.

---

[108] The 'circle' is a dish the mother is washing.

Z 383 Tamen zuo yixie shenmo shiqing?
he-PL do 1-C:PL what matter
What are they doing?

Z 384 S: Zhe $_{II}$xiaohair gòu $_{I}$shenmo ne?
this child grab what Q
What's that child grabbing?

Z 385 Gòu $_{III}$nǎge ne...
grab which-C ASP
Which is he grabbing...

Z 386 E: Mm. Nage shi shenmo?
AFF that-C be what
Hm. What is that?

Z 387 S: $_{II}$Chǒubuchulai, kan, *$_{II}$kanbu-ϕ-lai shi $_{I}$shenmo.
see-not-out-come see see-not(-out-)come be what
I can't tell, see, can't make what it is.

Z 388 E: Mm.
AFF
Um-hm.

Z 389 S: $_{III}$Zheige shi... shi bu shi $_{II}$naqu le, ba.
this-C be be not be hold-go ASP SUG
This is.. isn't he taking it away?

Z 390 Shi bu shi... shi bu shi na $_{III}$zheige ba?
be not be be not be hold this-C SUG
Isn't... isn't he taking this?

Z 391 E: Mm.
AFF
Hm.

Z 392 S: Shi ba?
be SUG
Isn't that right?

Z 393 E: Shi.
be
Right.

Z 394 S: Shi ba?
be SUG
Right?

Z 395 E: Shide.
be-EMP
That's right.

Z 396 S: Na le,, shi ba?
hold ASP be SUG
He's taking it, right?

Z 397 E: Ta gan ma?
she do what
What's he doing?

Z 398 S: Ta gen ta yao ba.
she with him want SUG
She's asking him for it.

Z 399 E: Ou, gen ta yao.
EXC with him want
Oh, she's asking him for it.

Z 400 S: Dui ba.
right SUG
Right.

Z 401 E: Mm, mm, mm. Na zheige dongxi?
AFF then this-C thing
Mm-hm, mm-hm, mm-hm. And this thing?

Z 402 S: $_{II}$Dèngzi, $_{IV}$dēngzhe gòu ya.. gòu a.
stool-NOM ascend-ASP grab EXC grab EXC
The stool, he's climbing it to grab.. to grab.

Z 403 E: Mm, mm. Gan ma?
AFF do what
Mm-hm. What for?

Z 404 S: ∇Zou..zou zi∇ $_{II}$gòudezháo. ϕ[109] $_{II}$dengzi
?? grab-can-get (use) stool-NOM
??? he can get it. A stool

Z 405 $_{II}$gòudezháo ye hao.
grab-can-get also good
it's easy to get it.

Z 406 $_{II,III}$Haogoudezhao, dui bu dui? Dui, ba
good-grab-can-get right not right right OBJ
It's easy to get, right? Right, he's taking

Z 407 $_{III}$zheige... gē $_{III}$zheige, qu naṙ gou $_{III}$zheige.
this-C move this-C go there grab that-C
this...moving this, and going there to grab that.

Z 408 E: Mm, mm.
AFF AFF
Mm, mm.

Z 409 S: Dui, ba?
right SUG
Isn't that right?

Z 410 E: Dui, dui, dui.
right
Right, right, right.

Z 411 S: Jiu $_{III}$zheige, jiu bu $_{III}$zhidao le,.
just this-C just not know ASP
Just this, I just don't understand.

Z 412 E2: Jiezhe jiang ba.
continue-ASP speak SUG
Keep talking.

Z 413 S: Zhe bu $_{III}$zhidao shi $_{I}$shenmo le,.
this not know be what ASP
I don't know what this is.

Z 414 E: Mm-mm.
AFF
Uh-huh.

Z 415 S: Zhe $_{I}$shenmo zhe..zhe.. ◇ye◇[110] you $_{I}$shenmo
this what this also have what
This what this..this..what either there is here

[109] The coverb *yong* 'use/with' is deleted here.

Z 416		jiu	bu	$_{III}$zhidao	le$_{,}$.				
		just	not	know	ASP				
		I just don't know							
Z 417	E:	Bu	zhidao	le,	ho.				
		not	know	ASP	EXC				
		Oh, you don't know.							
Z 418	E2:	Ta	zai	zuo	shenmo,	zheige	ren?		
		he	ASP	do	what	this-C	person		
		What's she doing, this person?							
Z 419	S:	$_{III}$Zheige	ren	na	*$_{III}$zheiϕ..	*$_{III}$zheiϕ..			
		this-C	person	hold	this(-C)	this(-C)			
		This person is holding this..this..							
Z 420		$_{III}$zheige..	$_{III}$zheige..	$_{III}$zheige	ne...	*$_{III}$zheϕ	$_{II}$quanr.		
		this-C	this-C	this-C	Q	this(-C)	circle-NOM		
		this..this..this... this circle.							
Z 421	E:	Uh-huh.							
		AFF							
		Uh-huh.							
Z 422	S:	Bu	$_{III}$zhidao..	bu	$_{III}$zhidao	gan	$_{I}$shenmo	ne.	
		not	know	not	know	do	what	ASP	
		I don't know.. don't know what she's doing.							
Z 423	E:	Ou.							
		AFF							
		Oh.							
Z 424	S:	Bu	$_{III}$zhidao	le$_{,}$.					
		not	know	ASP					
		I don't know.							
Z 425	E:	Xiamian	zheige	ne?					
		under-side	this-C	Q					
		And this under here?							
Z 426	S:	Zhe	bu	$_{III}$zhidao	shi	$_{I}$shenmo	le$_{,}$.		
		this	not	know	be	what	ASP		
		I don't know what this is.							

[110] The subject should have used another word for 'also' (i.e., *hai*) in this context.

Z 427 E: Nage shi shui.
this be water
That's water.

Z 428 S: Ou, $_{III}$nage ϕ shui a.
EXC that-C (be) water EXC
Oh, that water.

Z 429 E: Ei.
AFF
Uh-huh.

Z 430 S: Bu $_{III}$zhidao. Ou zhe shi shui.
not know EXC this be water
I didn't know. Oh, this is water.

Z 431 E: A. Shide. Shui zenmoyang?
AFF be-EMP water how-kind
Mm. Right. What about the water?

Z 432 S: Zhe shui $_{II}$chulai. Chu $_{II}$waibiar...
this water exit-come exit outside
This water's coming out. Going ouitside...

Z 433 dao zher lai.
arrive here come
going over here.

Z 434 E: Shide.
be-EMP
Right.

Z 435 S: Dao zher, shi ha?
arrive here be Q:EMP
Going here, right?

Z 436 E: Shide.
be-EMP
Right.

Z 437 S: Ou.
AFF
Oh.

Z 438	E:	Ni	kan	zhei	sange.
		you	see	this	3-C

Look at these three.

Z 439	S:	Ta	$_{III}$zheige	ne?	Zhe	gan	ma	ya?
		he	this-C	Q	this	do	what	EXC

And this? What's this doing?

Z 440	E:	Ei.
		AFF

Uh-huh.

Z 441	S:	$_{III}$Zheige	shui	ben	zhe	$_{II,III}$quanrli	lai	la.
		this-C	water	rush	here	circle-in	come	EXC

This water is rushing onto this circle.

Z 442	E:	Mm.
		AFF

Mm-hm.

Z 443	S:	Zhe	$_{II}$quanr	ben	$_{III}$zheli	qu,	shi	ba?
		this	circle	rush	here	go	be	SUG

The circle's rushing over here, right?

Z 444	Bu	shi	ba.	Na	bu	shi	le,.
	not	be	SUG	that	not	be	ASP

No. That's not it.

Z 445	E:	Zhei	sange	ren	guanxi	shi
		this	3-C	person	relation	be

What's the relation between these 3

Z 446	shenmo?	You	meiyou	guanxi?
	what	have	not-have	relation

people? Is there any connection?

Z 447	S:	Zhei	$_{III}$sange	ren,	ta	$_{III}$zhege...
		this	3-C	person	he	this-C

These three people, him over here...

Z 448	E:	You	meiyou	shenmo	guanxi?
		have	not-have	what	relation

Is there any connection?

Z 449	S:	Na	ke	bu	$_{III}$zhidao	le,.	Jiu	
		that	indeed	not	know	ASP		
		That I don't know at all. It's just						

Z 450	$_{III}$nage	jiu	bu	$_{III}$zhidao	le,.	
	that-C	then	not	know	ASP	
	that that I don't know.					

Z 451	E:	Nage	bu	tai	you	guanxi,	shi	ba?
		that-C	not	too	have	relation	be	SUG
		There's not much connection there, right?						

Z 452	S:	Bu	$_{III}$zhidao.
		not	know
		I don't know.	

Z 453	E:	Nage	shui	zai	manchulai,	shi	ba?
		that-C	water	at	fill-exit-come	be	SUG
		That water's overflowing, right?					

Z 454	S:	A.
		AFF
		Oh.

Z 455	E:	Na	ta	zenmoyang?	Ta	yinggai	zenmoyang?
		then	he	how-way	he	should	how-way
		And what about her? What should she do?					

Z 456	S:	Ou,	shui	$_{II}$chulai	la.
		AFF	water	exit-come	EXC
		Oh, the water's coming out.			

Z 457	E:	Shide.	shui	bu	shi	chulai	de	ma?	
		be-EMP	water	not	be	exit-come	EMP	Q	
		Right. Isn't the water coming out?							

Z 458	S:	Ou,	shui	$_{II}$chulai	le,.	Shui
		EXC	water	exit-come	ASP	water
		Oh, the water's coming out. The water's				

Z 459	$_{II}$chulai	ta	$_{III}$neige...
	exit-come	he	that-C
	coming out and that...		

Z 460 E: Ta yinggai zenmoyang?
he should how-way
What should she do?

Z 461 S: Yao bu yao...yao $_{IV}$goule$_v$... yao...mm...
want not want grab-ASP want
Shouldn't she grab... should...mm...

Z 462 [boa]... bu dui le$_s$.
not not right ASP
nuu... not right.

Z 463 E: Mm.
AFF
Mm.

Z 464 S: Aiyou.
EXC
Darn.

Z 465 E: Mei guanxi. Manman lai. Hai you meiyou
no relation slow-slow come still have not-have
That's ok. Easy does it. Is there

Z 466 qita de shiqing?
other MOD matter
anything else?

Z 467 S: Bu shuo le$_s$.
not speak ASP
I'm not saying any more.

Z 468 E: Ni ganggang shuode bucuo. Jiu shi
you just speak-ADV not-bad only be
You just talked well. It's just that

Z 469 youde shihou shuobuchu hua lai.
some time speak-not-exit speech come
sometimes you can't get it out.

Z 470 S: Ei, jiu $_{II}$shuobuchulai, dui le$_s$.
AFF just speak-not-exit-come ASP
Yeah, I just can't get it out, right.

Z 471 Jiu shi zhei $_{II}$yangr.
only be that way
That's just the way it is.

Z 472 E: Ni neng jiang shenmo jiu jiang shenmo.
you able say what just say what
Say whatever you can.

Z 473 S: Ni jiang $_{I}$shenmo $_{II}$shuobuchulai,
you say what speak-not-exit-come
I can't say what I want,

Z 474 $_{II}$jiangbuchulai ya.
talk-not-exit-come EXC
I can't get it out.

Z 475 E: Jiangbuchulai.
talk-not-exit-come
You can't get it out.

Z 476 S: A. Ta bu shi dou [suō][111] ∇_{II}dùihùa∇.
AFF he not be all say dialog
Uh-huh. It's not that he always siz dialogs.

Z 477 Zhe $_{I}$shenmo xie $_{I}$dongxi, hua wo
this what M:PL thing speech I
These things, I

Z 478 quan hui shuo...
complete can say
can say all of them...

Z 479 E: Uh.
AFF
Oh.

Z 480 S: Ta jiu shi bu f-.. $_{I}$xianzai wo $_{I}$meiyou le$_{s}$!
he just be not now I not-have ASP
He's just that f-.. now I don't have them!

[111] For *shuō*.

Z 481	E:	Ou,	zhei	yangzi.		
		AFF	this	way		
		Oh, is that right.				

Z 482	S:	A.	Zhei	hua	$_{II,IV}$shuochulaile$_v$,	zhī
		EXC	this	speech	speak-exit-come-ASP	know
		Uh-huh. These words, when I say them, I know				

Z 483	shi	bu	dui.
	be	not	right
	they're wrong.		

Z 484	E:	Ou.
		AFF
		Oh.

Z 485	S:	Bu..bu..bu	shuo	le$_s$.
		not	speak	ASP
		I'm not..not..not saying any more.		

Z 486	E:	Mm.	Jiu	bu	shuo	le.
		AFF	just	not	speak	ASP
		Oh, you're not saying any more now.				

Z 487	S:	Dui	a!	A	dui	le$_s$.
		right	EXC	EXC	right	ASP
		Right! Right.				

Z 488	E:	Ni	zhidao	shi	cuo	de,
		you	know	be	wrong	MOD
		You know it's wrong,				

Z 489	suoyi	ni	bu	jiang.
	so	you	not	talk
	so you're not going to talk.			

Z 490	S:	Dou	bu	jiang	le$_s$,	dui,
		all	not	talk	ASP	right
		I'm not saying a thing, right,				

Z 491	dui,	bu	neng	shuo	le$_s$.
	right	not	able	speak	ASP
	right, I can't talk anymore.				

Z 492 E: A.
AFF
Oh.

Z 493 S: $_{I}$Keshi ye $_{II}$guoqu $_{III}$yidiar, wo
but also pass-go 1-bit I
But after awhile, I

Z 494 jiu bu $_{III}$zhidao le,.
just not know ASP
don't know.

Z 495 E: Ou, bu zhidao le.
EXC not know ASP
Oh, you don't know.

Z 496 S: Bu $_{III}$zhidao le,, jiu.
not know ASP only
I just don't know.

Z 497 E: Ou.
AFF
Oh.

Z 498 S: ??? bu $_{III}$zhidao le,.
??? not know ASP
[??] don't know.

Z 499 E: Ou.
AFF
Oh.

Z 500 S: Jiu... bu hao ting.
only not good listen
It just... sounds bad.

Z 501 E: Ni xiaohair you meiyou lai kan ni.
you child have not-have come see you
Do your kids come to see you?

Z 502 S: ∇chit∇.. Lai la! Lai la! Ai,
??? come EXC come EXC EXC
??? They come! They come! Yes,

Z 503 ${}_{IV}$laile$_v$ jian wo, a.
come-ASP see I EXC
they come to see me.

Z 504 E: You.
have
They do.

Z 505 S: Ei, ${}_{II}$mingr lai.
AFF tomorrow-NOM come
Uh-huh, they come tomorrow.

Z 506 E: Mingtian?
tomorrow
Tomorrow?

Z 507 S: Ei.
AFF
Uh-huh.

Z 508 E: Ou.
AFF
Oh.

Z 509 S: ${}_{II}$Mingtian ${}_{II}$xiawu lai.
tomorrow bottom-noon come
They come tomorrow afternoon.

Z 510 E: Mingtian xiawu lai.
tomorrow bottom-noon come
They come tomorrow afternoon.

Z 511 S: A, a.
AFF
Uh-huh, uh-huh.

Z 512 E: Na ni yinggai hen gaoxing.
then you should very happy
So you should be happy.

Z 513 S: A.
AFF
Uh-huh.

Z 514	E:	Neng	kanjian	tamen.			
		can	look-see	he-PL			
		You can see them.					

Z 515	S:	A, a.					
		AFF					
		Uh-huh, uh-huh.					

Z 516	E:	Tamen	shi	qí	che	lai	
		he-PL	be	ride:straddle	vehicle	come	
		Do they ride their bikes					

Z 517	haishi	zou	lu	lai?
	or	walk	road	come
	or walk here?			

Z 518	S:	H.. uh	you	qí	che	de	you..you
		HES	have	ride:straddle	vehicle	MOD	have
		H.. uh some ride bikes and some.. some..					

Z 519	zou..zou..zou	lu	de.
	walk	road	MOD
	.. walk..walk..walk.		

Z 520	E:	Liangge	dou	you,	shi	ba?
		2-C	all	have	be	SUG
		They do both, right?				

Z 521	S:	Uh	DOU	QUAN.. quan	dou[112]	hui.	
		HES	all	complete	all	able	
		Uh they both can..can do either.					

Z 522	E:	Suoyi	ni	zhu	de	difang,	ni	jiali,
		so	you	live	MOD	place	you	home
		So is where you live, your home,						

Z 523	li	zheli	yuan bu yuan?
	from	here	far not far
	far from here?		

[112] ZYJ self-corrects her word order mistake.

Z 524	S:	Bu	yuan.				
		not	far				
		Not far.					
Z 525	E:	Bu	yuan.				
		not	far				
		Not far.					
Z 526	S:	Bu	yuan.	$_{IV}$Zanmen	$_{I}$keshi	lí	nahar[113]
		not	far	we-PL	however	from	there
		Not far. But, we're only					
Z 527		jiu	shi	◇$_{II}$sanshiwu	lu◇[114].		
		only	be	thirty-five	road		
		route 35 from there.					
Z 528	E:	Ou,	sanshiwu	lu.			
		EXC	35	road			
		Oh, route 35.					
Z 529	S:	Zhào	$_{III}$zheige...	∇jīng...jīng shī∇			
		according	this-C	startle teacher			
		According to this... startle.. startle teacher					
Z 530		zhe	∇jīng shī∇...	uh...			
		this	startle teacher	HES			
		this startle teacher... uh...					
Z 531	E:	Ei.					
		AFF					
		Uh-huh.					
Z 532	S:	Xin...	$_{II}$qishiwu	lu...	wo	???	
		new	75	road	I	???	
		New... route 75... I ???.					
Z 533	E:	Ou.					
		AFF					
		Oh.					

[113] Colloquial Pekingese for *nar* 'that place'.

[114] Both the general context and the presence of the word *lí* 'to be distant from' indicate that what should appear here is a number of miles, rather than the number of a bus route.

Z 534 S: Ta ye shuo $_{IV}$duile$_{v}$, jiu...
she also say right-ASP just
She also says it's right, then...

Z 535 E: Dui, wo zhidao nide yisi.
right I know you MOD meaning
Right, I know what you mean.

Z 536 S: Shi ba?
be SUG
Isn't that right?

Z 537 E: Hai you, ni de maobing wo hen qingchu.
still have you MOD defect I very clear
Also, I'm clear about the nature of your illness.

Z 538 S: Ou.
AFF
Oh.

Z 539 E: Jiu shi shuo, ni suiran zhidao shi cuode...
just be say you though know be bad-MOD
That is to say, although you know it's wrong...

Z 540 S: $_{II}$Shuochulai jiu..jiu a.. jiu cuo le$_{s}$.
speak-exit-come then HES then wrong ASP
I say it and..and uh.. and it's wrong.

Z 541 Wo cuo.. ni $_{II}$shuocuo bu $_{III}$zhidao $_{I}$zenmo
I wrong you say-wrong not know how
I'm wrong.. when you say it wrong and you don't know how

Z 542 shuo le$_{s}$, ye bu $_{III}$zhidao cong nar lou...
say ASP also not know from where EXC
to say it, and you don't know from where uh...

Z 543 ye bu $_{III}$zhidao nar $_{III}$cuode. Zhe bu
also not know where wrong-MOD this not
and you don't know where you're wrong. This isn't

Z 544 ???... $_{I}$Zenmo hui dé zhe bing le$_{s}$ ne? Aiya.
??? how can get this sick ASP Q EXC
???... How did I get a sickness like this? Darn.

Z 545	E:	Ou.							
		AFF							
		Oh.							
Z 546	S:	$_{II}$Sanshiwu	lu.						
		35	road						
		Bus route 35.							
Z 547	E:	Ou,	sanshiwu...	tamen	zuo				
		AFF	35	he-PL	ride				
		Oh, 35... they take							
Z 548		sanshiwu	lu,	shi	ba?				
		35	road	be	SUG				
		route 35, right?							
Z 549	S:	$_{II}$Sanshiwu	lu	lai.					
		35	road	come					
		They come by route 35.							
Z 550	E:	Mm.							
		AFF							
		Mm.							
Z 551	S:	???	zai	shuo	jiu	$_{II}$shuobulai	le$_{,}$.		
		???	again	speak	then	speak-not-come	ASP		
		??? I say it again then can't say it.							
Z 552	E:	Ou.	Tamen	hai	yao bu yao	zhuan	che	le?	
		AFF	he-PL	still	want not want	change	car	ASP	
		Oh. Do they also have to change busses?							
Z 553	S:	A,	dui	le$_{,}$.					
		AFF	right	ASP					
		Oh, right.							
Z 554	E:	Tamen	hai	yao	zhuan	che.			
		he-PL	still	want	change	car			
		They also have to change busses.							
Z 555	S:	Dui,	hai	zhuan	che.	ZHUAN	CHE		
		right	still	change	car	change	car		
		Right, they change busses. They change bus onto							

Z 556 *III*NEIGE *II*SANSHI... liu[115].
that-C 30 6
that thirty... six.

Z 557 E: Sanshiliu. Sanshi ji..ji lu, shi ba?
36 30 several road be SUG
36. Route thirty... something, right?

Z 558 S: Ji lu, a.
many:Q road AFF
What route?

Z 559 E: A, sanshi ji lu.
AFF 30 several road
Oh, thirty something.

Z 560 S: ??? 'ji lu... ji lu' *IV*laizhe.
??? several road several road come-ASP
??? 'route something...' What 'route something'?

Z 561 E: Na bu suan hen jin. Bu suan tai jin.
that not count very close not count too close
That's not very close. Not too close.

Z 562 S: Ye bu suan tūi[116] yuan.
also not count too far
It's not too far, either.

Z 563 E: Ye bu suan tai yuan.
also not count too far
Also not very far.

Z 564 S: Ye bu suan tai yuan.
also not count too far
Also not very far.

Z 565 E: Tamen zou lu lai haishi...
he-PL walk road or
Do they walk or...

---

[115] The order should be *Zhuan neige sanshiliu che*.
[116] Pekingese dialect for *tài* 'too'.

Z 566 S: Zou..zou..zou bu xing.
walk not good
Walk..walk..walking's no good.

Z 567 E: Ou zou bu xing, tai yuan.
AFF walk not good too far
Oh, walking's no good, it's too far.

Z 568 S: $_{IV}$Zouzhe bu xing, $_{IV}$zoule$_v$..
walk-ASP not good walk-ASP
Walking's no good, walking..

Z 569 $_{IV}$zoule$_v$ bu xing. Zuo...zuo che.
walk-ASP not good ride vehicle
walking's no good. They take...take a bus.

Z 570 E: Ou, zùo chē a.
EXC ride vehicle EXC
Oh, they take the bus

Z 571 S: Zùo ϕ qí chē a.
ride (vehicle) straddle:ride vehicle EXC
Take the bus ride bikes.

Z 572 E: Ou, qí chē a.
EXC straddle:ride vehicle EXC
Oh, ride bikes.

Z 573 S: A, yǒu qí chē dė
AFF have straddle:ride vehicle MOD
Uh, some ride bikes

Z 574 yǒu zùo chē dė.
have ride vehicle MOD
and some take the bus.

Z 575 E: Tamen ye zuo neige gonggong qiche, shi ba?
he-PL also ride that-C public car be SUG
They also ride that bus, right?

Z 576 S: ??? ye ϕ $_{III}$gonggong $_{II}$qiche,
??? also (ride) public car
??? also the bus,

Z 577 ye ye [zi-].. ɪshenmo...
also ride what
also also ri-.. whatever...

Z 578 E: Tamen you yuepiao meiyou?
he-PL have month-ticket not-have
Do they have monthly bus passes?

Z 579 S: You a.
have EXC
Yes.

Z 580 E: You a. Tamen mai yuepiao. Ni
have EXC he-PL buy month-ticket you
They do. They buy monthly passes. Do you

Z 581 you meiyou yuepiao?
have not-have month-ticket
have a monthly pass?

Z 582 S: Wo ɪmeiyou.
I not-have
I don't.

Z 583 E: Meiyou yuepiao.
not-have month-ticket
You don't have a monthly pass.

Z 584 S: Wo gēn[117] jia... zuo fan.
I at home make food
I'm at home... cooking.

Z 585 E: Ou ni zai jiali.
EXC you at home
Oh you're at home.

Z 586 S: Ker hai yao zuo fan chi.
but still want make food eat
But I still have to make things to eat.

---

[117] Colloquial Pekingese for *zài* 'at'.

Z 587 E: Ou. Zuo fan de. Zai wo jia, wo
AFF make food EMP at I home I
Oh, you cook. At my home, I

Z 588 zuo fan. Wo airen bang wo xi panzi.
make food I spouse help I wash dish
do the cooking. My wife washes the dishes for me.

Z 589 S: Ou, xi $_{II}$panzi, ou. $_{I}$Dagai
AFF wash dish-NOM EXC probably
Oh, she washes the dishes. That's probably

Z 590 gen $_{III}$neige $_{II}$Zhongguo ren bu $_{I}$yiyang le,.
with that-C China person not same ASP
different than the Chinese do it.

Z 591 E: Dui.
right
Right.

Z 592 S: $_{II}$Zhongguo nahar ... you shi $_{II}$Zhongguo.
China there again be China
In China... once again it's China.

Z 593 Zuo..zuo..zuo fan le,.
make food ASP
Make..make..making food.

Z 594 E: Ei, shaowei bu yiyang.
AFF little not same
Yeah, it's a little different.

Z 595 S: Wo ??? gen ???...
I ??? with ???
I ??? with ???...

Z 596 E: Mm. Na ni zuo de cai yinggai
AFF then you make MOD food should
Hm. Well, the food you make probably

Z 597 hao haochi.
very good-eat
tastes really good.

Z 598 S: $_{III}$Haochi! Dui, dui, dui, dui, dui.
good-eat right
Tastes good! Right, right, right, right, right.

Z 599 $_{III}$Haochi shi $_{III}$haochi a.
good-eat be good-eat EXC
It tastes good, alright.

Z 600 E: Mm.
AFF
Mm.

Z 601 S: ??? $_{I}$xianzai wo bu guan le,.
??? now I not manage ASP
??? now I don't take care of that.

Z 602 E: Xianzai bu guan, yao xiuxi, shi ba?
now not manage want rest be SUG
Now you don't take care of it, you want to rest, right?

Z 603 S: Dui le,. Wo $_{II}$erzi $_{II}$nuer, zuo fan le,.
right ASP I son daughter make food ASP
Right. My son and daughter do the cooking now.

Z 604 E: Tamen ziji zuo.
he-PL self make
They do it themselves.

Z 605 S: Ei, xing le,. Shi ba?
AFF good ASP be SUG
Yeah, that's ok. Right?

Z 606 E2: Ta bu jiangde ting hao de?
she not talk-ADV very good EMP
Doesn't she speak well?

Z 607 Jiang chang pian de bu xing.
talk long version MOD not good
Talking a long piece she doesn't do so well.

Z 608 S: Chang..chang..chang pian ϕ $_{IV}$shuobuliao.
long version (MOD) speak-not-able
A long..long..long piece I can't say.

Z 609	E2:	Shi	ba?	Jiang	ge	gushi.	Jiang	yijian	shi.
		be	SUG	speak	C	story	speak	1-C	affair

Is that right? Tell a story. Talk about something.

Z 610	S:	Wo	$_{II}$jǐgėr[118]	xiang.
		I	self	think

I'll think of it myself.

Z 611 E: Mm.
AFF
Mm.

Z 612	S:	Shuo	$_{II}$gushi...
		say	story

Tell a story...

Z 613 E: Ei.
AFF
Uh-huh.

Z 614	S:	TING	$_{III}$YIGE	GEI	*$_{II}$XIAOϕ...
		listen	one-C	give	small(-child)

Hear one to the chil...

Z 615	gei	$_{II}$xiaohar	ting	$_{III}$yige[119].
	give	child	listen	one-C

let the children hear one.

Z 616	E:	A,	dui.
		AFF	right

Um-hm, right.

Z 617	S:	$_{I}$Keshi.. $_{I}$keshi	ne...	xin	???	xiang	nar	a?
		but	ASP	heart	???	think	where	Q

But..but where is my mind ??? thinking?

[118] Colloquial Pekingese for *zìjǐ* 'self'.

[119] Preverbal *gei* (*gei NOUN VERB*) means 'for the benefit of', and marks the *NOUN* (indirect object) with benefactive case. Postverbal *gei* (*VERB gei NOUN*) means 'to', and marks the *NOUN* as dative (Teng 1975, A. Li 1990, pp. 100-103). In Mandarin, the verb *ting* ('listen, hear') may take a benefactive, but not a dative indirect object. The subject realizes this, and self-corrects.

Z 618 $_{II}$Zuotian na $_{II}$xiaohair lai war. Wo he na
yesterday that child come play I to that
Yesterday that child came to play. If I told that

Z 619 $_{II}$xiaohar shuo, $_{II}$xiaohar jiang..jiang
child speak child talk
child, told..told

Z 620 $_{II}$gushi lai jiu hao.
story come then good
a story, that'd be ok.

Z 621 E: Zuotian jiang de, a?
yesterday talk EMP Q
You told it yesterday?

Z 622 S: $_{I}$Meiyou a. $_{III}$Xinli a, wo xiang..xiang
not-have EMP heart-inside EMP I think
No. In my mind I'll think.. think of

Z 623 $_{III}$yige. ??? Bu hao kan. ??? bu dui. ??? ...
1-C ??? not good look ??? not right ???
one. ??? It doesn't look good. ??? wrong. ???...

Z 624 Jiang dao nàr a, 'you
talk arrive there EMP have
When I got to that part, 'once there was

Z 625 $_{II}$xiaohair...', wo jiu gen ta shuo.
child I then with him talk
a little boy...', then I talked to him.

Z 626 E: Wo xianzai you xiaohair, youde shihou shuo
I now have child some time speak
I have a child now, sometime I tell

Z 627 gushi gei ta ting. Tai xiao.
story give him hear too small
him stories. He's too young.

Z 628 Ta tingbudong. Ta meiyou banfa.
he listen-not-understand he no way
He doesn't understand. There's no way.

Z 629 S: Bu hui, bu hui. ... $_{II}$Nanhair ba?
not able not able male-child SUG
No, no. ... It's a boy?

Z 630 E: Nanhair.
male-child
A boy.

Z 631 S: Zhen hao.
real good
Really great.

Z 632 E: Youde shihou renwei ting mafan de, xiaohair.
some time believe very trouble MOD child
Sometimes I think they're a lot of trouble, kids.

Z 633 S: Bu $_{I}$mafan.
not trouble
They're no trouble.

Z 634 E: Bu mafan? Wo yao zuo shiqing, ta
not trouble I want do matter he
No trouble? When I want to get things done, he

Z 635 ku le. Ta lao ku wo zenmo ban?
cry ASP he always cry I how do
cries. When he cries all the time, what do I do?

Z 636 S: Jiu hǒng a. Hǒng a. Bao ta.
just amuse EMP amuse EMP hold him
Just amuse him. Amuse him. Hug him.

Z 637 E2: Dou ta.
play him
Play with him

Z 638 S: Dou ta wanr.
play him play
Fool around and play with him.

.... end....................

Name Index

Subject Index

STUDIES IN THEORETICAL PSYCHOLINGUISTICS

1. L. Solan: *Pronominal Reference.* Child Language and the Theory of Grammar. 1983 ISBN 90-277-1495-9
2. B. Lust (ed.): *Studies in the Acquisition of Anaphora.* Volume I: Defining the Constraints. 1986 ISBN 90-277-2121-1; Pb 90-277-2122-X
3. N. M. Hyams: *Language Acquisition and the Theory of Parameters.* 1986 ISBN 90-277-2218-8; Pb 90-277-2219-6
4. T. Roeper and E. Williams (eds.): *Parameter Setting.* 1987 ISBN 90-277-2315-X; Pb 90-277-2316-8
5. S. Flynn: *A Parameter-Setting Model of L2 Acquisition.* Experimental Studies in Anaphora. 1987 ISBN 90-277-2374-5; Pb 90-277-2375-3
6. B. Lust (ed.): *Studies in the Acquisition of Anaphora.* Volume II: Applying the Constraints. 1987 ISBN 1-55608-022-0; Pb 1-55608-023-9
7. G. N. Carlson and M. K. Tanenhaus (eds.): *Linguistic Structure in Language Processing.* 1989 ISBN 1-55608-074-3; Pb 1-55608-075-1
8. S. Flynn and W. O'Neil (eds.): *Linguistic Theory in Second Language Acquisition.* 1988 ISBN 1-55608-084-0; Pb 1-55608-085-9
9. R. J. Matthews and W. Demopoulos (eds.): *Learnability and Linguistic Theory.* 1989 ISBN 0-7923-0247-8; Pb 0-7923-0558-2
10. L. Frazier and J. de Villiers (eds.): *Language Processing and Language Acquisition.* 1990 ISBN 0-7923-0659-7; Pb 0-7923-0660-0
11. J.A. Padilla: *On the Definition of Binding Domains in Spanish.* Evidence from Child Language. 1990 ISBN 0-7923-0744-5
12. M. de Vincenzi: *Syntactic Parsing Strategies in Italian.* The Minimal Chain Principle. 1991 ISBN 0-7923-1274-0; Pb 0-7923-1275-9
13. D.C. Lillo-Martin: *Universal Grammar and American Sign Language.* Setting the Null Argument Parameters. 1991 ISBN 0-7923-1419-0
14. A.E. Pierce: *Language Acquisition and Syntactic Theory.* A Comparative Analysis of French and English Child Grammars. 1992 ISBN 0-7923-1553-7
15. H. Goodluck and M. Rochemont (eds.): *Island Constraints.* Theory, Acquisition and Processing. 1992 ISBN 0-7923-1689-4
16. J.M. Meisel (ed.): *The Acquisition of Verb Placement.* Functional Categories and V2 Phenomena in Language Acquisition. 1992 ISBN 0-7923-1906-0

STUDIES IN THEORETICAL PSYCHOLINGUISTICS

17. E.C. Klein: *Toward Second Language Acquisition.* A Study of Null-prep. 1993
    ISBN 0-7923-2463-3
18. J.L. Packard: *A Linguistic Investigation of Aphasic Chinese Speech.* 1993
    ISBN 0-7923-2466-8

KLUWER ACADEMIC PUBLISHERS – DORDRECHT / BOSTON / LONDON

9 780792 32466

GPSR Compliance

The European Union's (EU) General Product Safety Regulation (GPSR) is a set of rules that requires consumer products to be safe and our obligations to ensure this.

If you have any concerns about our products, you can contact us on ProductSafety@springernature.com

In case Publisher is established outside the EU, the EU authorized representative is:

Springer Nature Customer Service Center GmbH
Europaplatz 3
69115 Heidelberg, Germany

Batch number: 10761588

Printed by Printforce, the Netherlands